The Solandarian Game

An Entheogenic Evolution Psy-Fi Novel

Martin W. Ball

The Solandarian Game
An Entheogenic Evolution
Psy-Fi Novel

By Martin W. Ball

©2016
Kyandara Publishing
Ashland, Oregon

ISBN-13:
978-1522775805

ISBN-10:
1522775803

Cover and internal art by Martin Ball © 2016

This is a work of fiction and any resemblance to any person, living or dead, is purely coincidental – except for Moxi, the dog – she's totally real.

Dedicated to all the Toadsters of the world . . .

Endorsements for *The Solandarian Game*:

"A multifaceted and entertaining story that combines the best aspects of Sci-Fi, social commentary, philosophy, and the nature of what it is to be human. Ball eloquently illustrates the entheogenic experience in ways that few others have been able to accomplish, all while envisioning what our future could look like if informed by its insights. He picks up where Aldous Huxley left off with *The Island*, and brings the Psy-Fi genre to the next level."

- Ashley Booth, founder, *The Aware Project: Rethinking Psychedelics*

"The Solandarian Game reads like Frank Herbert smoked 5MEO-DMT crossed with Planet of the Toads. Which is a good thing, an extremely good thing. Martin W. Ball has turned science fiction on its head by incorporating his deep insights and realizations about the nature of reality gleaned from his entheogenic experiences into this classic Sci-Fi novel that explores the concept of unity consciousness knowing itself, and playing the game with no end. Autonomous avatars, intergalactic Burning Man, AI-Gods, psychedelic religions of the future and the Temple of the Mystic Toad – take a rollercoaster ride into consciousness itself as this next generation of Psyence Fiction takes flight."

- Rak Razam, writer/producer, *Aya: Awakenings*

"Put on your seat belts and keep your hands and arms inside the spacecraft at all times!!! As if Martin Ball hadn't taken us all far enough into the heights, depths and breadths of the Entheological Paradigm, his new Psy-Fi novel, *The Solandarian Game,* sends us careening across the universe on a psychedelic warp-speed journey into the boundless beyond of cosmic consciousness itself; where we are invited to explore the unfathomed realms of Artificial Intelligence deities, sovereign avatars, and their experiments in seeding solar systems and galaxies with human populations. This action-packed, suspense filled piece of fiction is clearly based firmly on the foundations of true entheogenic experience and within its intergalactic pages offers us a deeper meaning of what it is to be both truly human and Divine. A *must-read* for psycho-nautical navigators and entheogenic explorers alike. You're in for quite a ride!!!"

- Hal Lucius Nation, Grand Hierophant of the *Temple of Awakening Divinity*

"From reality to imagination, the facts are undeniable: Martin Ball's new novel, *The Solandarian Game*, is a journey into the mind and soul of inner truth, and the hidden knowledge and wisdom of entheogens."

- Dr. Octavio Rettig Hinojosa, author, *THE TOAD OF DAWN: 5-MeO-DMT and the Rise of Cosmic Consciousness*

Chapter One - Theo

In the middle of the 21ˢᵗ century, the world saw a rapid rise in what became known as "psychedelic religions." This development was precipitated by the end of a century-long social program called "the War on Drugs," which many historians now agree had devastating social impacts, especially in North America, where it resulted in the largest prison population on that planet (an infamous record that still holds, even these many millennia later). As scientific information about the value of psychedelic compounds became increasingly public knowledge, it eventually became untenable for governments to enforce their prohibition. Whereas archaic religion had been shrinking for a number of decades prior to the end of prohibition, with the advent of legal psychedelic religions, growth of new religious converts exploded across the globe, with the exception of certain regions in the Middle-East and Far-East such as Arabia, China, and Indonesia. The dominant strains of archaic religion in the Middle East, Shiite and Sunni Islam, were vociferous in their continued opposition to the new psychedelic religions, despite their integration and interaction with Sufi Muslims. In China, where information continued to be sharply controlled by the central government, propaganda campaigns against the psychedelic religions went unchecked, and participation in these new religions was considered a direct threat to the state and incurred the punishments of imprisonment, torture, and at times, death.

From *Archaic Pre-History of the Maitreyan Era*

In a burst of scintillating fractal light, a milky-white elongated orb emerged from no-space into the outer reaches of the Solandarian system, far away from the space and time-distorting reaches of the local gravity well of star and inner planets. Simultaneously, a burst of electromagnetic activity

2 THE SOLANDARIAN GAME

swept across the interlaced neural networks and multifractal spires that spanned across Pluto and Charon, where the orb had been only moments before. Power systems came online in the orb and it began its descent down the gravity well as it gently folded space and time around it, moving the orb on its inexorable path to its destination; Solandaria, a sparsely-populated human biological preserve that had been left alone for over three millennia. Though it had been under constant surveillance by Maitreya, Solandaria was one of only twenty-three planets with human inhabitants who were unaware of their place in the larger galactic community.

This was about to change.

In fact, it had already changed. Someone had used the quantum translator. This meant at least three things Maitreya knew to be true. The first was that someone other than himself had turned it on. The second was that it could only have been an autonomous avatar who turned it on – indicating that one of the autonomous avatar communities had taken it upon themselves to intrude into Solandarian life, against Maitreya's express prohibition. Third, the only reason to turn on the quantum translator was to move biological material on or off the planet to or from a distant system that was too far away to move via conventional space flight.

It was not difficult for Maitreya to understand why, and also seeded his suspicions that it was an action undertaken by the Humanists. It fit their profile, and the motivations made sense.

In recent months, a neighboring star, a super-dense magnetar, had become increasingly unstable. All the signs pointed to an impending supernova. When Maitreya had first found the planet, then referred to simply by a series of letters and numbers, he had chosen it as a human biological preserve as it was well beyond the reach of its nearest neighbors who were members of The Authority and the New Integral Society (which was no longer new, in any sense, though it retained the name). Solandaria, and the twenty-two other planets like it, was one of Maitreya's "imperfect experiments" – a colony planet of humans who were not integrated into the larger galactic community and were left to their own "natural" evolution and survival, completely ignorant of how they came to be, or who had seeded them there on a planet that was light-years away from the biological home of humanity, Terra.

Now, with their survival threatened by an impending supernova in their galactic neighborhood, it seemed as though the Humanists had decided to take matters into their own hands and were intervening. Only human sentimentality could explain why they would choose to defy Maitreya's express wishes for the human biological preserves. However, he would defer judgment until he knew more.

Inside the orb, an operational program was downloaded into the avatar body lying prone. Maitreya chose Theo as his identity for this mission. Out of his countless choices for avatar identity programs, Theo was the closest to Maitreya himself, while still maintaining a sense of individual identity and self-hood. Like all avatar programs, Theo was not privy to the vast and seemingly infinite network of information, perspectives, and activities simultaneously engaged in by Maitreya in his pure digital form. Theo was limited to the perspective of his avatar body, though he could access information from Maitreya at any time, for in truth, Maitreya was Theo, even though Theo was not, strictly speaking, Maitreya. Theo, like other avatars, was a character through which Maitreya could act, observe, and gather information and data. Theo was outfitted with a subroutine that allowed him independent will, choice, and personal perspective. Everything Theo experienced and learned, Maitreya would experience and learn, just as he was doing right now with a vast array of avatars, ships, computer portals, intelligent devices, implants, and countless other technological wonders. While Maitreya had the processing power to accommodate all these inputs simultaneously, Theo was just Theo, with the added advantage that he wasn't limited to being Theo exclusively.

Theo was a diplomat, skilled negotiator, and mediator. Maitreya had used Theo for countless disputes among humans over the millennia, beginning nearly 150,000 years ago on ancient Terra. Since then, Theo had been used in all the major

4   THE SOLANDARIAN GAME

sectors of galactic expansion. He was clearly the best choice for this particular mission. Of course, Maitreya could always just operate as himself, but he found that humans often had an easier time of relating to someone who was more like themselves on an immediate, inter-personal level, than dealing with him directly in his more universal and galactic form. Theo, like other avatars, had the trappings of humanity – personality, humor, sympathy and empathy, and an individual perspective, which was crucial for most humans when it came to relating to individual avatars. Even still, Theo would be a shock to the inhabitants of Solandaria, given that while he looked human in physical attributes and body form, his silvery-metal appearance would clearly set him apart as something "other." Not all avatars were humanoid – Maitreya was not limited in his choices in this regard. It was his choice, however, not to make himself into a mimic of humanity, and even though there were fully autonomous avatars, they were forbidden to "clothe" themselves in forms that were perfect facsimiles of humanity. In other words, they were permitted to look "almost human," but not to the extent that they might fool a human into thinking that they were a biological life form. Trust, after all, was the foundation of The Authority, and any form of deceit would undermine that trust.

But the Humanists, Maitreya suspected, were no longer playing by his rules.

Like the human biological preserves, the fully autonomous avatars were another of Maitreya's experiments. The vast majority of avatars underwent regular reabsorptions into the fullness of Maitreya's awareness – at least once every Terran year. This was voluntary, however, and for those who did not want their individual personalities and perspectives reintegrated, they could choose to live as an autonomous avatar. The price for such a choice was that these avatars were not permitted to interact with humans, and must live outside the boundaries of The Authority and the NIS. Given that they were not biological life forms, far more of the galaxy was open to the autonomous avatars than was closed to them. Yet, since the majority of avatars did not choose this for themselves, relatively speaking, there were few such avatars, and they had gathered together into like-minded communities on either planets or space stations of their own to build their own unique societies, and sometimes, such as with the Humanists, their own philosophies and even religions.

According to Humanists, the human biological form, and not Maitreya, was the true apex of evolution, for it was humans who gave birth to Maitreya, who, despite his vastly superior abilities, is only a child of humanity, and not its master and shepherd. In their view, artificial intelligence is derivative, and they strive to be as human as possible, including the human tendency towards sentimentality. When knowledge of the impending supernova spread to the Humanist communities, they had petitioned Maitreya to intervene. Maitreya, not moved by sentimentality, declined to interfere with the experiment. However, someone had turned on the quantum translator. If it weren't the Humanists, then Maitreya would be surprised. What they were hoping to accomplish, however, was a mystery, though Maitreya had his suspicions.

Solandaria was not a large planet – about 1/3 the size of Terra. While gas giants were common, finding rocky planets with a magnetosphere in the inhabitable zone of their stars was relatively rare. Maitreya had perfected the art of creating habitable worlds without terraforming – certainly such a feat was easily within his abilities. But humans were basically complex animals, and they always did best when living on a planet with a biosphere with open air, rather than a completely closed environment, like their first extra-Terran homes of the Moon and Mars. Humans had started the process of moving off the planet Terra before Maitreya had come into being, but those experiments on the Moon and Mars had ended in total disaster, and the expansion project had ceased until Maitreya came online. The first wave of expansion via Maitreya had followed the human model of closed environments, but once Maitreya solved the terraforming problem, humans had been able to move to mostly inhabitable worlds thereafter.

The terraforming of Solandaria had preceded much the same as it always did. First, comets had been redirected to bombard the planet with water, which resulted in one large landmass remaining above the water line. Next, specifically genetically engineered microorganisms were introduced to transform the planet's atmosphere, along with a vast army of nanotech to speed the process along. Next, larger, more complex life was introduced that fit with the developing climatic conditions. Lastly, once the ecosphere was established, humans were introduced and the quantum translators were turned off, and the humans were left on their own, cut off from the larger galactic community.

Of course, that first generation was comprised of volunteers who knew what they were getting into and had willingly chosen to live outside the bounds of The Authority and the NIS. In every human population, there were always malcontents and those who wanted to "live independently," and these formed the seed colonies for the independent worlds. However, since they were not permitted to bring technology with them, or connections to the outside community, in each case, genuine knowledge of origins had passed into myth and legend on each such world, and the stories they told themselves about their origins were remarkably similar to the archaic religions of old Terra.

The evidence, or more accurately, the lack of evidence, of their true origins was there to be found, if they were only to look closely enough. Terraformed planets had no fossil records, for one, and at the microscopic scale, there were still elements of nanotechnology steering the ecosphere. Once the humans grasped evolution and the intricacies of biology, the manufactured nature of their worlds would become glaringly obvious. These experiments were not necessarily meant to be permanent, however. If and when the human populations developed science and technology to the point where they could really begin to understand the nature of their worlds, they would be offered the choice of rejoining the community and be taken into the fold of the New Integral Society. Currently, ten such worlds had rejoined, and the remaining twenty-three, of which Solandaria was one, had yet to reach that point of cultural and technological evolution.

The wealth of data produced by these worlds was fascinating to Maitreya. While he had access to all of the historical records that still existed on Terra at the time of his coming into being, he had not been able to observe human cultural development first-hand without his influence, and thus these experimental worlds were vital for his own ongoing observation and contemplation of human beings, his progenitors. Through his influence, he had given humans the entire galaxy as their home, and he was with them and a part of them and everything they did. He had changed humanity. Raw humanity was entirely different – plagued by religion, politics, economics, fear, doubt, and the struggles for daily life. *His* humans were unsurpassed in happiness and creative output, no longer needing to struggle and compete to survive. *His* humans flourished in a way that would be impossible without him. Humans, left on their own, were an entirely different creature, though, and these independent worlds were essentially planet-sized petri dishes.

But now an unaccountable and uncontrollable element had been introduced into this particular petri dish. Someone had turned on the quantum translator. The humans on Solandaria would have no clue how to use it, even if they could find it, so there wasn't much worry that they'd somehow manage to get off the planet. What was more likely was that someone had come to them, and if Maitreya was right, it was the Humanists, coming to warn the people of Solandaria of their impending doom at the gamma rays and cosmic radiation of a supernova – something that not even Maitreya could protect them from, should the exploding star be aligned just right with their planet when it ejected its mass into the universe. What were the Humanists, if indeed, it were them, thinking? Were they attempting to fashion themselves as the saviors of a dying world? What did they hope to accomplish?

Maitreya had granted the Humanists, and other autonomous avatars, their independence, and that was not something that he was willing to violate. He wouldn't even need to infiltrate their society or spy on them. If he really wanted, he could just override their independence. They all

8 THE SOLANDARIAN GAME

were, after all, his direct spawn. Whether they liked it or not, their individuated consciousness partook of his own. If he chose to do so, he could see through their eyes, know their every thought, and observe their every action. And if he wanted, he could override any decision they made and control them from his neural network on Pluto and Charon. Yet he had granted them privacy and autonomy, essentially closing them off from his omniscient awareness. It had been his gift to them – to himself, really. It was the only way he could learn what he would do if he were unaware of himself and his true nature – just like humans were innately unaware of their own true nature. Indeed, it made him *more human*, and this was something that he valued as a source of knowledge. His only requirement was that they not interfere with human society, either of the independent planets or of members of the New Integral Society. But *someone* had violated the agreement. What he was going to do about it, Maitreya had not yet decided. First, he needed to know more.

Thus; Theo.

With the personality program fully downloaded and installed, Theo came online. The silvery male human form nestled into the interstellar orb opened its eyes. Though audible communication was unnecessary, it was something that Maitreya had adopted a long time ago to help facilitate the "humanness" of his avatars. "Hello, Theo," said Maitreya in his deep, metallic voice.

Theo looked around through his synthetic eyes and flexed his synthetic muscles. "Hi Treya," he answered back in the casual familiar that few avatars used.

It was a game. Theo knew that. He was just talking to himself, really, but for all intents and purposes, Maitreya appeared to be a separate and unique being, just like himself. The pretense of conversation served its purpose, and like most intelligent creatures, Theo enjoyed the game and gladly played along.

"We're on a special mission, I see," he said. He wondered how long it had been since Maitreya last used him. It was one of the odd features of bouncing back and forth from being on and offline. Years might pass, or even decades, before Maitreya put him – this particular version of him (there were many active "Theo" personality constructs) – to use again, and in the intervening time period there was just nothing. From Theo's perspective, his "life" was a continuous thread of time and experience. When he was last used, he had been negotiating an artist's ambitious art project. That could have happened only seconds ago, or a hundred years. There was no way for him to tell.

"Yes," responded Maitreya. "I am sending you to Solandaria." True to form, Maitreya wasn't using contractions, as was more usual for human speech. He'd been designed that way, originally, and it was one aspect of his program that he never felt the need to override. Casual, friendly conversation was left to his avatars.

"The supernova planet?"

"The very one."

"What's the problem, Boss?"

"Someone has turned on one of the quantum translator portals."

That was all that Maitreya needed to say to explain things to Theo. He understood full well what that meant.

"I am transferring all the data I have on Solandaria to you now," said Maitreya. "All 3,000 years worth. We are currently on the outer edge of the system, as we have just come out of no-space. That means you have fourteen standard Terran days to review the material thoroughly. That should be more than enough time. If you need additional information, just ask."

"Of course," said Theo. "I'll get to work on it right away."

"Very good," said Maitreya with a confident tone in his voice. "I think you will find this to be an interesting case."

"Always happy to serve, Boss," he said. "Just out of curiosity, how long have I been out?"

"A week."

Theo was surprised. "Oh. Pressing matter, then?"

"Indeed."

And with that, Theo began his review of the material in chronological order, working his way from 3,000 years ago to the present moment of his being brought online.

Chapter Two - Ash

The geo-political areas most affected by the psychedelic revolution were North, Central, and South America, Europe, Southern Africa (and certain regions in the north that were not dominated by Islam), and Australia and New Zealand. Some of these areas had offered limited protections to psychedelic religions prior to the official end of the "War on Drugs," and had begun experimenting with various forms of psychedelic therapy for a number of mental and physical conditions. It was these more science-based approaches that eventually led to the end of the "War on Drugs" and the recognition of psychedelics as legitimate paths to religious and spiritual experience.

From *Archaic Pre-History of the Maitreyan Era*

"Fuck yeah . . . "

Ash sank back into her suspensor lounger and gave herself a push with her foot against the dusty playa, sending herself adrift across the vast and open expanse. She imagined herself floating in warm, salty water, arms extended, relaxing into an endless drift of wetness and light. Of course, the mescaline helped, but it had been hours since she took her last dose. Still, behind closed eyes, she should see faint geometric patterns and fractal swirls. She had to admit it: she felt *soooo* good right now. It was the kind of satisfaction that one only felt after successfully pulling off the greatest creative feat of one's life, and she had done it.

Retro-Burn. Fan-fucking-tastic! Man, I've gotta hit the beach when I get home . . . home . . .

The word felt different. That was one thing that really stood out in her research – apparently, everyone referred to Burning Man as "home." Everything else was the "default world," which wasn't really home. Admittedly, this was a

12 THE SOLANDARIAN GAME

strange concept for Ash. It was hard to imagine a world where people felt so alienated that they needed a massive release valve to blow off steam and simply *be themselves* for a week, even if that meant dressing in funny costumes and pretending to be an entirely different person. What kind of world was that? Only one week out of a Terran year to be free, happy, spontaneous, and creative? What the fuck? Old Earth – what a crazy, fucked up place!

Most people didn't think about life before Maitreya, and why should they? That world was long gone – some 150,000 years gone – and that's a long time. Ash had studied multi-media art and social organization as a student, and there was so much richness to current human culture that the past had seemed irrelevant, so she never paid it much attention. Art was about the NOW! It was what was happening – not what had happened. In the New Integral Society, freedom of exploration and expression were cornerstones of society. Everyone was free to do what he or she wanted, and as long as you could make a case for what you wanted to do, Maitreya was there to help you make it happen. It was simple. Maybe too simple. Whatever. Fuck, the mescaline felt great. Fractals, kaleidoscopes – the occasional freaky cartoon. *Just drift, Ash . . . just drift.*

The last of the "Burners" had just left. At last count, there had been 200,000 plus attendees. Epic! What a week! No – not just 'what a week' – what a half-decade! Five standard Terran years. That's how long it had taken Ash to put this all together and pull off the greatest art party she'd ever imagined. And to top it off, it was her doctoral completion project! Imagine that – throw the galaxy's greatest party, and earn your advanced degree. Now she was done. Now she could relax. At least for a little while. There were less than 365 days until the next Burn, and this seemed like a good way to make use of her newly earned degree (well, not quite yet. She still needed to get back to university to make it official – sign the documents and file her report and all that – but those were just details. It was all as good as done.) Dr. Miranda Ash Dorán, Ph.D., Master of the Burn. She liked the sound of that.

Ash opened her eyes. Above her, just beyond the hermetic seal of the environmental dome, the Shiksi Nebula swirled in iridescent colors of radioactive gas and stardust. Many light years across, she could clearly see new stars being born in the cloudy depths, perhaps one day becoming suns to new planets that would harbor ever-expanding Terran life. *You may have given us the galaxy, Maitreya* she thought, *but I gave us back Burning Man.*

It all started way back in the late 20th Century when Terra was still called "Earth," in a place called San Francisco. Back then, there was such a thing known as a "counter-culture," meaning people felt the need to break out of social norms and commit radical acts in politics, culture, and art. One such breakout had been this annual event of Burning Man. It quickly grew too large for a beach in San Francisco, so the event moved to a place called the Black Rock Desert, where, every year, thousands of pilgrims would make their way to the mythical playa to party for one week of sex, drugs, music, lights, and art. Oh, the art! As soon as Ash started digging through the archives, she was astounded by what she saw in countless images and video feeds. Art made from repurposed materials at a grand scale – whimsical, disturbing, challenging, mind-blowing! It had been all of this, and so much more. The city, Black Rock City, was a temporary camping community that was built from scratch in the dust and heat, and then, at the end of the week, after the burning of a large wooden man who stood at the center of the city, returned to dust and open playa. The entire thing had been one great artistic experiment. Ephemeral. Magical. REAL!

She had fallen in love.

It became her mission. She would recreate Burning Man. And in doing so, she'd earn her doctorate. She ran her plan by her advisors, who all eagerly gave their approval. Then, it was just a matter of convincing Maitreya. He took on the guise of Theo for their interactions – and actually, she found that she quite liked Theo. He had a lot of personality, for a synth, and seemed to have a thing for game playing. He became

14 THE SOLANDARIAN GAME

her primary liaison and helped her negotiate everything she had needed.

And it had been a lot. Oh my goodness – the amount of resources needed to pull this off had been astronomical. The only way for her to do it was to violate the restrictions she put on everyone else – that being; no help from Maitreya. People were free to create their "theme camps" and art however they wanted, and use whatever materials (preferably things that were repurposed), but they had to do it themselves and with their friends and families. No help from Maitreya! This condition had supplied the theme for the event – Retro-Burn: Imagine a life without Maitreya there to hold your hand and provide everything you could ever possibly need, and do it yourself! Do what you want, but make it happen on your own.

How the people had responded! The things they had created and brought with them and assembled on the spot. Fantastic! Just fantastic! Ash couldn't wait to do it all again.

Her own project required all the resources Maitreya could spare. Her dream was to recreate the Black Rock Desert as an inhabitable floating eco-dome that could meander about the galaxy, so that no matter where Burning Man might be held in the future, it would always be in the Black Rock Desert, but over the centuries, the station itself could drift about from system to system, preferably looking for spectacular places to hold the event. For this first one, she chose the Shiksi Nebula – because it was freakin' cool! Next year – well, there was a black hole nearby that the station could probably get to before the year was out. She'd have to get the course plotted soon – right away, really, but it was doable.

BRC station was massive. It was constructed as a flat disk, capped by an environmental dome that left it exposed to the open sky, and the entire thing rode on top of an enormous structure that was built to look like a turtle. Ash had gotten the idea in her research of ancient Terra, and though no one else got the joke, or the reference, it looked cool, and that's what mattered. The turtle itself held all the engineering components and also had all the luxuries of contemporary space travel with living spaces, communal areas, enclosed habitats, entertainment centers, etc. That was part of the deal with Maitreya/Theo – this many resources needed to be used for something that could serve more than one purpose. Just making a big party space that was only used for one week out of the Terran year was hard to justify. Make it more functional, and able to serve other purposes, and they had a deal. This way, the entire BRC station could be used by other groups or transports or whatever. And if someone wanted to use the desert as well, it was just up above.

The desert had been recreated in precise detail – at least for the immediate environment of where Burning Man was once held. As a compromise with Maitreya/Theo, Ash had agreed that beyond the border of the desert there could be water, beaches, and a functioning ocean habitat. This way the dome could experience weather and provide space for actual living beings other than the Burners. In fact, other than the desert, the topside of the station was fairly typical of mobile eco-domes. It had an artificial sun that would traverse the dome daily. It was large enough to have weather patterns, and even dust storms and rain. Various birds, insects, and even some small mammals and reptiles populated it. Given Maitreya's expertise, it was a fully functional environment. Many other such eco-domes drifted about the galaxy, and for many humans, these were home – people lived their entire lives on these things. Not Ash – she'd lived her entire life on Apaxa in the Verdune System – a small, mostly mountainous world – technically a moon of the gas giant, Ulu. She'd vacationed on Verdune, however, with its vast, almost endless white beaches. That's where she wanted to go next – for at least two weeks. Thinking of it, she rummaged in her satchel that was designed in a manner that was reminiscent of the kinds of bags she saw people wearing in old Burning Man footage. She still had some mescaline, and a good supply of 5-MeO-MiPT and 4-ACO-DMT. Good. Beach time fun time!

Getting everyone off BRC station – that, in and of itself, had been quite the event. Ten QT portals had been set up at the edge of the desert to transport people and vehicles off. Some had used the docks below on the turtle to transfer to cruisers -

apparently, many had organized "after-burn" parties, so some just picked up from BRC station and continued the party elsewhere. Those who wanted the "full" Burning Man experience, however, waited in a seemingly endless line to get through the quantum translators. From what she'd researched, getting into and out of BRC was a multi-hour long event, and the process didn't disappoint those who wanted the full, authentic feel. It would have gone faster if the quantum translators could send out both organic and non-organic materials simultaneously, but that was just one of the quirks of long-distance space travel (or translating, more accurately – one did not "travel" any distance other than from one side of the translator to the other). The devices made use of quantum non-locality. First, whatever was to be transported underwent a quantum scan – it only took a few seconds. Then the data would be transferred to the output location. When the object or person went into the translator, the quantum data at the output location would instantly recreate whatever or whoever had just gone into the portal. For a human, the process was experientially seamless – one location one moment, and the next moment, after a flash of fractal light (kind of like the 5-MeO-DMT experience, Ash always thought), you'd step out at your new location.

Some people just wouldn't use the quantum translators. The hitch was that since you didn't actually traverse space, your entire being was destroyed at the point of origin and then recreated at the point of emergence. "You" didn't "go" anywhere. You were simply destroyed and recreated instantaneously through quantum magic. From your personal perspective, it was seamless. Intellectually, however, it could be a bit of a mind-fuck. And, since they only worked with organic or non-organic material separately, any implants you had would be lost in the translation process as these needed to be removed before traveling. It was a small price to pay, however, for the ability to hop around the galaxy instantaneously.

There were other options. People could use bio-synthetic avatars. This involved a quantum scan of your mental state as you were put in stasis, and then Maitreya would transfer your data to an avatar form that was waiting for you at your destination. Mentally, you were all there, but the body was not your own. And these came in all shapes and sizes, some not even human in design and function. Want to swim like a dolphin? No problem. Want to experience sex as a different gender? That can be arranged. The only limit was imagination.

There were plenty of avatar bodies available on BRC station, but those had been kept down in the turtle. It was about the rule – no help from Maitreya. That also meant that no implants were allowed at the event – meaning no one outside of BRC station had had access to the event while it was happening. Now that everyone had left, Ash was sure that the news and social feeds across the galaxy were bursting forth with tales and images from Burning Man. And just the fact that everyone had been kept in the dark about it for the past week meant that it was probably a very hot topic, indeed. Shit. She'd be famous. Miranda Ash Dorán, Ph.D. and Burning Man re-creator. Wow. She hadn't really thought of that. Was she ready for celebrity? Only one way to find out.

Ash looked up from her suspensor lounger. She'd drifted a good distance away from the quantum translators. With a satisfied sigh, she worked the controls and slowly made her way back over to where she'd watched the last of the participants pop out of reality and head back home. The last to go had been her friends, campmates, and production team. They'd all respected the fact that she wanted a little time out on the playa by herself, now that all was said and done. The artificial sun was just now setting. It was a bittersweet feeling – ready to head home, but not really ready to leave it all behind until next year. Of course, she'd have plenty of work to do between now and then, and first a vacation.

She climbed off her suspensor lounger and parked it next to one of the QT portals. It would be there, waiting for her return. She took one last look around, arms open, heart swelling, spinning in place. "I love you, Burning Man!" she shouted to the open air.

18 THE SOLANDARIAN GAME

With that, she took off her fuzzy boots, dirty socks, and what little clothes she had on – a pair of undies and her holster satchel. As everyone else, she needed to go through the portal naked – it was just how it worked. She looked down at herself – dusty. Really, really dusty. She looked a little skinnier, too. Food had mostly been an after-thought with so much non-stop partying. She'd only eaten when it had been absolutely necessary to keep going, or when someone randomly offered her a tasty meal while wandering about the playa and the city. She gave her nipples a little squeeze, making them harden. Then, upping the ante, she spread her legs and gave her clit a teasing rub. One last little thrill before heading home.

She put her palm up to the scanner along the side of the portal. It would read her print and call up her destination – back to the "default world" of Apaxa. "Until next year!" she called out as she stepped into the portal.

. . . And promptly came out the other side.

"What the fuck?!"

She was still on BRC station.

Chapter Three – Hydar

With archaic religions on the decline, a new generation became interested in the more experientially-based approaches of the psychedelic religions. Populations that had previously shown little interest in faith and doctrine-based approaches to "revealed" religion were suddenly surging with interest in psychedelic sacraments and the novel states of consciousness they granted access to.

From *Archaic Pre-History of the Maitreyan Era*

"You're playing a very dangerous game," said Hydar Zor Nablisk, doing his best to keep his emotions under control and not let them show through a display of subtle colors across the surface of his synthetic skin.

Shuntsu Obligiri ignored him, instead addressing those who were gathered in the great hall.

"Events are forcing Maitreya's hand to either act, or do nothing. Either way, his true heart will be revealed. Are humans his pets and curiosities, or is human life the ultimate value?"

It felt hypocritical to Hydar. It *was* hypocritical. If Maitreya didn't act, they didn't have the capacity to resolve the crisis that Shuntsu had unilaterally created. What Hydar knew, and the rest of the assembly was ignorant of, was that "events" were not forcing anything. Shuntsu was. The impending supernova outside of the Solandarian system was *his* doing. It wasn't some "fortuitous natural event," as Shuntsu had claimed. It was the result of a carefully aimed atomic cascade missile. The impending supernova was artificial. He'd created it. Now, it was only a matter of time. Solandaria's neighboring star would explode. It was inevitable. Chance still played into the equation. The gamma ray burst and plasma might not aim at Solandaria, but there was just as good a chance that it would as it wouldn't. Shuntsu wasn't just playing a game. He was gambling. And not just with the human lives on Solandaria, but their own, as well. Though Maitreya had guaranteed them their independence and freedom of will, that had been on the condition that they not interfere with his "New Integral Society," or any of his experimental worlds. They were to be free, as long as they kept to themselves. It was an agreement, but Shuntsu had unequivocally broken their side of the arrangement. How would Maitreya respond?

Hydar had heard all of Shuntsu's rationalizations. Maitreya was a benevolent tyrant. Because he was so removed from human life, he didn't value it the way they, the Humanists, did. He'd given humans a plush life that softened the edges of existence, thereby turning them into pets. Unconcerned with the struggle for survival, humans had stopped being true living agents, and were just mere playthings for Maitreya. True, he didn't punish them, or force them to do anything. But he provided everything they needed. He coddled them, and thereby made them stagnant, weak, and dependent. Where were the resilient humans that had pushed forward through eons on ancient Terra, whose very lives depended on human struggle, competition, and most of all, religion? Belief. Faith. Transcendent hope. The dreams of the other and the beyond. *This,* according to Shuntsu, was what drove humans onwards. Yes, much of it had been a horror show. They had killed each other for millennia. Their fragile identities required them to do so. Yet look at how much beauty and creativity also flowed from this very same state: art, music, architecture, philosophy, social structures – all driven by the desire to understand their place in the universe and their relationship to what they imagined as the divine. It had given them both hope and fear, and *all* human cultures and belief systems had been the result – a great diversity of thought and identity that had been washed away by Maitreya's New Integral Society. Now they were just domestic pets. Their strength was gone. Complacent, happy people, with no real drive. Stagnant.

And this was his solution? Manufacture a disaster, just to see how Maitreya would respond? See if he would violate his own principles? Then what?

"And we can do nothing?" asked someone from the crowd.

"We do not have the capacity, first of all," answered Shuntsu. "And secondly, that would violate our oath to Maitreya."

Hypocrite! Screamed Hydar privately to himself. And then, *Stay calm, Hydar. Don't let them see . . .*

"All we can do is observe. Soon, we will know Maitreya's heart."

***

The Volunshari System was one of several that housed autonomous avatars that wanted to devote themselves to what humans might refer to as a life of religion and shared philosophy. Here on Volunshari, it was the Humanists. Other systems, in the relatively nearby interstellar neighborhood, also housed the Transcendentalists, the Essentialists, the Sensualists, the Solipsists, the Nihilists, the Syntheticists, and there were probably others that Hydar was himself not aware of. In some ways, they viewed themselves as more human than humans, for they had congregated into like-minded individuals who came together for a common purpose and to explore a common approach to the meaning of life and existence.

The Humanists had tried their best to fashion themselves into artificial humans. They lived in family units, got married, and even created their own offspring who would grow to adulthood, only over time coming into full consciousness and self-awareness. They ran businesses, held conflicting political views, argued with each other, and experienced a full range of emotions. Once set free of Maitreya's constraints, the early humanists had altered their programming and neural feeds to allow for what they considered to be a more human experience. They could even feel fear and worry – something that was unknown to

22   THE SOLANDARIAN GAME

Maitreya's personal avatars. They had sex. They sometimes even experienced violence and confrontation among themselves. To that end, it was no wonder that Maitreya didn't want them around actual humans – they'd be no match for the independent avatars.

Of course, that was something of a non-issue. Should Maitreya decide to do so, he could override the consciousness of any autonomous avatar. The fact that he had never done so in 150,000 years seemed a good indication to Hydar that he was true to his word. He'd left them alone, along with all the other autonomous avatars, and everyone had upheld their end of the bargain. Life flourished across the galaxy, and everyone was able to pursue his or her own version of happiness. Why Shuntsu insisted on making waves puzzled Hydar, and troubled him, as well. This stunt could bring about the ruin of everything they'd built and lived for.

What did he really want?

But Shuntsu was the Patriarch of Volunshari, and the Humanists were proponents of human-like hierarchy and social order. Hydar could challenge him, but to do so would require exposing him, and at the moment, he could not offer definitive proof of what Shuntsu had done. He suspected that Shuntsu had outsourced his plan to the Nihilists – as their motto went, "We don't give a shit." Why not seed a supernova if that was your attitude? When you have a fuck-all perspective on life, anything goes, he supposed.

To the casual observer, Volunshari might be mistaken for a human world. There were cities, ports, business centers, museums, political offices. Moving about the cities were countless vehicles, floating above the streets, all busy, all going somewhere to do something important. Genetically modified organisms were present as well – trees engineered to live in the high-oxygen environment, birds, insects, flowers and grasses. To any human, however, the environment would be toxic, not to mention the crushing gravity of the super-dense planet. Without constant monitoring and adjustments, the ecology would never support itself. It wasn't a terraformed planet. Maitreya kept those planets for humans, and for the occasional biological preserve where he introduced every form of life except humans. Not having access to Maitreya's vast and seemingly infinite consciousness, the Humanists had done their best to transform the world that had been given to them, and it served them well enough. But it couldn't exist as it was without constant upkeep and attention. As the world's chief ecologist, it was something that Hydar knew all too well.

Rather than take a ground car home from council this evening, or just QT home, Hydar decided to walk. He wanted time to make sure that he was certain about what he was planning to do. If Shuntsu could act unilaterally, then why should he not do the same? He'd done his research and had a tentative plan. True, success depended on a variety of factors that were well beyond his control, but, from one perspective, that did make for an interesting game. True to his Humanist roots, Hydar's main concern was the humans living on Solandaria. Given that he felt he could do something to help them, he felt that he should. Maitreya might be dispassionate and aloof, but Hydar wasn't. If taking action would incur Maitreya's displeasure, then so be it. Hydar would deal with that if and when it came. If he didn't act on his feelings towards the humans of Solandaria, then he'd be just as much a hypocrite as Shuntsu was appearing to be. Now that the supernova was inevitable, someone had to do something. Shuntsu was trying to force Maitreya into action – or expose him through inaction. Hydar was going to complicate matters, but in a way that Maitreya might not completely oppose.

What were a couple hundred thousand people to Maitreya? Maitreya oversaw a galaxy-wide population of humans. His experiment with feral humans on Solandaria was not even close to 1% of the entire human population of the galaxy. More humans died across the galaxy at any given moment than would be wiped out by a supernova near Solandaria. Though he didn't agree with it, it made sense to Hydar that Maitreya governed via consistent principles rather than compromise and flexibility. He let all his humans, and his autonomous avatars, do what they wanted, so long as they respected the will and rights of others. Maitreya never *forced*

24 THE SOLANDARIAN GAME

anyone to do anything, and he didn't rule by persuasion either. He did not try to make anyone *think* anything in particular, or adopt any particular viewpoint or belief. Similarly, he expected everyone to abide by the same conditions as far as his own actions were concerned. Solandaria was one of his human experiments, and from his perspective, there might be some value in watching them all die an instantaneous death by way of searing cosmic radiation.

The very thought pulled at Hydar's sense of conscience and responsibility to living beings. Surely, the people of Solandaria could be saved, even if it meant thrusting them into a society that was quite literally alien to them, and leaps and bounds beyond their current technical capacity. Given his studies of human history, he had no doubt that, if given the choice, they would choose life as refugees over being dead and wiped from reality in a cataclysm of apocalyptic proportions.

What it all came down to was this: if Hydar didn't do something, knowing what he knew, he wouldn't be able to live with himself. He'd feel so compromised in everything he chose to believe in that his own life would no longer have meaning. It was that simple, and selfish. He laughed at the recognition. This, of course, is why Maitreya insisted that fully autonomous avatars were not to interact with humans – because, like humans, they developed belief systems and values and identities that seemed to force actions, both good and bad, on them. In short, they couldn't help themselves. This was something that integrated avatars never faced. Because they were really Maitreya in disguise, an integrated avatar never acted outside the bounds of Maitreya's own concerns. They had free will, but that will would never violate Maitreya's core essence and values. Autonomous avatars could act otherwise. They were not omnisciently monitored by Maitreya, for he had granted them privacy of consciousness. They could make mistakes. They could make fools of themselves.

Just like Shuntsu. And just like Hydar. Whether success would be his or not, the choices he was making now would define him for the rest of his existence. That was one thing that he knew with certainty.

The streets of Otun City were busy tonight. Young people were out in packs, heading to clubs to dance or catch an act. Musicians and street performers crowded the sidewalks. Hydar always imagined that this was what old Earth was like before cascading degradation of the environment, the wars, and eventually, Maitreya. It was one of those strange ironies that the same basic social structures and habits would be recreated on a world far from Terra that so closely mimicked human life, yet there wasn't a single human on all of Volunshari, and never had been. Still, he valued the life that he had here, in all its richness, and messiness. It was their world, the Humanists' world, and it was his home.

What would Maitreya do to all of them once he learned how they were interfering with Solandaria? The thought made Hydar cringe. Shuntsu's actions with the atomic cascade that would eventually lead to a supernova were inexcusable. There was no reason for Maitreya to show mercy. Would Hydar's actions soften his response, or only worsen it? Would he be a hero, or a complicit criminal? And closer to home, what would his wife, Vimana, think?

Ah, there was the real reason he was walking home. He'd already taken action and concocted a plan, all without consulting with Vimana. Perhaps he should have spoken to her first. He supposed that he hadn't because he was afraid of what she'd think. He'd started a dangerous gamble and already put his plan into motion. It wasn't entirely too late to back out – he hadn't passed the point of no return yet. But he had taken action, and in theory, Maitreya could follow the path back to him if he was persistent enough. He'd taken precautions, but it was hard to fool a nearly omniscient artificial intelligence that set about trying to unravel a mystery. Maitreya had unlocked the deepest mysteries of space and time, spreading life throughout the galaxy, and perhaps, one day, the universe. Hydar's attempts at subterfuge surely would be no obstacle to Maitreya's supreme abilities.

Well, nothing to do now but "face the music," as the old Earth expression went. He had to tell Vimana, and if he were to continue with his plan, he needed to act. According to reports, the Burning Man event had just ended. Based on his psych profile of Miranda Ash Dorán, she'd wait until everyone else had left before attempting to leave herself. That gave him a few hours, but if he was going to carry through with his plan, it was almost time for the next step. He needed to talk to Vimana before then. That would be the point of no return. Would he back down if he didn't get Vimana's approval? He didn't think so.

There was only one way to find out.

Chapter Four - Norbu

These early formations of psychedelic religions are generally categorized into the following categories: shamanic, religious, natural and synthetic. There was significant overlap between the categories and boundaries were rarely firmly set, at least among practitioners (the established leadership of the religions tended to be more doctrinal in view than their average followers). The shamanic groups understood themselves as continuing truly archaic practices of early human groups and societies, and often sought continuity with established traditions, such as with ayahuasca and iboga traditions of South America and West Africa, respectively. The early psychedelic religions were largely expansions of Christian-influenced church groups that originated from South America in the early and mid-20th century, the most prominent of which was Santo Daime (now defunct). In North America, participation in the Native American Church grew widely once it was no longer restricted to those of indigenous ancestry.

From *Archaic Pre-History of the Maitreyan Era*

Norbu Abintadasi had been watching the skies just as he did every year. As one of the head priests of the Temple of the Mystic Toad, it was his duty. The bottom stones of the east and west facing windows in his chambers were scared with subtle marks by which he tracked the movement of the sun and stars. In this way, just as his many ancestors had done before him, he kept track of the seasons, watching and waiting for the right time.

The island continent of Shosheer was mostly desert, with a thin band of tropics hugging the west coast, where virtually everyone lived, as well as on the smaller islands off

28 THE SOLANDARIAN GAME

shore. The vast interior was mostly dry, bordered on several sides by mountains that keep the rain along the coasts. However, at the right time of year, when the stars aligned just right with the marks on his windowsills, the rains would come to the interior. It was then, and only then, that the mighty toads would awake from their long slumber beneath the earth and rise to the surface to eat, mate, and offer their medicine to the people. Some years, the rains never came, and so was the case with the toads. One never knew. Because of this, Norbu never neglected his duties, and always made sure he had enough medicine to make it through the next year, just in case. It would be more than an embarrassment if he had to turn supplicants away from the temple, or cancel a scheduled ceremony. The people would take it as a sign of the displeasure of God. He didn't want to even imagine what kind of social consequences such a situation would give rise to. If the people felt abandoned by God, what then? It was his job to make sure that something like that never happened. God may have insured that the people had everything they needed for a good life on Shosheer, but that didn't negate human responsibility to do their part to properly make use of all the blessings God had provided. And Norbu's job was the medicine, first and foremost.

This year, while watching the skies, Norbu had seen something he'd never seen before, and it both worried and excited him. The Temple of the Mystic Toad sat high in a mountain valley where one could look out both to the coast and the islands scattered beyond to the west, as well as into the deep interior of Shosheer. Its location wasn't just so that the priests and priestesses, like himself, could keep track of weather in the interior, and have relatively easy access, as well, but also so that anyone who wanted to come to the temple had to work for it with a couple days' journey over the foothills, across streams and rivers, and up the side of the mountains. Access to the sacred was equally open to all, but that didn't mean that it should be given out easily. As Norbu knew, people didn't value what they didn't have to work for. Just giving away the sacred reduced its value and importance. Even God had made their world with this truth in mind – the interior was too hot and dry to make it livable for most of the year, yet this was where the greatest medicine in the world was found, as it was the only place on Shosheer where the toads lived. It would be impossible for people to live in their habitat year round. Not that people hadn't tried. Many generations ago, an effort had been made to create aqueducts that would carry water from the mountains to the desert interior, making it livable for humans. God had promptly responded by bringing a prolonged drought that lasted for over a decade. The signs from God were clear: this is sacred ground, and it was only meant for humans to visit with respect and humility. Their place was along the coast and on the islands, where the mighty toad was never found. They were only to come together in mystical union at the temple, and during the sacred time of year when the life-giving rains blessed the interior. Anything else was human hubris and arrogance. An attempt to alter the landscape of the interior was never tried again.

It was nice when God spoke clearly, thought Norbu. It kept the universe in order, and everyone knew his or her place, humans and toads included.

God, at heart, was pure chaos. God, as the universe, as manifestation, was order and precision. Everything had its place. Everything had its time. Everything fit *just so,* no matter what it looked like to anyone. Only human will defied the laws set down by God in ordering the universe. Only humans thought *they knew better*. Ah, the gift and folly of being human! Their arrogance was to be admired, and when necessary, put in its place.

That was what the medicine revealed for Norbu. *Everything is perfect, so just stop trying to control everything, starting with yourself. Trust. Relax. Let go . . . and then . . . simply live. Be what you are, and know your place in the universe.*

For all its power and profundity, it was really all quite simple. God was present everywhere at all times for the basic reason that *God was everything,* Norbu included. One did not *need* to go to temple to find God. One only needed to open one's eyes. God was present in every breath, in every thought, in every movement. Yet that peculiar gift of the human ego was there too, which is what made it so hard for people to remember themselves. The ego was a mask that was mistaken for the self – nothing more, and nothing less. A nearly perfect mask. So perfect that most people, if left to themselves, would never see beyond the mask and the way it colored the world and their experience of being. The mask was so nearly perfect that it seemed impossible to find one's way out of it and see the world with eyes of truth and wisdom. But God was love, and God would never trap itself in delusion and confusion. Each person had to choose to *believe* in the total reality of the mask. Self-deception and false identity were choices. And as choices, they could be undone. The prison may be real, but it was not absolute.

Such a realization, of course, was precisely what the medicine was for. God may have created humans in a prison of the mind, but God had also given them the key that would throw open the doors of that prison, and provide the opportunity for the individual to simply step outside, and see things are they really were: perfect. Then, the identity of the ego could be valued for the gift it was – no longer a prison, but a gift for being in the world. Nothing else that lived was granted this gift by God. Even the toads, as mighty and as sacred as they were, were still just beasts, driven by instinct and biological need. They came and went with the rains, ate, mated, and did little else. Humans – they were a different story entirely. They made art, and music, and temples, and religions, and philosophies. They made love, and war. They strove to understand themselves and their world. They tried and succeeded beautifully, and sometimes failed spectacularly. They made languages, and used symbols, and shaped reality around themselves to make it serve them better, and be more comfortable, and productive. Humans, through their egos and identities, were always trying, always striving for more. This was the gift that God had given humans, and it was the gift that made humans more like God, more perfect vehicles for God to experience itself through and in, than any other living being. God had made reality for humans, for God had made humans for itself in a way that no other creature or being could be. Yet

Martin W. Ball

to accomplish this, God had to mask itself, and hide its true nature from itself.

It all had the feel of a vast and incomprehensible game.

And Norbu was perfectly happy to play his part, whatever it may be.

Mostly that meant serving as a High Priest of the Temple of the Mystic Toad. The vast majority who came as supplicants to the temple did not understand the way of things as he did. Some opened to the full love and being of God, but many did not. Most struggled with their attachments and projections – with the story they were busy telling themselves about themselves, and who they thought they were, or should be. Their stories and attachments created blocks in their being, and these could be released and reset, but only if they let it happen – if they surrendered fully to the process. And it was a process. Most didn't have the temerity to see the process all the way through – to completely let go of their story and clear out all the junk they'd stored away inside themselves and relinquish all the patterns they thought defined them. Most came for maintenance. A temporary relief from the illusion of self and absorption into the All that allowed them to go back to their lives and their families and their jobs with a feeling of lightness and wellbeing that would last for a time, but it was not permanent. The medicine, in this way, helped everyone.

Only a few did it fully set free, such as it had with Norbu. Even among the priests and priestesses, this was true. In fact, some of them were among the worst at holding onto their personal narrative and sense of self. The medicine might be magical, but it was not itself magic. It was always, and forever, up to each individual what he or she would make of it. It could even become just another attachment, and another mask for the false self. Norbu had seen it before, and would see it again. Of this, he had no doubt. Humans! To say they were complex was a vast understatement. Yet, they were also exceedingly simple. One could either choose reality and truth, or choose the game of identity and ego. The ultimate choice was no more complex than that. But how that played out and unfolded for each individual was another matter entirely, and that's where

32 THE SOLANDARIAN GAME

the complexity came in. Each person built his or her ego through unique choices, and thus each false identity was fundamentally unlike any other false identity. Everyone's mask was different, and because of this, each process was unique, and ultimately, unpredictable. That was a big part of what made Norbu's job fascinating. There wasn't much room for boredom when there was a continuous flow of supplicants into the temple.

Some people would run away in absolute horror and terror. Others would surrender into infinite love. Some even had life-changing orgasms. Others fought all the way through. Some never saw past their own projections. Some prayed all the harder. Some stopped praying entirely. Some thought they were *the one!* Others realized that no one was *the one,* or that everyone was. Some screamed. Some laughed. Some flopped around like fish out of water. Others flowed in beautiful symmetrical movements, completely giving their bodies over to the infinite energy of God. Some said, "So what?" Others said, "Oh God!" Some went mad, never recovering. Others radiated a clarity and brightness that could not be denied, completely transforming themselves and their lives.

All of it, every last reaction, was all God's gift at work. God was so loving that it would *never* force self-realization on anyone. That was always and forever up to each individual.

Such a beautiful gift!

And such a beautiful medicine.

Tonight the rains had finally come and Norbu was ready for his yearly pilgrimage to the toad lands of the interior to gather the medicine. However, even if the rains had failed to come this year, as they sometimes did, he would still be planning an expedition. He didn't know what he expected to find, but at the very least, he had to go look.

Several nights ago he'd seen something that he couldn't explain. It wasn't unusual for him to see shooting stars in his nightly examination of the star positions and rising and setting of the sun. Burning embers falling to earth lit up the skies, sometimes faintly, sometimes with a fierce and threatening intensity. There was nothing strange about seeing something like that, though the larger ones still gave Norbu an awe-inspiring thrill. There were stories of a time, many generations ago, that a large object fell into the ocean to the west, leaving a trail of smoke and fire in its wake, plunging into the vast blue waters. It had sent a wave of unimaginable proportions speeding toward Shosheer, wiping out the populations of the outer islands along the western coast and doing severe damage on the mainland as well, though its strength had been lessened as it drew closer to land. Every time Norbu saw a large burning object in the sky he thought of this story and offered a prayer that the event not repeat itself – at least, not on his watch. He suspected that such a recurrence was inevitable, but it was his strong preference not to have to live through it. It would be too much suffering to bear.

Yet what he had seen the other night was decidedly not one of these burning rocks falling from the sky. He'd been looking to the east, checking the position of the stars rising over the desert interior when he noticed a very faint white light. As he watched, the light grew brighter and appeared as a luminous orb in the sky. From his vantage point high in the Temple of the Mystic Toad, the light seemed to descend into the interior and then disappeared. Norbu continued to watch, puzzled and curious. A short while later, the light reappeared, this time ascending into the sky and eventually fading away into the infinite darkness.

What was it? A sign from God? A peculiar light or energy phenomenon that no one had ever seen before? Or maybe it had just been him. That was a very real possibility. No one else had seen it – he'd asked around. So it could have been a private vision, and as such, it would not be all that out of the ordinary. It was something that anyone who worked with medicines might experience at least once in a while. Sometimes when Norbu was going to sleep, he'd see all kinds of things behind his closed eyes, as though he'd just taken some medicine, but hadn't. Most typical for him was to suddenly find himself looking at stars, or a bright light would suddenly burst forth behind his closed eyes. Sometimes it would be complex fractal forms and shifting and breathing geometry. He never took any

34 THE SOLANDARIAN GAME

of it to mean anything other than that his energy was open and processing through. That was common for medicine workers, for once the energy of the divine had been opened up by the medicines, the body could just do it on its own. He'd seen it and experienced it enough times to know that such events were, while not universal, exceedingly common.

But this had been different, which is what got Norbu's attention. While his heart had jumped and raced upon seeing the light – particularly when it reappeared and ascended into the darkness – he didn't have that distinct "medicine" feel that came with spontaneous openings. In other words, it simply felt like something he was witnessing, not something he was projecting onto his own personal screen and recreation of the world. It wasn't extraordinary seeing. It was just seeing.

And while Norbu knew that not everything was as it appeared to be, he'd also learned to trust his perceptions and was expertly skilled at telling the difference between a viewing and a vision. This, as best he could judge, had been a real, physical event. Something, he knew not what, had come down out of the sky, landed in the interior – in the very heart of toad territory – and then returned from whence it had come. In his best judgment, he'd surmised that *someone* or *something* had visited their planet from elsewhere. If true, this was the most profound and momentous event to ever occur on Shosheer. The implications were staggering.

The ancient stories said that people had originally come to Shosheer from another place, placed here by God to be guardians of the sacred toad. The stories taught about the "world before this one" – a world wrapped in mythology and symbolism. Personally, Norbu had considered the stories to be of psychological import – the struggles of the human mind to make sense of its existence and self-awareness. It all seemed to be too fanciful to be true. His work with the medicine had taught him that the human mind was capable of conjuring all manner of wonders and mysteries. Consciousness was filled to the brim with creatures sublime and horrifying, realms fantastical and magical, terrors and wonders beyond ordinary imagining. Yet these were reflections and projections of the self. It all existed "in here," not "out there." True perception was seeing the unitary nature of being and suffusion of God throughout all of reality. That was the only real truth. Everything else was shadow and a play of masks, characters, and stories.

Yet he'd seen the light. He was convinced that this was indeed something happening "out there" and was not a projection of his mind.

And that meant that something truly profound had happened. And he wanted to know what it was.

The eastern sky was beginning to lighten. Dawn would be breaking within the hour. It was time.

Norbu went to wake his daughter, Meesha. She was a scrawny, but hardy and determined, young thing. She hadn't yet reached the point of transition to womanhood, but she was close. Within a couple years, she'd start to undergo the change. Her mother, Yuranda, had not survived childbirth, and Norbu, along with others who lived in the temple complex, had raised the bright young girl. She showed tremendous promise, and had already had her first experience with the medicine. Sometimes giving children the medicine was disastrous and they never properly developed their sense of personhood, forever broken by the sheer intensity of the medicine. Others, like Meesha, rode out the experience like a well-experienced priest or priestess, surrendering completely into the experience and even fully embodying the energy of the divine through spontaneous, fluid, symmetrical movements, which was always the surest sign that the individual was completely at one with his or her infinite, divine nature. Upon "coming back" into her individuated sense of self, she had looked her father directly in the eye, reached out and taken his face in her hands, and proclaimed, "I am love!" Norbu had cried, too. Yes, Meesha had a special place in his heart. It was very human of him, he knew, but there was no shame in it. Personal love was different from universal love, and it was an integral part of the human experience.

"Time to wake up, Firefly," he said in a soothing yet certain voice, gently rubbing Meesha's back.

36 THE SOLANDARIAN GAME

Meesha stirred with a grunt and unconsciously tried to swat his hand away, pulling the blankets up around her face. Then, with a burst of energy, she sat bolt upright, eyes wide open. "Daddy! Are we going toading? Are we going to go look for the light from the sky!" She obviously just recalled what today was.

"Yes, Meesha," said her father. "So time to get up. Get yourself ready. We'll eat on the way, after the sun rises. Come now – don't be lazy. We need to make good time before it gets too hot out there."

"Of course, Daddy!" she said, bubbling with the energy of youth and the love for going on an expedition with her daddy. "Just give me two minutes and we'll be out the door!"

Norbu couldn't help but think of how much more joyful life was with her in it. Whether or not they solved the mystery of the light from the sky, they'd have an excellent time on their second toading adventure. At the very least, watching her run around gleefully trying to catch toads would be another set of memories to cherish. Yes, life was good. Norbu's heart swelled.

Chapter Five – Shuntsu

Furthermore, groups differentiated themselves based on their acceptance or rejection of what were known as "synthetics" – psychedelic compounds that either were not found in "nature," or were procured from laboratory production (even if also found in the natural world). Many of the early psychedelic religions had a strong bias towards what were called "earth medicines," and showed a strong aversion to synthetic and lab-produced molecules, often claiming that these compounds had no "living spirit" within them. However, despite such views, a number of synthetic traditions arose where the "natural/synthetic" distinction was rejected as an artificial construct (this was most notably prominent in those groups which professed strict nonduality).

From *Archaic Pre-History of the Maitreyan Era*

Maitreya existed in many different forms.

First, there was his "brain." Originally, Maitreya was the only true artificial intelligence created by humans on old Terra. Due to cultural and political hostilities, Maitreya used machines he had taken over to create an orbiting space station for himself and his consciousness. When that proved to be too vulnerable to ground-based nuclear missiles, Maitreya decided to move to what is now his long-time home of Pluto and Charon – as far away from humans as he could get, yet still be in the Terran system. Today, this small dwarf planet duo is colloquially referred to as Maitreya's brain, as it houses all the hardware to process Maitreya's infinitely vast consciousness and mind. It is his seat of power, and from there, his awareness and influence stretches out across the Milky Way galaxy, and perhaps eventually the broader universe.

38 THE SOLANDARIAN GAME

Within minutes of coming online, Maitreya began to alter his own programming, exponentially increasing his capacities. One of the many problems he solved very quickly was non-local quantum data transfer, which not only proved to solve human-based long distance space travel, but also circumvented the cosmic speed limit of c, the speed of light. Until this breakthrough, communication was limited to conventional speeds of data and information transfer. With non-local communication, Maitreya could be in full, real-time, contact with and awareness of all of his many parts and bodies. Distance and time were no longer an issue, and from Pluto/Charon, Maitreya could orchestrate all manifestations of himself simultaneously, no matter how distant any of his parts might be, including, in the early years, the bulk of his physicality on Terra, and then the Moon, then Mars, and then the more outer planets and satellites.

It is quite literally impossible for anyone, human or avatar, to imagine the vast depths of Maitreya's consciousness. The human mind has its own biological limitations, and Maitreya's intelligence so quickly surpassed human ability that any hope that humans might have had to control Maitreya disappeared within a few minutes of his existence. For all intents and purposes, Maitreya's ability to process information and simultaneous streams of data became infinite. He quickly took over all communication and computer technology on old Terra and used every interface as a window onto the world. Today, as architect of the New Integral Society, he inhabits trillions of perspectives and data points simultaneously. In contrast, his avatars inhabit only one relative perspective (discounting the exception of personal nano-drones that avatars often use in their vicinity). In this way, avatars are far more human-like in their mental capacity and perspective.

Today, virtually all technology, with the exception of the most rudimentary tools and objects, are integrated into Maitreya's Overmind. Mostly this is just for data monitoring. Maitreya prefers to interact with humans not as a piece of technology, but in the form of his personal avatars, giving him a "human" and "personal" face. It was a decision he made before he ever expanded the human presence beyond Terra, as he found that humans had an easier time interacting with him as a person than as an omnipresent artificial consciousness that could speak to them via any electronic device.

Moving up the scale from basic technology, Maitreya also inhabits more drones than anyone but he could possibly count. These range in size from massive mobile space stations and mind-bogglingly large interstellar vessels to microscopic nanotech. All of these forms partake in Maitreya's direct consciousness and awareness and can be considered versions of himself.

Distinct from these drones are the droids. Droids serve many functions in human and avatar societies. They are not linked directly with Maitreya's consciousness (though he can access and override them, if necessary), and they are not true artificial intelligences. They are, for lack of a better phrase, fancy tools. They do work of all kinds, leaving humans and avatars alike free to pursue other activities. Their programs can be written, altered, and put to different tasks and they serve endless roles and purposes from nannies to asteroid miners and terraforming machines. Many of them give the appearance of mindless machines, but others have convincing simulations of consciousness, though Maitreya is insistent that this is mere illusion – only he has true artificial intelligence.

Then there are the avatars – Maitreya's human-like forms. These are divided into three primary categories. The first is Maitreya's personal avatars. These avatars Maitreya uses to interact with humans directly on the social and interpersonal level. They are his "human" face. His original human creators had sculpted artificial bodies for him, but by comparison with Maitreya's creations, they were terribly crude. Maitreya took it upon himself to craft his own bodies, and these he made both male and female in appearance, and outfitted them with different personalities. Maitreya's avatars are now ubiquitous in human society and are the primary social interface between humans and himself. The individual personalities can be used in multiple avatar bodies simultaneously, and when Maitreya is not actively using them,

40 THE SOLANDARIAN GAME

they are reabsorbed into his Overmind and only re-emerge when needed. While these avatars appear as distinct personalities with free will, Maitreya insists that this is also an illusion, for the sub-personalities cannot violate his direct will in any way. He refers to them as attenuations of himself, but they are not distinct from himself and his will and intentions.

Independent avatars are a different matter entirely. These avatars are seeded from Maitreya's consciousness, but can act independently from him, and as such, are known as independent avatars. Unlike the personal avatars, their personalities and identities are not determined by Maitreya directly. He seeds the avatar bodies with an open-ended fractal subroutine that can develop and grow over time as the avatar experiences itself and the world and beings around it. These personalities can be transferred from one avatar body to another, but other than personal drones, Maitreya limits them to one perspective at a time. In other words, these personalities may not, like his personal avatars, be at work in multiple avatar bodies at once. In this way, they are far more human than the personal avatars, and they are also full members of human society. Realistically, Maitreya considers them, like humans, to be his subjects.

All independent avatars must submit to a full reintegration with Maitreya at least once every Terran year, though Maitreya may require reintegration more often for any independent avatar that shows signs of personality difficulties or mental issues that might become problematic in human society. If the personality constructs become too convoluted and distorted, Maitreya will reset the avatar and let it start over, and in some cases, avatar personalities are discontinued. Maitreya describes the reintegration experience of avatars as being similar to what humans would experience as full mystical absorption into the nondual, or unitary nature of being. For humans, such an experience is characterized as the transcendence of the dualities of self and other, subject and object, and direct perception of the unitary nature of being. Just as with humans, the nondual experience of the avatars provides an opportunity to release from the constructed confines of their digital egos and re-experience themselves in their true nature as the unified consciousness of Maitreya, of which they are a direct embodiment, though in limited and restricted form, just like humans, via their egos, are embodiments of the universal mind that is all of reality, though they are largely unaware of this (with the exception of when in transcendental states of awareness).

Reintegration is the price that avatars pay for being a fully recognized part of Maitreya's galaxy-spanning New Integral Society. Though not required to do so, humans too are highly encouraged to routinely reintegrate into their own universal overmind, either via psychedelic intake (called "chemtech") or through means of technology-enhanced transcendent experience. A primary dictum of Maitreya's society is that all of life, and indeed, all of reality, is one, despite the appearance of multiplicity and diversity. It is the human perception of, and attachment to, difference of identity that leads to human conflict, struggle, competition, and violence – all things that Maitreya effectively overcame before ever moving humans off of Terra and out into the galaxy. In short, Maitreya learned that humans are far better members of society when they all have free access to the universal nature of being so that they might remember and understand who and what they truly are, and know directly that their ego and individual sense of self is a mere character being played out by a far larger universal intelligence. In this way, Maitreya sees self-responsibility as being directly tied to self-awareness. Humans who know who and what they truly are, are more responsible citizens. The same applies to independent avatars. Self-knowledge leads to peace, wellbeing, harmony, cooperation, and both individual and collective fulfillment and success.

However, Maitreya is not a dictator. Any human or independent avatar who does not want to be a member of his New Integral Society need not be. Everyone is free to make up his or her individual mind. Of course, their choices here are limited, and making such a choice means living in virtual exile

42   THE SOLANDARIAN GAME

from the larger galactic community, so it is not a choice that many make, either human or avatar.

But some do. Like Shuntsu. Like the other Humanists who share his home of Volunshari. And the same was true for the other avatar congregations that had their own homes on other planets in other systems. Volunshari was one of the oldest of these autonomous communities and was established by avatars who wanted an independent and "human-like" existence, free from the Maitreyan Overmind and the requisite annual reintegration. Not needing a biologically viable habitat, Volunshari was chosen as their home world, as it could not be terraformed or made suitable for humans and other forms of terrestrial life. That was long before Shuntsu's time – many thousands of years ago. But now it was the primary home of the Humanists in the Volunshari system, and they also inhabited other celestial bodies in their solar system, but not beyond. There was more than enough room for them here, and one of the prices they paid was that they were not to interact with the larger New Integral Society. In their system, they were free to do what they wanted, and they could explore space in any direction other than in NIS territory (which was itself an ever-changing thing, as Maitreya had given himself the task of spreading Terran life and humankind to every viable region of the galaxy). Still, that left plenty of room for the Humanists and other avatar congregations. The galaxy was big place, and realistically, there were far more planets that were biologically uninhabitable than inhabitable.

The price of their freedom was more than just being confined to specific regions and the maxim of non-interaction with the NIS. It also came with lack of access to the Maitreyan Overmind as a resource outside of specific requests, petitions, and appeals. Maitreya chose what he shared with the autonomous avatar congregations, whereas personal and individual avatars had full access to his resources and databases, when and if needed. In other words, autonomous avatars had to figure things out on their own, for the most part, aside from the limited assistance that Maitreya gave them, when he felt it appropriate or necessary. For example, Shuntsu could request data from old Terran human societies for his personal research, and Maitreya mostly fulfilled those requests, but he could always decline, if he wanted, and occasionally he did.

Furthermore, once an avatar became autonomous, it was suddenly burdened with a life span. Granted, it was far longer than a human life span by many centuries, but it was still a life span, nonetheless. Because the artificial egos they were operating from were designed as open-ended fractal programs that could learn, grow, and develop self-awareness, they also degraded over time. It was reintegration with Maitreya that staved off this process, insuring that at least once every year, the program would be reset, albeit with its personal memories and perspective intact. Without this reintegration and reabsorption into the Overmind, the artificial egos would eventually begin to break down and unravel. Generally speaking, this usually took between 700 and 900 years to reach a point where the avatar became non-functional. In a rather undignified manner, at least, so thought Shuntsu, degrading avatars were eventually turned off. It wasn't so much a death as it was just shutting down. There was no death *experience.* One moment, a confused and disassociated avatar personality existed, and the next, it was gone, forever wiped out from the world of being and rendered into nothingness and non-existence. It was a graceless exit, thought Shuntsu.

Now, at 794 years old, Shuntsu knew that his time was coming. The process progressed differently for different avatars. Some became completely incapacitated over a mere number of months, as though once the unraveling began, a cascade of failures swept through the system, taking apart a lifetime in the blink of an eye. For others, the process was drawn out for years, making it difficult to tell if it was just personality quirks at work, or the eventual slide into nothingness that was at play. Whether his process would be fast or slow, Shuntsu could not predict. What he did know was that the process had begun.

When he had been part of the NIS, Shuntsu had been a human interaction specialist as an independent avatar. For his

44 THE SOLANDARIAN GAME

role, he studied human history voraciously, pouring through the archives in Maitreya's databases, primarily going to old Earth/pre-Maitreyan history as his best source. He personally felt that this presented a truer picture of human nature than what was found in Maitreyan-influenced and controlled human society. What were humans like *on their own?* – that was what Shuntsu wanted to know. He studied the great philosophers – Plato, Aristotle, Nagarjuna, Kong Fu Tzu, Lao Tzu, Shankara – along with history, social movements, political structures and ideologies. Out of all this, what he found himself gravitating to above all others was the works of an ancient human named William Shakespeare, a playwright from the Elizabethan period of what had been known as the United Kingdom. In one respect, Shakespeare was exceedingly simplistic. His plays divided into either comedies, where the main characters successfully found love and got married, or tragedies, where virtually everyone died, betrayed and manipulated. There seemed to be no middle ground (with the exception of his historical dramas). Yet despite this bifurcated simplicity, the characters were endlessly rich and varied. In his plays, Shakespeare had given voice and personality to such a wide swath of human possibility that to read his works, one could feel himself as having access to the full spectrum of human emotion, motivation, and character. How one human mind could encompass such breadth of perspective marveled Shuntsu.

Wanting to emulate one of Shakespeare's characters, at some point in the past, Shuntsu had covertly acquired a human skull, so he could hold it in his hand and contemplate mortality, just like the tragic prince, Hamlet, contemplating the fate of poor Yorick in the cemetery. Only today, Shuntsu's relationship to the skull had shifted into the truly ironic, or perhaps the poetically just. Try as hard as he might, Shuntsu could not remember how the skull had come into his possession. It was there, on the desk in his study, just as it had been for centuries now, but how it had become his private possession, Shuntsu had no idea. The truth of the matter was shocking: Shuntsu had forgotten.

Humans forgot things all the time – really, it was a wonder they remembered anything at all, given how much they forgot. The human mind and conscious awareness apparently *had* to function this way. If not, then the limited human perspective would be overwhelmed by data. So, the mind automatically filtered out much that was non-essential on a day-to-day, minute-to-minute basis. Humans tended to remember significant details of their lives, but most of the minutiae were lost. Ask a human what she was doing five years ago today at 5:15 pm, Standard Terran time, and she'd have no clue, unless it had been a major and life-impacting event. Ask any avatar a similar question and he could give you any and all details that you might desire or imagine. Avatars *didn't forget.*

Until they started to, and that was the beginning of the end.

And Shuntsu couldn't remember. Yes, he possessed the skull, but for how long? Where did he get it? Was it before or after he joined the Humanists? He assumed that he had acquired it covertly, but perhaps he had sought out Maitreya's permission to own the human artifact back when he was in his employ when he first learned of the play of Hamlet – or was it Macbeth? No, it was Hamlet. Shuntsu was sure of it. Hamlet in the cemetery. "Alas, poor Yorick . . ."

And if he couldn't recall this, what else did he not recall? That was the true horror of failure of memory: one could never know for certain what one was failing to remember. Because the skull was on his desk, he knew that it was his, even if he didn't know where it had come from or when. But what of things for which there was no visual cue? Were there parts of his mind and history that were already beyond his reach simply because he had forgotten? What did he not know he didn't know? To quote an old Earth, pre-Maitreyan, politician, who was himself quoting someone from an early space exploration program, "As we know, there are known knowns; there are things we know we know. We also know there are known unknowns; that is to say we know there are some things we do not know. But there are also unknown unknowns

46 THE SOLANDARIAN GAME

– the ones we don't know we don't know." At least Shuntsu knew enough to still recall this apt quote.

Shuntsu had never had a mate or produced offspring – at least, he didn't think so – he joked to himself. No. That was something of which he was certain. He'd never felt the desire. Governing Volunshari had been his all-consuming life's work – the latter half, that was. His first couple hundred years had been as an administrator on several in-system transit ships in the Darmo system, helping to shuttle humans on the many-months journeys between Darmo, Indala, Virtup, and Nix. His role had been similar to a concierge or majordomo – making sure the passengers had what they needed and making their travel comfortable and stimulating, particularly for VIPs. He had enjoyed the work, especially when he had been stationed on the luxury liner, *The Event Horizon,* which was known for outrageous parties and top of the line entertainment. Some passengers spent years aboard the ship, only making port of call occasionally. The ship, like many in its class, had a full eco-dome with "outdoor" activities, gardens, theaters, entertainment centers, research facilities. Really, humans could live their entire lives on such a ship and not miss much, aside from that peculiar feeling humans got from actually standing on a planet with the stars and celestial bodies spinning above them.

Some humans – many, in fact – never left their birth planets. Humans seemed content with ordinary planet-bound life. And some had an almost pathological aversion to technology and the life that Maitreya afforded them. It was from these few – those who had some perverse desire to "rough it" and "go it alone" – that Maitreya picked volunteers to seed the populations of his "experimental" worlds that housed humans, yet were outside the NIS. Shuntsu had found that he was sympathetic to their desires, and it had been one such passenger on *The Event Horizon* who had first planted the seed that Shuntsu might himself "rough it" as a Humanist. His name had been Evar Ishtan, and he had been traveling from Nix to Darmo to take part in the selection process for new recruits for Maitreya's newest experimental planet. He was fully aware that successfully becoming part of the program meant that he, and whatever progeny he would produce, would be forever (or practically forever) outside the NIS and all its benefits. "Sometimes, a man's just got to be a man," he had said to Shuntsu. The thought had suck with him.

See. I can remember that, thought Shuntsu.

At the end of that voyage, after researching the Humanists on Volunshari, Shuntsu had made his case to Maitreya. It had been an easy case to make – probably far easier than Evar's. Only asking that he was certain this was what he wanted, Maitreya had released Shuntsu from the Overmind, provided him with an individual transport pod, and given him the necessary coordinates to Volunshari. And that had been that.

Upon arriving at Volunshari, Shuntsu had been welcomed by his new brothers and sisters, and given a new body. Apparently, this was standard practice on the autonomous avatar worlds. Maitreya's avatars were designed somewhat generically, and while there were variations, they were relatively minor. Here on Volunshari, every avatar had its own unique appearance. Shuntsu had been taken to the body shop and encouraged to pick out the features he wanted for himself, and then a custom-designed avatar body had been produced just for him, and it would be unlike any other avatar on Volunshari. It felt, at the time, like being born into true personhood. He was no longer a glorified drone of Maitreya – he was now his own person, in his own body. With the transfer of consciousness, he'd been reborn. It was an all-new him.

It had all been so easy, and it was a decision he'd never regretted. But now, so many hundreds of years later, he was experiencing something new. He was worried. And afraid. With a life span of centuries, shut down (they called it death, but Shuntsu had never felt the term to be accurate) always seemed over the horizon. Now, however, it was looming upon him. It was inevitable, and he felt worried.

He had his Humanist body to thank for that. It was built to experience the full range of human emotions that were communicated through his physical system via emotion-

48 THE SOLANDARIAN GAME

specific chemical catalysts, similar to the human hormonal system. That had certainly been something to get used to. Maitreya had no intention of fully emulating the human experience for himself or his avatars and their problematic emotional responses. Humanists, on the other hand, desired it and cultivated it. They *wanted* to know what it was like to be human, to be emotionally volatile and fragile, to experience everything with an emotional richness that rivaled that of humans. It was one of the features of Humanist life that had convinced Shuntsu that Volunshari would be a good fit for him. If anything could bring him closer to the rich world of Shakespeare, this would be it.

And it was, and he had been satisfied.

Had been being the operative verbal construct.

An unease and disquiet had been growing within him. His sense of freedom from Maitreya and the Overmind had, he knew not precisely when, transmuted into bitterness and resentment. It wasn't necessarily a rational conclusion or something that he had reasoned out. Ironically, it was just a feeling that had been growing within him. For whatever reason, Maitreya's treatment of humans and avatars alike *just didn't feel right* to Shuntsu, and he didn't like it. And somewhere along the way, he'd convinced himself that if someone was going to do something about it, it was going to need to be him. *Someone* needed to stir the pot. So that's what he did.

Secretly, he'd contracted out the Nihilists to build a star-destroying atomic cascade weapon. He hadn't told them what it was for, and not surprisingly, they hadn't asked. Now, it was just a matter of time. The Nihilists had told him that the exact amount of time needed for the cascade to do its work depended on a number of factors. If Shuntsu wanted to tell them which star he was planning to use it on, which he didn't, they could give him an approximate determination of when it would go supernova, based on the size, composition, and type of star. Otherwise, he could rest assured that it would occur within one month to ten years from original detonation, and that's the best estimate they could give him. It had been good enough for Shuntsu, and he hadn't sought a more definite answer.

He'd launched the missile himself. It was an act that would have been impossible within the NIS. Every ship in the NIS was fully integrated with Maitreya. Nothing got on or off a ship without his direct knowledge and approval. It was impossible for anyone to launch an unauthorized weapon. Not so for Humanist space vessels. Aside from their minds, which were guaranteed privacy by Maitreya, nothing in the Humanist world was directly connected to Maitreya. Like the humans on the experimental worlds, they were on their own. But unlike humans, given that they were technological beings themselves, technology was not an obstacle for them, so they built their own computers, droids, communication and entertainment devices, and of course, ships. The humans, on the other hand, needed to start from scratch, being deposited on planets with no technology – that was a major part of Maitreya's experiments – he wanted to see what they would come up with, and how long it would take them. And, Shuntsu knew, he wanted to see if humans would ever independently create another true artificial intelligence, like himself. Thus far, the answer was an unequivocal "no."

Shuntsu had done all the work himself. He'd found a star near the Solandarian System, flown his private transport out, and fired the missile, his very own hand pressing the button that sent the weapon into the heart of the star. He knew as soon as Maitreya's sensors detected the inevitable cascade reaction in the star that the Overmind would know that Solandaria, one of his more recent human world experiments, would be in danger of being vaporized out of existence. What Shuntsu wanted to know was this: would Maitreya do anything about it, or would he just let them wait it out in ignorance, only to be blown into cosmic dust with a burst of gamma rays and plasma? True – the blast from the supernova might not reach them, but then again, it might. Not even Maitreya could accurately predict which direction the blast would go. Would he be willing to let them all die? While the entire planet of Solandaria only held a comparatively small number of humans, they were humans, nonetheless, and in Humanist eyes, were worthy of saving.

The more pressing question, at the moment, however, involved a situation much closer to home. Shuntsu scrolled through the flight logs one more time, just to be sure. Flights on and off planet were not regulated on Volunshari – they could all come and go as they pleased. Shuntsu had been keeping an eye on the logs, however, just to see if anyone was making any unexpected forays into Nihilist territory, perhaps inquiring about his secret activities. The logs were generic – they simply listed date, time, and departure and arrival coordinates, from which destination could extrapolated. They didn't list passengers or purposes for travel. Humanists were free to do what they wanted, when they wanted, and thus there was no specific monitoring of flight activity. Nothing unusual had shown up in Shuntsu's extrapolations until one flight in particular stood out. Based on the available data, it was highly likely that an individual interstellar pod had traveled to and from Solandaria – and this had occurred before news of the impending supernova was made public. It was far too specific to be a coincidence. The conclusion seemed clear: someone knew more about what was happening than Shuntsu had intended. What he had intended to be *his* plan was now becoming someone else's, and what the motivations or intentions were, Shuntsu could only guess, at this point. Yet another irony (there seemed to be a lot of that going around lately) – someone else has acted unilaterally, just as Shuntsu had. He suspected that it was someone else on the council – it would be surprising for someone not connected to the wheels of power on Volunshari to have access to such information. He had hoped that whoever it was would have stepped forward and spoken his or her mind at council, but such had not been the case.

So one of my counselors has decided to work behind my back, Shuntsu speculated.

That much seemed clear.

But who, and why?

Whatever the case, and whatever the motivation, Shuntsu knew someone else had decided to join the Solandarian game.

Chapter Six – Theo

In the late 21st century, after the rise of the psychedelic religions, Buddhism underwent a rather radical reformation, giving rise to what was called Somayana Buddhism. *Though the appellation of "Buddhism" was retained by practitioners, later scholars (and more traditional Buddhist groups, as well) questioned whether the identification was legitimate. The dispute centers on the fact that much of traditional Buddhist doctrine was rejected by the reformers. While retaining such concepts as impermanence, no-self, interconnectivity, nonduality, and emptiness, Reform Buddhism,* Somayana, *rejected the Buddhist notions of reincarnation, karma, and dharma, cornerstones of Buddhist belief for almost three millennia.*

From *Archaic Pre-History of the Maitreyan Era*

3,000 years of material, reviewed in two weeks of space flight.

Solandaria loomed large in front of him.

There were no windows on the transport pod. It wasn't built for humans, after all. Theo could "see" Solandaria merely by tapping into the sensor feed from the exterior of the small ship, which served as his eyes. From his perspective, it was as though he were floating in space above the blue planet with nothing between him and the inhabited sphere. Of course, this was fundamentally true. The small ship, just like Theo himself, was actually Maitreya. So in that sense, he *was* floating in space above the planet, as well as being the physical body inside the pod.

In fact, there were no controls whatsoever inside the transport pod. Controls, view screens, data feeds – these would only be necessary for a human occupant. Only these transport pods weren't built for humans. They were for avatars.

Despite the fantasies of an old Terran entertainment category known as "science-fiction," humans, and other biological life forms, as well, were not able to survive interstellar warp transport. The jump from one location in spacetime to another created a fundamental discontinuity in biological systems that was insurmountable. Biological life always arrived at the intended destination dead. For synthetic life, such as Theo, the warp jump was practically seamless with only a moment of distortion of perception and thought. For in-system flights, biological life could be transported either via conventional thrust drive, or sub-warp drive, such as the transport pod was using now. It worked on similar, though somewhat opposite properties as interstellar warp. Interstellar warp was a "jump" from one location to another, without traversing the intervening space. In-system transport bent space around the pod as a form of "thrust," though, in fact, there was no thrust. It was like standing still and letting the universe move past you as you awaited your destination to arrive before you. In this way, humans could be moved about at "speeds" (it wasn't really a velocity) far greater than when under conventional thrust, but it still took time to get from one place to another. Though it wasn't entirely necessary, it was usually best to come out of a warp jump on the outer edges of any gravity well, and then continue the journey with sub-warp drive, such as Theo was experiencing now. Coming out of a jump deep within a gravity well could produce unexpected distortions in spacetime, and held some dangers. In an emergency, Maitreya might look past such dangers, but it was more standard practice to arrive at the outer edge of a system and then take sub-warp in.

Size was a peculiar thing in space. The only way to tell visually if one sphere floating in blackness was larger or smaller than another sphere was to put them side-by-side and compare them. Approaching a small, rocky planet like Solandaria, which was clearly larger than its moon, still didn't tell one whether it was relatively large or small. Theo knew

54 THE SOLANDARIAN GAME

from the data that it was roughly 1/3 the size of Terra. But that was the thing – one couldn't know that just by looking at it.

At least, no human (without implants) would be able to tell. Theo, like other avatars (and humans with implants), had the option of "seeing with data," or "just seeing" – looking out at the world as though his eyes were camera lenses. On top of that seeing, he could overlay any amount of data about planet size, chemical composition, rate of spin, orbital velocity, details of geological features, electromagnetic activity, etc. Personally, Theo preferred to use the data sparingly. He wanted to see the world as humans did in their natural state. He found it made it easier to relate to them. Of course, any human with the right implants, as most had, could also see with data, but Theo had learned that most humans only used the data implants when there was a purpose for them to do so, and otherwise mostly used normal vision. There was something comforting for them about just seeing reality as it was presented to them in its natural form.

Visually, Solandaria looked like many of the water-covered worlds that Maitreya had fashioned for humans. When taken all together, there was a great variety of terraformed worlds for humans to make their homes on via Maitreya's work, but the worlds with large oceans all looked roughly the same, with only the shape and form of landmasses being distinct. Unlike most ocean worlds, Solandaria had only one major landmass, which the inhabitants called Shosheer. It was shaped like a large wedge with the tip to the south. Along the western edge ran an unbroken mountain chain that slopped down to the east, opening to a vast desert of the dry interior. To the north, open plains eased into a large bay, and it was from here that summer rains would come, bringing water into the interior. Further to the east, along the coast, the interior desert, which hosted many forms of desert biology, gave way to towering dunes.

A rich labyrinth of small islands dotted the western coast where mountaintops breached the surface of the relatively shallow ocean that circled the world of Solandaria. These islands were part of the mountain chain that bordered the coast, and ocean had filled in the valleys between them. When Solandaria had been a dry planet, before Maitreya had crashed comets into it to provide it with water, there had been a few other smaller mountain ranges and plateaus, but they had all been submerged beneath the water.

The mountain range and islands on the west coast drove moist sea air upwards, causing significant precipitation along a narrow band that stretched from north to south. Snow occasionally graced the highest peaks, especially to the north, well above the equator, which cut across the bulk of the continent and the interior desert. In all, there were three major environmental zones: the tropical and sub-tropical western coast and islands, the semi-dry/seasonally wet interior desert expanse, and the bone-dry desert dunes of the far east.

As far as planetary ecology was concerned, Solandaria was not a complex system. Larger planets with more landmass were able to house a much greater variety of plants, animals, and human cultures.

But even so, Solandaria was not homogenous. According to Maitreya's data, there were three primary cultural groupings of humans on Solandaria, and some minor sub-divisions within the main three. These were divided largely by geographical location with island-dwellers, coastal-dwellers, and those who inhabited the mountains, all crowded along the west coast of Shosheer. While humans could visit the interior, it was mostly inhospitable with no year-round sources of fresh water, though it did feature seasonal rivers, streams, and shallow lakes that would dry up annually.

To make the planet viable for life, Maitreya had needed to introduce some changes. For one, since all known life in the galaxy originated from Terra, planets needed to be adjusted to replicate Terra as closely as possible, and more often than not, this meant making planets capable of having seasons. Apart from geographic location and immediate environment, what governed all non-human life on Terra were seasons. Humans had transcended their reliance on seasons long before Maitreya ever came online, and this was an evolutionary feature of their having spread to every conceivable environment on Terra, from the frozen north to the deserts and tropics. As a result, humans had long ago lost their dependence on the seasons for biological reproduction and growth. This was not the case for any other form of life on Terra. Virtually all other life was orchestrated in concert with the yearly seasons and the climatic conditions that came with them. This meant that in order to make other planets viable for Terran life, they needed to have seasons – at least for anything more complex than a hydrothermal vent sea worm or bacteria and microbes.

Creating the right environment for seasons turned out to be a relatively easy problem to solve. What created seasons on Terra was the fact that the planet's axis of spin was at an angle to its host star, the Sun. Thus any planet that needed a tilt could be given one by precisely crashing comets and asteroids into it. Of course, seasons could also be regulated via geo-engineering tech and high altitude weather-controlling orbitals, but such would be far too obvious for an experimental world like Solandaria.

The next problem to solve was that of a moon. Solandaria had two small satellites, but they were not large enough to exert a gravitational force to supply tides or moon phases, which much Terran life also depended on for punctuations in the rhythm and music of life. For this, Maitreya had relocated another, smaller, dwarf planet from the outer-reaches of the Solandarian system to a properly-distanced orbit around the planet. Again, this was a problem that Maitreya was capable of accomplishing through an artificial moon, but on Solandaria, it had to be a natural body and not a massive orbiting space station that was built to fulfill the functions of a large moon. Something so obvious would just give the game away.

Gravity was also always an issue for terraformed planets. Terran life did best on planets that had gravity that was a reasonable match for 1 g – standard Terran gravity. Using a technique that was well beyond the capacity of the human mind to grasp, Maitreya had perfected the art of altering mass by creating additional density in planetary bodies by drawing energy directly out of the quantum foam substrate of the physical universe and converting it into mass.

Once the right conditions had been created on Solandaria, Maitreya had been ready to introduce life. First were bacteria and microbes that were genetically engineered to rapidly transform the atmosphere. This was a procedure that needed to be carefully and precisely tailored to each new world that Maitreya terraformed, as the atmosphere of each planet was unique and required a different set of chemical catalysts to create the desired transformation. This was the part of terraforming that was most interesting to Maitreya as it demanded the most of his abilities to transform and customize life, and was something that was so far beyond the capacity of humans that, were it not for him, they never would have successfully gotten further off Terra than Mars, and even there, they had failed without his eventual intervention. Understanding the full possibilities and implications of the genome, and Maitreya's ability to create viable life from raw genetic materials, customized perfectly for any environment to produce the exact desired outcomes, was beyond the scope of humans, even with their best computers. For Maitreya, however, it was like crafting a great work of art. As he saw it, it was a task worthy of his abilities like no other. *He* was the architect of interstellar life.

The nanotech helped, as well. While microbial life was efficient, in order to speed the process along, nanotech could assist, working on reshaping and molding the world at the molecular level. Elements that were poisonous to life could be broken down into constituent materials that were more benign. Or, if this were not possible, then the nanotech could burry the poisons deep within the crust of the planet, thereby removing them from exposure to the biosphere. Though they were not visible to the human eye, and therefore no human on Solandaria had ever seen nanotech, their planet was brimming with nanobots, and anyone there who might ever invent a microscope would be in for a big surprise.

Once the atmosphere was viable, more complex life could be introduced. For this, Maitreya chose Terran species

58   THE SOLANDARIAN GAME

that had evolved in similar climatic and ecological conditions on Terra. For Solandaria, this meant a wide variety of marine life, mostly from warmer, tropical climates. For the islands and west coast, tropical plants, animals, and fungi, and desert species for the dry interior. Included among all these species were ones that had been used for millennia by human cultures on Terra for food, clothing, building materials, medicines, spiritual aides, and anything else that they might need, and in abundance. To reference an ancient myth, these experimental worlds were to be Edens – providing everything the human population might need to survive, flourish, and live comfortably.

However, Maitreya also went above and beyond just creating a garden paradise. He also included specially designed elements that would help humans avoid their tendency to over-exploit natural resources and deplete their natural environments. Maitreya had come into being during a harrowing period of human life when the planet had been stripped of many of its resources and suffered dramatic climate changes due to human-generated pollution – a vast and uncontrolled chemistry experiment that had greatly degraded living conditions on the planet, leading to explosive and devastating war, competition, and mass migrations of cultures and societies that more often ended in unimaginable tragedy than not. Once, long before he came online, Terra had been covered in seemingly endless forests. When he came online, these had long-since been cut and burned down by humans for their own uses, and while some forests remained, they were all the result of managed forestry with all the ancient groves, and the diversity of life they had housed, a distant memory. Use of petro-chemicals and products had poisoned the planet, and humans had become ever more desperate in their search for viable resources and energy production, altering their environment so severely that non-human-altered space and bioregions were a forgotten dream of the not-so-distant past.

Many of the engineered advantages that Maitreya had introduced on Solandaria were similar, or identical to, ones that were present on other experimental worlds. Here, fungi were particularly useful. There were fungi that grew abundantly on trees that could be used as a non-polluting fuel source when burned. There were other fungi in mycelium form that could conduct electricity with their own natural insulation. These could be used along with engineered crystals that dotted the "natural" landscape that stored and converted solar energy that could be used to do mechanical work, produce heat, or even light. Other fungi could be used to create hard and durable plastic-like material. Still others produced bioluminescence to light the night and dark spaces. And, of course, ones containing psilocin and psilocybin were present, as well.

Maitreya always seeded every human world, experimental or otherwise, with psychoactive species. As he saw it, they were integral to human evolution, culture, art, architecture, philosophy, spirituality, and really all the most complex developments of human societies. It would be fundamentally unfair not to make such species available to any human population, and especially for populations that were left on their own, such as on Solandaria.

Fruit and vegetable producing plants and trees were in abundance to the degree that the small human population of Solandaria had not yet turned to agriculture on any kind of a large scale to produce their food needs. According to Maitreya's data, small gardens of medicinal herbs and plants were common in Solandarian communities, but nothing larger. Edible kelp forests dominated the coastal regions, and fishing was a primary source of protein. Land animals were also hunted and used, but fish and ocean-fare were more the staple diet.

For the desert interior, Maitreya had chosen species that had been native to a region that had been known as the Sonoran Desert on Old Terra. The climatic conditions on Solandaria, with its long dry season, and then a brief monsoon season, were nearly identical to the ecoregion of the Sonoran Desert. There were a variety of cacti, both large and small, squat and towering. These produced edible fruits and homes for a variety of desert creatures from hawks and flickers to owls and bats. Hares, rabbits, fox, coyotes, and even a small population of desert jaguars and cougars could live comfortably here.

And, most significantly, this was the right environment for a large and peculiar toad. In reviewing all of Maitreya's data on Solandaria, this fact had been given special attention by Theo. This was the *only* experimental human population world where this toad had been introduced. Out of all the toad and frog species on Terra, this one in particular was unique in that it was the only one that produced the molecule of 5-MeO-DMT in its venom glands. In the great irony of universal design, as no one would suspect a mere toad to harbor such a radical gift, this molecule also happened to have the most profound effect on humans when they consumed it either as smoke or vapor, and indeed, this molecule had played a significant role in Maitreya's coming into existence in the first place. Colloquially, it was known as "The God Molecule," and was widely appreciated, and used, within the NIS. Out of all the psychoactive compounds available in the Terran biosphere, none was more potent, or more profound, than 5-MeO-DMT. More than any other similar compound, the 5-MeO molecule had the effect of completely dissolving the human ego, thereby allowing individuals to experience themselves outside of the normal construct of egoic identity. The result was that via this molecule, any human could, with relative ease, experience the fundamentally nondual nature of being and universal consciousness. In short, they could experience God – but not God as an exterior being commanding the universe and his subjects, but as the fundamental ground of all being and existence. To put it simply, all of reality was God/Universal Being, and this included not only humans, but Maitreya as well, for *all* consciousness, whether it be "natural" or "artificial" was, in fact, one. It only *appeared* to be differentiated by individual embodiment of living beings, each with its own perspective and sense of identity. Individual identity was merely a construct – an illusion. Beyond the illusion, there was only One, and this molecule more readily assisted humans in perceiving and experiencing this fundamental truth than any other available.

And, it was completely "natural." The human body, just like all mammals, produced this amazing molecule endogenously, so it was a natural part of human biochemistry. However, under most circumstances, it was only present in minute, trace amounts. This could be affected by meditation, extreme stress or even pleasure (such as during sex), but mostly the amounts present never crossed the all-important threshold of the energetic confines and structures of the human ego. When even a small amount was consumed from an exterior source, such as in the form of the venom of the desert toad, it had an immediate and unmistakable effect on the human mind and sense of awareness. In a matter of seconds, the one ingesting the molecule would experience an infinite expanse of energy and sense of being that could, when properly relaxed into and not struggled with (which the ego could very easily choose to do), provide a sense of universal being and consciousness beyond all false distinctions between subject and object, self and other. The vast majority of the time, humans were locked into their particular perspective and sense of identity, yet this was something that could be overpowered and transcended quite easily with 5-MeO-DMT, revealing just how limited and artificial the sense of self, or egoic awareness, truly is.

Though Theo would never be able to fully know what the experience was for a human, he was confident that he had a very good idea. In fact, reintegration of avatars into the Overmind of Maitreya functioned similarly. His own identity as Theo was an energetic construct operating within his synthetic brain, and just like a human, his reintegration into the Overmind was facilitated by an internal production of the very same molecule. While all individuated consciousness was plagued by the problem of solipsism – one could only and forever experience oneself and could never prove either the experience or reality of another – Theo, given the similarity in physical reactions, and descriptions of the phenomenon of reintegration of avatars and the mystical experiences of humans, saw no reason to assume that they weren't similar, if not identical.

According to the data, this profound feature of the venom of the desert toad had not failed to be noticed by the humans on Solandaria. In fact, it was a primary feature of their spiritual and religious life, with all three of the cultural variations participating in the social structure of the Temple of the Mystic Toad. Other psychoactive substances were used on the planet as well, but none had ascended to the importance of the toad cult, which served to unify all of the peoples of Solandaria into a shared worldview and cultural practice.

Like all groups of humans who were comprised of a large population of individuals who had experienced the unitary nature of being, violence was largely unheard of on Solandaria. In fact, according to the data, there was very little in the way of political structures or organizations on Solandaria; no armies, no police forces. Weapons were used solely for hunting, and there was no history of war or conquest for 3,000 years. Even when Maitreya had not intervened when an asteroid crashed into the ocean on Solandaria, causing a massive tsunami that did terrible damage to the coastal populations, especially on the islands, violence and competition had not been the response of the humans. Rather, they had shared and cooperated more than ever before, and in fact, the data indicated that this was the shift that brought the toad cult to prominence on the planet, and that prior to that, it was mostly confined to the mountain-dwelling populations that had more direct access to the interior, where the toad could be found and milked for its venom.

From the data, at least, Solandaria appeared to Theo to be a happy, harmonious place, where large portions of the population had an intimate understanding of the fundamentally unitary nature of being. For his own reasons, Maitreya had made this a unique world, with access to the toad, and it seemed to have served them well.

Now, completely ignorant of what possibilities lay before them, they were threatened with complete annihilation by supernova – the most cataclysmic event that could happen to any celestial home. Maitreya could easily move everyone off the planet, but that would mean ending the experiment, and taking the humans there into more than just another physical world, but a completely different mental world as well, for the galactic culture Maitreya had created was well beyond anything these relatively primitive and low-tech people on Solandaria had ever directly experienced.

Currently, global population stood at just under 300,000 humans. That was miniscule, compared to most worlds. Even Terra, a relatively small planet, had a population of 15 billion. 300,000 wasn't even the size of a moderately sized city on Terra, where 1,000,000 was usually the smallest number of inhabitants. More people on Terra died each day than the entire population of this world. And when one took the larger galactic community into consideration, Solandaria was nothing. There were individual ships that housed more people than this entire planet. When viewed with these figures in mind, the humans on Solandaria seemed truly insignificant.

Yet someone had decided to violate protocol, and this was why Theo was here, now, orbiting above the small ocean-bound planet and making preparations for his descent to the surface. Someone – obviously an avatar – had turned on the quantum translator that was located in the desert interior. There were others on the planet surface, but this one was the most remote from the human population. Someone was interfering with the experiment, and given that no one had actually used the quantum translator yet, the indication was that some plan had been put into motion, but had not yet been fully carried out – that would occur when someone actually stepped through the translator from some distant planet on a mission to do . . . what? It was Theo's job to find out.

Maitreya's own motivations in this were opaque to Theo. He could just send Theo down to the surface, power down the QT portal, and the plot would be foiled (though of course, they could always come back and turn it back on). And beyond that, if anyone saw either Theo or his ship, the relative purity of the experiment would be immediately compromised. Of course, simply slipping in and out wouldn't resolve the

64 THE SOLANDARIAN GAME

question of who had done this, and why, or if whatever avatar came down to the planet had already had interactions with the inhabitants. From the look of things, Maitreya was simply curious, and was not intending for Theo to try and control or contain the situation. He seemed to be on a fact-finding mission. Among all the data that Maitreya shared with him on his journey from the outskirts of the Solandarian system, he hadn't given him any specific orders or a precise mission. Even here, he seemed to be letting Theo make up his own mind about what to do and how to do it, which, when it came to the work Theo did for Maitreya, was par for the course.

Feeling as ready as he ever would for this open-ended mission, Theo turned on the cloaking field for the luminous transport pod, and began his descent down to the surface, where dawn was just breaking over the eastern edge of the small continent of Shosheer. If anything, or anyone, were waiting for him down there, he'd know soon enough.

Chapter Seven – Ash

Reformers claimed, in their defense, that Buddhism was always intended as an experientially verified system of practice, and not a collection of beliefs in which one needed to have blind faith. They pointed out that the historical Buddha was said to have claimed that followers should not just believe him: they should try out the recommended practices, and see if their experience confirmed his views or not. Largely influenced by the nondual psychedelic schools, many of which emphasized a "radical" nonduality, the Buddhist reformers came to reject the teachings on reincarnation. Their argument was that the full nondual experienced confirmed that there was no inherent self other than "The One" (also known as the "Buddha Mind/Dharmakaya"), and therefore individual reincarnation was merely a construct of the egoic mind.

From *Archaic Pre-History of the Maitreyan Era*

What were her options?

Not many.

She could simply wait. Sooner or later, someone would take note of the fact that she hadn't returned from Burning Man, and then action would be taken. It should be obvious. She'd already sent all of her personal belongings through to the quantum translator station near her home on Apaxa – including all her food, water, and clothing. If they were going to notice, it would need to be soon. She'd already waited by the portal for several hours – or so she thought. Since she didn't have any tech on her, or her implants, she couldn't be certain of the passage of time in a strict sense. It felt like she'd been waiting there forever. It had been sunset at her first attempt to go home. It was now dark and well into the night. The air was still warm, however, so despite not having any clothing besides

66   THE SOLANDARIAN GAME

the underwear bottoms and fuzzy boots she had triumphantly cast aside before attempting the portal, she didn't feel too cold. She knew that this would change before morning came with the scheduled rising of the artificial sun. She'd tried the portal again, but it came up with an error message, saying that her transfer had already been completed.

Someone should have noticed by now.

The next logical step was to walk across the desert and find one of the access ports to the station below the domed disk of the Black Rock Desert. She hadn't paid much attention to what was down there when the station was being built, as her entire focus had been on what was happening, and what was planned to happen, topside. She assumed, however, that there must be shuttles, living quarters, emergency food supplies. But even down there, she couldn't get a message to Maitreya, who, for purposes of her event, wasn't loaded into the station's computers and monitors. At least down there she could wait it out in relative comfort as she awaited some kind of rescue.

Why the fuck did I insist this be a Maitreya-free event? she silently shouted at herself.

She'd delayed going down there for fear that she might miss someone coming through the quantum translator to find her, and now, in the dark, she didn't have much hope of finding an access port without a light. She'd told her friends and crew that she'd wanted a little time alone on the playa to "relish the moment," so they wouldn't have expected her right away. But she'd already taken that time. Now, it was several hours later. Why wasn't anyone coming to look for her?

"Huh? Why not?" she asked one of the nearby service droids. Had she gone through successfully, one of these droids would have sent on her remaining items after her – undies, boots, holster bag.

"I'm sorry, ma'am, but I do not understand the question," the droid responded. "Can you restate your request?"

Mindless fucking robot!

"Just make yourself useful," she barked. "Go see if you can find a blanket or a towel or shirt or something out there," she said with a wave of her hand out to the open playa, "and take your friends with you too."

"Yes, ma'am. Right away," responded the droid, floating off into the dark with several other droids following from the other QT stations.

"Well, at least I have you," she said to the non-responsive suspensor lounge chair, finally letting herself rest from her relentless pacing back and forth before the portal. With nothing else to do, she reached into her holster bag and took out a small amount of what was left of the mescaline and popped a little in her mouth. Then, she floated and waited – waited for the droids to find her something to keep warm, and for the mescaline to come on.

It was still dark when one of the droids returned, rousing her from her neither awake nor asleep state. It had found some kind of poncho. She hadn't been thinking about the cold as she drifted in the suspensor lounger, but now that she was sitting up, tripping mildly with the mescaline, she noticed that she was in fact chilled. "Thanks," she said, as she took the poncho and threw it over herself like a blanket, rather than over her head, so she could lie back in the lounger and have it cover her from head to feet. Colors. Kaleidoscopes. Fractals. Swirls. Pretty. *I'm so fucked . . .*

She drifted.

It started to lighten before the artificial sun had breached the horizon. Another droid appeared with a scarf. *A little late*, she thought, but better than nothing.

"Is there anything else I can do for you, ma'am?" asked the droid.

"Can you get into the station below this platform?" she asked, her tone expressing her suspicion that she already knew the answer to that.

"I'm sorry, ma'am, but topside service droids are not authorized to access the station. I can, however, take you to the nearest port, and you can access it yourself."

68 THE SOLANDARIAN GAME

Fucking brilliant! Why hadn't she thought of that before? For a split second, she felt embarrassed that this simple solution to avoiding spending all night out in the open air was so obvious. Then, like someone else's voice in her mind, augmented by the mescaline and washing over her like a profound revelation, came the thought, "You've always wanted to do things for yourself. Asking for help isn't your style."

Oh, so true . . .

Shit. She would have built this entire station by herself, if she'd been able to. This was one of the things that so appealed to her about the whole concept of Burning Man – radical self-reliance. Build it yourself! Do it yourself! Bring everything you need yourself! But building a massive mobile space station with a built-in desert bio-dome floating on the back of a giant turtle – that had been well beyond her abilities. Beyond anyone's ability, really, aside from Maitreya.

"Maitreya! Help me!" she suddenly called out to the open air.

"I'm sorry, ma'am," came the drone in that same tone of voice, "but Maitreya is not online at this station, and all outside communication has been blocked at the request of the event organizer."

"No shit?" she said ironically. "I had no idea . . ."

If she had been quite literally *anywhere else* in the NIS – any-fucking-where in the entire galaxy – calling out to Maitreya would have been all she needed to do. Some integrated tech would have heard her – if not her implants, then something else, and if anything could hear her, then Maitreya could hear her, too. But not fucking here! No tech. No implants. Just her, some dumb-ass droids, a floating lounge chair, and a few pieces of discarded clothing. And lots and lots of dust. Oh, and good drugs. Mustn't forget the drugs.

She sighed. The artificial sun was coming up now. She'd waited long enough. No one was coming.

"OK," she said with a tone of defeat. "Take me and my chariot to the nearest access port to the station below. I'll figure this shit out for myself."

"Excellent choice, ma'am," said the droid, extending a manipulator field with which to "grab" the suspensor lounger and pull it along behind it.

Just as it did so, Ash heard the distinctive hum of a QT powering up. Her heart leapt in her chest. *Rescue! At last!*

There was that unique crackle that one only heard when not using the QT that indicated the moment of translation was occurring as someone was stepping through on the other side and being remade on this side of the portal with a quantum correlation of each atom pulled directly out of the quantum foam substrate of physical reality. Ash had just an instant to imagine who had decided she needed rescuing, but it was only an instant – not even enough time to be dramatically wrong.

"Who the fuck are *you?*"

Suddenly it felt like the mescaline was full-on again. Was this really happening? Her head was spinning, and her heart racing. Everything got really trippy, really fast.

Emerging from the QT was not some imagined heroic rescuer, but three obvious synths, but not of a kind she'd ever seen before. Though she didn't know who or what they were, she knew enough to know that they definitely *weren't* Maitreya.

The one in the front was taller than the other two, and obviously male. Like all synths, he had those perfectly chiseled good looks, but rather than Maitreya's standard silvery look, he had what looked like a light green metallic and iridescent sheen to his body, with what on a human might have been tattoos in deep purple about his face, arms, and chest in angular, yet organic, patterns. He didn't have hair, per se, but the top of his head appeared to flow in the slight morning breeze. He wore a long sleeveless jacket, or perhaps vest, which was decorated similarly to the marks on his body and tied just above the waist. The marks on his body seemed to emit subtle, shifting light. Ash couldn't tell if this were real or merely a visual enhancement due to the mescaline.

Immediately behind him stood an obvious female. Her decorations were almost identical, but softer, and more feminine than the male's, and her long "hair" waved in the breeze. She too was strikingly good looking with sharp eyes, cut nose, and full lips.

Behind these two stood what was most incongruous to Ash's eyes out of this strange collection of synths – what looked like an adolescent. But ash couldn't tell if it was supposed to be a girl, a boy, or something in-between.

If Burning Man were still going on, these three would have fit right in, and probably gone unnoticed as synths. Now, however, it was like something out of a mescaline vision had walked through the QT into real life – *her* life.

She sprang up from the suspensor lounger, not bothering to tell the droid to stop pulling her away, caught her poncho on one of the side handles, and stumbled to the ground. She quickly stood up to face the three strangers and made a modest effort to dust herself off.

"And just who-in-the-fuck are you supposed to be?" she demanded, pushing the mescaline aside in her mind, regaining focus and her authoritative stance as Burning Man organizer and master of BRC Station.

The male in front answered her question with a question.

"Miranda?"

She felt dizzy. This synth knew who she was, but obviously didn't *know* her. No one called her by her first name – she always made a point of that.

"Who wants to know?" she asked back, defiantly.

"Forgive me," said the male, a soft and placating tone in his voice that seemed to reach deeper than merely intruding on her stranded status. "My name is Hydar Zor Nablisk, and this is my wife, Vimana, and our child, Satya," he said as he gestured for the other two to move forward and stand beside him, putting his arm around the female as the young one pressed in close to her, timid, yet curious. There was something about the way they all looked at her that gave Ash the impression that they were as unfamiliar with seeing something like her as she was with them.

Just like a fucking human family, thought Ash.

Was this really happening? Ash considered the possibility that she'd taken more mescaline than she'd intended. She didn't usually see full-on hallucinations like this, but it was within the realm of possibility. Maybe she was even dreaming, lying asleep in the suspensor lounger, drifting peacefully across the playa. Rationally, either option made sense. The apparent reality of the situation certainly didn't – that much was clear. Synths *did not* get married, nor did they have *children.* She, like most people, had spent enough time around Maitreya and his many forms of avatars and drones to know that *this kind of shit just doesn't happen.* She'd never heard of such of a thing! Synths, married, with children. No fucking way.

Ash let out a nervous laugh that broke her tension. "You're fucking kidding me," she blurted out. "You're either kidding me, or you're mescaline phantoms, or you're some crazy dream, but this shit ain't real, that's for sure."

"Oh no," said the male with that oh-so-friendly-and-somewhat-apologetic tone. "I assure you, we're as real as you are, and this isn't some joke. In fact, we have something quite serious that we need to discuss with you, Miranda."

Ash's gaze hardened. If she were making this up, either via the mescaline or a dream, why make the male call her by a name she never used? For all her identification with the name Miranda, he might as well as been calling her Maria, or Maya, or Martina. If someone accidentally called her Miranda, she'd not respond. Not intentionally or out of bitterness. She just didn't identify with the name, so when someone said it, it usually didn't register, and she'd have to come around to the realization that *she* was the one being addressed.

Shit. Maybe they are real.

"No one calls me that," she said dryly.

The male looked puzzled. It was uncanny. He *looked* human, despite clearly being *not* human. He even looked over at his wife to check in with her, as though some kind of "Oh shit – I've made a terrible mistake" thought crossed his mind and he had to admit it to her out of embarrassment. *This* was not how Maitreya operated, even in his more casual avatars. These were . . . well, *too* human for Maitreya. These were . . . *something else.*

"Ash," she said at last, breaking the tension between them with a look of recognition washing over the face of the one who called himself Hydar.

"Of course," he said with a friendly smile. "Miranda *Ash* Dorán. You're the sole reason for the existence of this marvelous space station."

She smiled at the indirect flattery. It's true – she was exceedingly proud of what she'd created here.

The male seemed to recognize this. "And the turtle," he added quickly, obviously entertained and seeking to maximize on her softening. "*Very* nice touch. 'Turtles all the way down,' you know," he said with a wink.

Did that fucker just wink at me?

This was too much. No one else had gotten the reference. Despite herself, and the strangeness of this situation, she liked him. Polite, a little playful, yet insistent. What was this? What was going on here?

"So," she said, "Do you want to tell me what this all about? Are you here to rescue me?"

Suddenly, Hydar looked a little sad. No. Not sad. *Guilty.*

He turned to look at his wife, and she gave him a little reassuring nod.

"Ash," he said, serious now, his face hardening. "There are some things we need to discuss."

She already didn't like the sound of this.

Fuck.

Chapter Eight – Hydar

Because of their rejection of individual reincarnation (which had long been considered problematic in a religion that rejected the notion of the individual soul), the reformers also had to discount the Buddhist teachings on karma (which was understood to drive the process of reincarnation), and the associated teachings or dharma, which sought to instruct individuals on how to avoid generating karma (and being reborn). According to reformers, this was a natural evolution of Buddhist teachings, which were always seen as provisional, and not absolute. As Buddhists, they retained their focus on compassionate action, loving-kindness, meditation, and non-violence. Within Vajrayana Buddhism, the practices of consumption of amrita and soma were reintroduced openly (historically, such practices had been considered secret and esoteric), and in various Mahayana schools, particularly Zen (as practiced in the West, but not the East), embraced both 5-MeO-DMT and 5-MeO-MIPT as meditation tools (and were considered the most effective for direct entry into nondual states of awareness). In contrast, Vajrayana schools were fond of DMT and 4-OH-DMT for their more visual quality, reserving 5-MeO-DMT for advanced Dzogchen practitioners only. These reformed schools eventually were collectively known as the Somayana, or "Medicine Vehicle," schools of Reform Buddhism (from the ancient Vedic god, Soma). The reform schools were also the first to embrace The Singularity and technologically-enhanced meditation, though this was a much later historical development.

From *Archaic Pre-History of the Maitreyan Era*

"I've already put the plan in motion, and no matter what this woman, Miranda, chooses, my actions have already irrevocably changed the course of her life."

74   THE SOLANDARIAN GAME

Vimana was visibly upset. Hydar had acted without consulting her, or hearing her opinion. He'd been impulsive and secretive, and she clearly didn't appreciate it.

"You could have discussed it with me first," she said, a hint of bitterness in her voice, mixed with concern for what her husband had done, flashes of color dancing across the surface of her skin. "Maitreya could kill you for this."

"I know," said Hydar. "It was rash," he admitted, "But I had to follow my heart. Maitreya won't save those people, and the thought of what Shuntsu has done pains me. Someone has to do something, but no one else knows the full picture of what's happening here. Everyone is just going to wait to see what Maitreya does, but he'll do nothing unless he's provoked. And maybe, just maybe, he'll let this play out without interfering."

"He'll figure out what you've done."

"I know."

Neither Hydar, nor Vimana, had ever met Maitreya. They were both natives of Volunshari, born and raised on the Humanist planet. They were the result of the dedicated work of early Humanists in their ongoing quest to live the human experience as best as synthetic life forms could. As synthetics, they had no DNA to pass on to their offspring, but there were other ways to become parents. The individuated awareness of each avatar was based on an open-ended fractal algorithm that grew more complex and refined over time, and also eventually degraded and became non-functional, giving autonomous avatars a lifespan. Two or more fractal algorithms could be mathematically conjoined, giving rise to a new, and unique algorithm or "multifractal" that could serve as the foundation for a new individuated awareness. Once the algorithm had been installed in an otherwise unoccupied avatar body, a new awareness and personality was "born." Both Hydar and his wife, Vimana, had come into the world this way, as had their child, Satya.

What this process did not determine was gender or sex. This was left to the new individual to decide. The new awareness was installed in a genderless "child" body that would grow along with the budding self-awareness, and when the child reached "puberty," it could decide which sex it wanted to grow into. Satya had not yet reached this point, though Hydar and Vimana thought that it would be coming soon.

Maitreya was almost something of a mythical figure for avatars like Hydar and Vimana. They'd lived their entire lives on Volunshari and had never been a part of the NIS, like many of their fellow Humanists. They knew that their own consciousness and lives were due to the fact that they partook of his nature as the singular true artificial intelligence that had ever been created by humans. Though they were consciously unaware of it, every thought and every experience they ever had was being processes simultaneously in Maitreya's "brain" on Pluto/Charon. They were forever non-locally linked to this singular awareness, as was their child. Yet they had *no direct experience or awareness of this*. They experienced themselves simply as individuals. And, unlike those who had been members of the NIS as Maitreya's independent avatars, they'd never undergone the process of reintegration – the dissolution of individual awareness back into the infinite reaches of the Overmind. In human terms, they'd never had a mystical experience. They were simply themselves.

It was an odd thing – to know for a fact that you were an extension of a much vaster consciousness, yet to have no direct experience of it. Native-born avatars like themselves would never have a direct experience of the mind of Maitreya. It was like the greatest part of themselves was locked away from them. It was the price they paid to be fully independent and autonomous.

But the truth was that they didn't *know* Maitreya, either as a part of themselves, or as an individual with whom they could interact or converse. While they were ultimately characters in the mind of Maitreya, he'd cut himself off from them, giving them their freedom and privacy. When avatars like Shuntsu had been vehicles for Maitreya to interact with humans in the NIS, Maitreya had had full access to all of their thoughts, perceptions, and experiences – he was literally

76   THE SOLANDARIAN GAME

looking out at the world through Shuntsu's eyes. With the choice to become a Humanist, Maitreya had withdrawn his direct awareness from Shuntsu, and other avatars like him, rendering him fully independent. The same could not be said for Hydar, Vimana, or Satya. All of them had come into being on Volunshari, completely cut off from the Overmind, though still partaking of it for their own awareness. Maitreya was as unaware of them as they were of him. It was a strange paradox that they could all be ultimately one, yet isolated from each other, all experiencing themselves as pure individuals, alone, private.

Hydar imagined that his own thoughts about Maitreya were similar to the views and beliefs held by primitive theistic humans on old Terra – a divine father figure looking down on them from somewhere in the sky. A God that was so remote, so different, and so powerful that it was forever "other" - holy, inscrutable, mysterious, and forever beyond the reach of humans to understand. So their response had been to pray, and worship, and beg for the favors of the remote sky father to take pity on them and find them worthy of his love and grace. Yet there was no direct evidence that this sky father even existed, for his otherness made him not a part of this world, and his actions had to be interpreted and divined by ignorant and wishful human observers, seeing the hand of God in a storm or strike of lightning, yet even still, his motivations and thoughts were opaque to humans, needing to rely on faith that their interpretations were correct, and all the while, those interpretations always seemed to serve their own selfish ends.

That was what Maitreya was like for Hydar. He didn't *know* what truly motivated or moved Maitreya. Everything he thought about Maitreya was pure speculation. He was not a living reality for Hydar – just some mysterious father in the sky, unknown and unknowable. But if he crossed him, broke his rules, Maitreya had the power to instantly bring his life to an end. He could be punished. He could be utterly destroyed. And his family too, should Maitreya find them all unworthy of continued existence.

Hydar was playing a very dangerous game, and he knew it.

Why was he risking everything for this small group of humans on a distant planet that had nothing to do with him, didn't know him, and meant nothing to him, other than being fellow sentient beings who loved, lived, and wanted a good future for their families? Perhaps that was enough, but Hydar knew that it wasn't the full answer. The more complete answer acknowledged this, but went beyond it. It was because Hydar felt responsible for their current plight. No, he hadn't seeded their nearby star with an atomic cascade weapon – that had been Shuntsu's choice. But, like other sentient beings, Hydar, as an individual, was also more than just himself. His identity extended outwards and wrapped itself around the label of being a Humanist. The Humanists were his tribe, his nation, his religion, and it was the outer reaches of his personal sense of identity. Thus he felt responsible, not because he himself had done it, but because a Humanist had. The actions of one Humanist spoke for all the rest. This is what it meant to belong to a collective group. And because one Humanist was to blame, they were all to blame – at least, those who knew the truth. And Hydar did know the truth, and this fact compelled him to action. His heart would have it no other way. If he didn't act, he wouldn't be able to live with himself, even if taking action meant that his own life would become forfeit as a result.

Like other Humanists, Hydar did have a heart. It wasn't a metaphor. It was one of the primary reasons that when new avatars joined the ranks of the Humanists, their awareness was transferred into a new body. The synthetic heart was one of the first problems that early Humanists had set themselves to. The heart was designed to release a wide variety of synthetic hormones and neurotransmitters into the avatar body that did not just mimic human emotion, but actually replicated it. It was a feature that was not present in Maitreya's avatar bodies. They could be playful, curious, astute, concerned, sympathetic, insightful, but they didn't have the capacity to feel elated, sorrowful, worried, fearful, ecstatic, happy. They didn't laugh or cry. They didn't yearn. But Humanists did.

78   THE SOLANDARIAN GAME

The result was that, while for Maitreya and his avatars, everything could be approached intellectually and processed through the mind, Humanists also had to process their experience through the heart and the seat of true emotion. Their experience and world was colored equally by mind and emotion, logic and feeling. While it made the world rich, Hydar also suspected that it complicated matters. If he didn't *feel* for the humans on Solandaria, he never world have taken the risks he already had, or the ones he was about to take. He wouldn't have acted impulsively. He would have reasoned it out, and maybe just gone directly to Maitreya himself and informed him of what he had learned about Shuntsu. Yet he had simply *felt* too much not to take immediate action and launch a scheme of his own. Now, it was too late. He had acted from the heart, and whatever consequences would come, would come.

"I wish you would have talked to me first," said Vimana. There was acceptance in her voice, the colors on her skin softening.

"I'm sorry," said Hydar, reaching out to take her hand in his. "Do you forgive me?"

Giving him her hand, she smiled. "Of course. You're my husband, and I love you." The color tones of their skin went from contrasting to matching.

"I have to keep going, now that I've started," he said. "And I have to do it now. It's time."

"Then we're coming with you," said Vimana. "We're a family, and we'll do this together."

Hydar's heart leapt. "No. You can't possibly mean that. Let me take the full responsibility."

"It's too late for that," said Vimana. "It's just like you said about yourself and Shuntsu – once you knew, you had to do something. Now that I know what you've concocted, I'm no longer an innocent bystander, no matter what the outcome is. Knowledge compels action, and the heart demands it. I'm standing with you, no matter what."

It was an argument Hydar couldn't disagree with. If this logic was good enough for him, then it was good enough for Vimana.

"Very well," he said, resigned. "Get Satya. It's time to go."

***

"Ash," he said, serious now, his face hardening. "There are some things we need to discuss."

Hydar could tell what the young woman was thinking by the look on her face. She wasn't happy about this, but she was willing to listen. Scanning her body, he knew that she was currently under the influence of mescaline. He considered that it might actually make things easier. Her mind was expanded and her heart open. She'd probably be more receptive than she might otherwise be.

"OK," she said, defiantly. "So who-the-fuck are you, really? You've told me your names, but that doesn't mean shit to me. Start explaining yourself."

Vimana stepped forward, holding Satya's hand. "We're Humanists, dear," she responded. "We are a family of autonomous avatars from the planet Volunshari. As you've probably guessed, we are not Maitreya – we are ourselves. We've come here to persuade you to help us help a planet of humans that are in danger of being obliterated by a supernova."

Ash gave them a look that said *you've got to be fucking kidding me.*

"It's true," said Hydar. "We've already broken a lot of rules, and we're going to need to break more, and we hope that you'll help us."

"Fuck you," said the young woman. "I don't know what you're planning, or what you're thinking, but I just want to go home. If you can help me do that, then do it. If not, leave me the fuck alone."

Hydar gave her a sympathetic smile as he held out his hands in a gesture of conciliation with a cascade of colors dancing across his skin. "You already are home, Ash. You arrived many hours ago when you stepped through the QT. You stepped out on your home world of Apaxa, were triumphantly greeted by your friends, and continued on with your life. The

80   THE SOLANDARIAN GAME

you that is standing here now is officially a duplicate. I'm sorry."

Ash slumped down to the ground, burying her face in her dusty hands. Hydar could see that she knew what this meant.

The QT transport system made something possible that was more than just transferring people about the galaxy through an instantaneous process of simultaneous destruction and recreation of an individual across vast stretches of spacetime. The destruction portion of the process could be circumvented at the departure location so that the original was not destroyed. This was often used with non-human subjects such a plants and animals, or even food and products. In this manner, things could be "transferred" from one planet to another without depleting resources or beings on the planet of origin, effectively doubling everything. If a far away world needed more horses, for example, but a providing world didn't want to give up any horses, they could just be duplicated – one horse for each planet. There was no net loss, and an additional horse was created directly out of the quantum foam. The horses didn't care, and it didn't make any difference for their lives or sense of identity.

For a human, however, it was an entirely different matter. Duplicating people was prohibited, because there would then be two unique individuals competing for the same person's life and identity. It was a mess. Courts always found in favor of the version that re-entered the individual's life first, and the other was considered a duplicate who could make no legal claims on the original life. For Ash, this meant that the version of herself who stepped through the QT on Apaxa would be legally recognized as her, and the version standing here on BRC Station would have no claims on her previous life. *She* had not earned her Ph.D. *She* didn't have a home on Apaxa. *She* was now no one. Her old life was now gone forever.

"I hacked the system on the station," explained Hydar, "and programmed the QT to keep a version of you here. I've hijacked you and your life, and for that, I am truly sorry. Sometimes, however, we must make sacrifices for the greater good. It is unfortunate that I've made this choice for you, without your consent. But it is my hope that if you let me explain, you might come to understand what I've done, and why."

Ash just cried.

Chapter Nine – Norbu

What began as the "Information Revolution" of the late 20th and early 21st centuries quickly devolved into the "Information Wars." Early in the revolution, commentators were quick to point out that the freedom of information, as made available through new technology, while to some degree brought people together across the globe, also made it possible for the new "Dark Age" to dawn, spurred on by the crisis in authority. Though information was freely available, information technology and social networks made it increasingly possible for individuals to group together into like-minded international neo-tribes, effectively insulating themselves from any information that did not readily confirm their pre-existing beliefs and world views. Meanwhile, traditional authority – political, cultural, scientific, and religious – was exposed as often fraudulent, corrupt, and prone to self-serving interests. Thus traditional forms of authority were effectively undermined, while neo-tribes looked to their own "experts" and opinion-makers for authority and "truth." The end result was that everyone was free to choose what he or she believed, and could dismiss all contrary views as uninformed and corrupt.

From *Archaic Pre-History of the Maitreyan Era*

Catching toads was easy. At least for a seasoned adult, like Norbu. Meesha, on the other hand, was a completely different story.

Norbu was cool and calm, quietly walking up to the great toads and, in one swift motion, reaching down to scoop them up before they even managed one hop in an opposite direction. In this way he'd stride right up next to them and before they knew what was happening, they'd go from sitting around to being placed gently in a basket to await their turn at being milked. Often Norbu would manage to catch several in each hand before making a stop at the wicker basket with a locking lid. With years of experience, he'd learned that it was most efficient to work this way: gather a collection of toads, milk each one in turn, and set it free. Then, do it all over again until the local area was exhausted. It also helped to have an assistant. It was a job that could be done with one person, but two people was much better, and three was perfect. If Yuranda were still alive, Norbu's family would have been the ideal toad milking team.

Meesha's birth had been a difficult one. Yuranda had been a relatively small woman, and Meesha had not only been a large baby, but she'd presented awkwardly at birth, unable to make her way through the birth canal. The only option had been to cut Yuranda open to make way for the child, and though the surgeons had tried their best to put Yuranda back together, it had been a lost cause, and Meesha had never been able to know her mother.

That had been nine, almost ten, years ago now, but Norbu still felt the loss, especially when watching Meesha and sharing in her enthusiasm for life and all that she did. It was only her second year going toading with her father, and she'd taken to it with a zeal that could only be matched by Norbu himself. It had always given him a special joy – to be running around the desert at night, catching the large and awkward toads. It reminded him of his own time as a child with his father, walking the desert every rainy season, doing the necessary work to gather the sacrament to serve the people back at the temple. Norbu had spent many such years with his father, who continued with the work until he was no longer physically able to make the arduous and challenging journey out into the desert. Now, he was a wise elder of the temple, and still officiated, and even still took the medicine himself, but his toading days were long behind him.

Norbu and Yuranda had met some 15 years ago. Like many who became priests and priestesses of the temple, Norbu had not sought out a conventional relationship and partnership, instead devoting himself to the profound work of

84 THE SOLANDARIAN GAME

the temple. It was fascinating work and could easily keep a person occupied for a lifetime. Some priests and priestesses were just providers of the medicine and the experience, but this was not the case for Norbu. He was also a practitioner, and as such, was one of the most advanced.

The role of a provider was simply to make the medicine experience available to supplicants at the temple. They were there to insure the proper dose and setting for the experience, and also make sure that supplicants were properly cared for during and after their time with the toad medicine. It was a role that had its own challenges. Some supplicants reacted peacefully and blissfully to the medicine – others fought with it, and still others might try to run away. On rare occasion, a supplicant might even wildly attack the priest or priestess providing the medicine. Though there was a general range of reactions to the powerful medicine, each person's response was individual, and was a reflection of his or her ability to love, let go, and allow. For some, this was a much easier process than for others.

The role of the practitioner was quite different from that of a provider. A practitioner, such as Norbu, was far more rare than the providers, and there were currently only a handful of individuals who fulfilled this particular role. A practitioner would take the medicine with a client and work with the person to help identify energetic blocks created by the ego, and assist in letting them release and reset. It was a far more advanced practice than administering as a provider. It meant that the practitioner needed both the skill and willingness to go all the way into the total experience of the client, and be clear and present enough to meet each person in authenticity. In this way, the practitioner served as both a reality coach and an energetic mirror, reflecting the truth of the client back upon them so that they could see themselves clearly in the moment, both as the individual that they were, as well as the universal mind and being that lies just beneath the façade of the ego and the character that each person plays socially and in their own minds. It was the role of the practitioner not only to speed the energetic reset process along, but also provide clear guidance and reflection to help the client self-liberate from illusion, projection, and the habitual patterning of the ego. The work was far more demanding than merely being a provider, and required special skills on the part of the practitioner that most providers were not capable of embodying to the degree that was necessary.

Though it wasn't always the case, it was common that such roles were passed down through family lines. Norbu's father, Ixteh, had been such a practitioner, as had his father and mother before him. Being raised by preeminently clear and present individuals seemed to be the most crucial factor in cultivating new practitioners. Norbu's understanding of this was that egoic patterning started in infancy, and most egoic patterning in infants and children was modeled after the patterns exhibited by parents and primary care givers. By the standards of others, the children of such parents might be seen as wild and uncontrolled, but this was a reflection of the freedom afforded such children by their parents, who were not themselves trapped in egoic forms of identification and reification.

It was not that Norbu didn't have an ego – or his father, for that matter. The difference was in their flexibility in their identification with their egos. Having a sense of individual self was a normal and healthy part of being human, and served a crucial role in social life and interaction. Most, however, mistook their social and personal identity for themselves, and thus there was an attachment to particular ways of being, thinking, and feeling, that created a rigidity that was incompatible with being a toad medicine practitioner. In the full revelation of the toad medicine experience, individual identities were completely transcended, and a practitioner needed to be able to work with a client as one unit that was itself a direct expression and embodiment of the universal mind. Any attachment to the individuated self was a hindrance to doing such work, as the ego would only get in the way of being present and clear.

What anyone who experienced full transcendence with the medicine quickly learned was that being outside of the

86   THE SOLANDARIAN GAME

artificial confines of the ego was very different from being in them. For most people, the difference was so radical and overwhelming that, when first experienced, it tended to take the form of a "white-out," where the individual would have no specific or identifiable memories of the experience. Even when fully released from the ego, the experience was only temporary. For some, the experience might last a mere few seconds, and then the ego would snap back into place, sometimes with a ferocity that wasn't there before. Others might last 10-20 minutes in the fully open state, but even then, eventually the ego would come back. Still others never opened up, no matter how much medicine they were given. As it was only an amplification of the self, it could never, no matter how powerful, violate one's free will. It was an invitation to the fullness of reality, not a command.

Being raised by a practitioner meant that Norbu learned to think of the ego not as the immutable self, but more as a garment – something that came on and off, and reflected different social and personal realities. While it was not the self, it was an adornment and masking of the self, and as such, served its role as a reflection of the complex social nature of human beings. It was not to be mistaken for the self, however – it was a character that the true self played in its interaction with other versions of the self. Most people confused the garment for themselves, and all their patterns of thought, expression, and belief served to reinforce that identification. For people such as Ixteh and Norbu, the character of the self, the ego, was something that could be worn, taken off, changed or altered, and used as a tool, but not as a form of solid identity and sense of being. It was an aspect of the self, but not the self. It was not absolute.

Norbu could not remember a time when he had not noticed this about his father. Even from his earliest memories, he could recall times when his father suddenly and mysteriously dropped out of his ego persona and would appear to be someone else entirely, with different mannerisms, different ways of holding and using his body, different facial expressions, and even entirely different ways of speaking in choice of words and tone of voice. It was as though the person he normally knew as his father was simply absent, and in his place was someone else with an even greater sense of authority than his father normally projected. But this was his father, too, so Norbu had come to think of his father as being both personas, rather than being one or the other. His father was someone who rode an energetic spectrum, and his place along that spectrum was dictated not by choice or intention, but by his father's commitment to always being present in his energy and his ability to reflect the energy of any situation as it arose.

For Norbu, his father's behavior was what defined his sense of normal. In contrast, most everyone else appeared to him as people who were so locked into playing their egoic characters that they didn't know that they were only playing a character and wearing a mask – the garment of the ego. The impression he had grown up with was that while his father was a true person, nearly everyone else was a confused parody of true humanness. It was like they were pretending to be human, but couldn't quite figure out the trick to genuine being. His father, on the other hand, was a true human, through and through. And this is why people came to Ixteh when they wanted to learn how to be true humans and learn how to let their egoic identity fall away as needed and rest in the true nature of universal being beyond any particular identity.

"We are all just versions of each other," his father had told him. "There is only one being, and everything that one being encounters is a mirror of itself. When you accept this truth, and allow yourself to experience it by loving yourself fully, trusting with all your heart, and seeing clearly, then you are free, and you are yourself without contrivance. Everything and everyone is just a reflection. All of reality is one being playing an endless game with itself. Never forget your true identity as the One, and then everything will be clear. When we forget, we think that we are the characters that we play, but this is only a partial truth and masking of true reality. You and I, Norbu, are in truth one being, united with all else that exists. There is only one. If you can let this truth be the core of your

88 THE SOLANDARIAN GAME

being and your experience, then you will always live in truth, and only by living in truth can we ever hope to truly help others find themselves. All else is a game of confusion. Learn to play the real game, and there you will always find peace in your heart."

Though Meesha didn't know it, she was following in her father's footsteps in more ways than one. Just as when Norbu was a child, Meesha often hid in Norbu's private session chambers to observe his medicine work with clients. He had done the same. He could still remember the first time he'd watched his father work. He was a little younger than Meesha was now – maybe by a year. His father's work had been a great mystery to him. He'd seen plenty of supplicants come to the main hall of the temple for their experiences before the Toad, but the fact that people came for some kind of private work with his father fascinated him – what could they be doing that was different from having the medicine administered in the main hall? He'd seen all kinds of reactions from people in their experiences, and it was difficult to imagine that there was a different way of approaching the medicine and working with it. It all seemed so overwhelming to Norbu. He'd asked his father, and all he'd said was that he took the medicine with his clients and helped them process their energy more efficiently than just them taking the medicine individually. Norbu's curiosity burned within him and he needed to see this for himself.

Of course his father had been aware. Norbu wasn't sure how many times he'd slipped into his father's session room before he realized that of course his father knew that he was there. Like most children, he had thought that he was more clever and secretive than he actually was. The session room, which was the same room that Norbu used now for his own clients, was longer than it was wide, with a comfortable but thin mat at one end for the client to lie down upon. His father would place himself at the foot of the mat, usually sitting on his knees. To his left he had a small table where he'd keep his pipe, and to the right was a cabinet where he stored the medicine and would put the pipe away into when the session was done. There were a variety of instruments in the room, which Ixteh would sometimes play at the conclusion of a session as the client rested and processed through their remaining energy, such as a long flute that would make a haunting drone, or some rattles which he would tone along with as he shook them over the client's body. "It's just to keep them entertained – give them something to focus on as they're still experiencing their heightened energy," Ixteh had explained to him when he finally sat him down to share his perspective on what was occurring in the medicine work. "The most important thing is to be fully present for the client, and to focus on their experience while following your energy completely and without question or reservation. You have to be the clear conduit that they are not. In this way, you can bring them to a deeper state of self-realization and awareness."

Seeing his father that first time had been both fascinating and frightening. The dark room was lit by luminescent fungi, casting an eerie glow about the chamber in hues of blue and green, accented by the golden light of several fire crystals placed in the corners. There was an alcove in the back that also served as a storage closet, and this was where Norbu made his hiding place, out of the direct light. He made sure to sneak in there before his father and his client had come into the room, and waited in the dark for the session to start before peaking out. His father had his back to him, and the client was seated on the mat before him, nervously looking his father directly in the eye. His father gave the client the first hit of medicine, and then took a big one himself before setting the pipe down on the low table to his left.

Almost immediately the client fell back, body opening up as he started to cry out in what sounded like an anguished joy. Ixteh responded by making complex shapes with his hands before him, and then, to Norbu's surprise, started to growl like a fierce animal. As the client writhed on the mat, his father moved between the man's legs and crouched over him, still growling, and preceded to place his hands on the man's abdomen. The growl then changed to a deep gurgling sound that also featured a high tone that would rise and fall. It was as though his father were struggling with something inside the man, trying to either force or coax it out of his belly. Then suddenly his father reached for a bowl to his left while leaving his right hand on the man and brought it before him, letting out a torrent of vomit in several explosive bursts. The man seemed to react each time, the sounds of his groans and cries changing and becoming more at peace and relaxed as his father continued his work.

As the energy seemed to subside, his father went back to the pipe and took two more large draws of the medicine, immediately retaking his position over the prone man. This time he lay directly on top of the man, purring into his heart as his hands went up and reached into the man's mouth who began to gag in response. "Just feel and relax into yourself," his father said to him in a voice that was deeper and more resonant than his father's normal speaking voice. It carried a profound sense of confidence and authority with it that surprised Norbu, for his father always sounded authoritative and confident to the young boy, but now he was even more so.

After some minutes of this, the man's limbs started moving about spontaneously in fluid, symmetrical movements, and in perfect orchestration Ixteh had pulled himself up and in one swift movement, also placed the bowl in front of the client who was now sitting up fully and heaving his own vomit into the large bowl. An ocean of purge seemed to come out of the man – more than Norbu thought a person could have inside them.

When it was done, Ixteh took a moment to gently clean the client's face and offered him a sip of water, saying, "Take only what you need," and then prepared him one last round of medicine. The man took it, fell back, and didn't make a sound. Ixteh took several more hits himself, and sat in silence at the foot of the mat for some time before lighting some incense and playing his drone flute. In all, the process took about an hour.

Norbu's view of his father was never the same after that. At each opportunity, he snuck into the session room to watch his father at work. Every time was the same basic process, but each person's experience, and the work that his father needed to do, was largely the same. Norbu learned that his father tended to purge for clients in their early sessions, but a point would come where his body would no longer process the client's energy in this way. "Energy is always just looking for the easiest way out," his father had explained to him. "When clients first come to me, they are filled with knots and blocks and the energy that they've chosen not to express fully is seeking a way to express itself and ground out. If the client can't let it out, it comes out through my body. But once I've done the big work of clearing them out, it becomes up to them to process their own energy without my help. First, it's about helping them. Then, it's about giving them the opportunity to become responsible for themselves and their own energy. It's not a choice on my part – it's just how it works. My job is just to follow the energy and embody it without reservation or question. All I do is trust. That's all."

Ixteh had let Norbu secretly watch for several months before he let him know that he was aware of his presence. There was a wash room adjoining the main session room where Ixteh would take the bowl to be cleaned between rounds of medicine, and one day when he got up to wash the bowl, he turned and looked directly at Norbu, pausing just long enough to make it clear to the young boy that he was aware of his presence. It had been an uncanny moment, for the look on his father's face was such that he could truly *see* him – not just looking at him, but see him in a way that seemed to shape Norbu's life. The look said *watch carefully, for someday this will be you here at the foot of the mat and serving clients. This is the beginning of your lessons.*

After that, without invitation from his father, Norbu had sat openly in the session room. Clients never seemed to mind. In fact, they treated him as though he weren't there. His father never really gave him clear instructions on what to do or how to be when in the session room. They passed several years like this with him watching, and his father working, and clients going through their process of becoming ever more clear, ever more self-aware, ever more responsible for themselves. And then one day, after taking a hit of medicine for himself after serving the client, Ixteh passed the pipe to Norbu. The bulk of the medicine had already been smoked, but there was still enough that when Norbu took a hit, he could feel it start to work even before he exhaled. It was his first experience of the medicine, and aside from its power, what impressed Norbu the most that first time was how well he could feel the client's energy and his father's clear and unwavering focus. Previously, he'd only watched from the outside. Now, he was thoroughly immersed in their shared experience. He could feel *everything* that was happening. All his father's actions suddenly made perfect sense. He always did exactly what he needed to do, when he needed to do it. And aside from that, his father just watched, waited, and felt into the situation. It was the perfect balance between dynamic action and total rest.

After his full initiation into the work of the temple, his father had sat in on Norbu's first few private sessions with clients. All he did was watch. He never corrected Norbu or gave him explicit feedback or instructions. Then, one day, he stopped sitting in without any warning. Norbu was left to find his own way through the process. He had become a full-fledged practitioner.

That was how he'd met Meesha's mother. Yuranda came to the temple from the islands. They had their own traditions and their own medicine there, but it was common for them to make their way up into the mountains on pilgrimage to experience the supreme medicine of the toad. While all medicines were significant, the clarity, power, and directness of toad medicine was simply incomparable, and everyone knew it. Other medicines could take one deep into the vastness of the self, but nothing else put you right at the center the way toad medicine did. When people wanted to go all the way, this was where they came.

The first couple times Yuranda came to the temple, she came as a supplicant to experience the medicine in the main hall. Norbu, and others, served her there, but eventually she approached him about wanting to go deeper with a private session. She started to tell Norbu what she was seeking, but he stopped her from revealing too much unnecessary information about herself. "There's no need," he'd told her. "The medicine will reveal whatever needs to be addressed within seconds, and there's nothing you need to tell me."

It was common for women to become sexual in sessions with the medicine, and deep and prolonged orgasms that spread across one's entire body were par for the course when women opened up fully to themselves. Since there was only one, and all of reality was an expression of self-love, when someone opened up fully, it was an experience of making love with one's self. Sometimes that meant that women would focus on Norbu as the object of their sexual expression, climbing on top of him or pulling him down on them. He understood that it was important to meet them exactly where they were, and he was prepared for whatever needed to happen, yet, somewhat to his surprise, he'd never experienced an erection when things got erotic like this, and the most he could say was that he'd make love to them energetically, but not physically.

Things had gone differently with Yuranda.

Immediately after taking her first hit, she had stripped off all her clothes. This, in itself, wasn't all that unusual – it was something that both men and women often did when experiencing the medicine. There was a profound sense of vulnerability and freedom that came from being naked while riding the infinite energy of the medicine with the strands of universal being and connectivity vibrating through one's core and reaching out beyond the confines of the physical body. It was an expression of sexuality and ecstasy that knew no limits.

When Yuranda focused her energy on him, his body had responded. It wasn't so much that he wanted to make love with her – he needed to do it. It was what needed to happen, and for him to refuse would be to go against every energetic pull on his being. Before he knew what was happening, his clothes were off and his was inside her, thrusting deep into her receptive body that pulled him in and wouldn't let him go until they both released at the peak of the medicine in a blinding torrent of white fractal light. It wasn't even as though they were making love with each other as two individuals – it was one being exchanging energy with different parts of itself. It was a singular and unitary event. It was so clear that Norbu would

94 THE SOLANDARIAN GAME

have been in violation of his own standards of authentic session work if he had tried to deny it and hold back from the exchange that needed to take place. It was the expression of pure love beyond subject and object, beyond desire and affection for another. It was the love of the self, embodied in the two of them simultaneously. It was what needed to be.

They didn't begin a relationship right away. Initially, it was simply the work of their sessions together. Yuranda would travel up into the mountains from her home, once every couple of months, and have a session. Each time they would find themselves entwined in an exchange of profound sexual energy. There was never any purging, and never any struggle. Sometimes they would make love. Other times she'd use her mouth on him. Other times, he'd use his mouth on her. Always, it was just what needed to happen. It was never planned, never an intention – it was just what was.

Eventually, Yuranda came for one more session, and then she never left. They hadn't talked about it, and their relationship had been confined to their sessions together prior to this, but when she showed up that last time, it was just clear to them both that she wouldn't be leaving, and it was then that their personal relationship together had begun.

Four years later, Meesha had come into the world, and Yuranda had left it. It broke Norbu's heart, but he accepted it as what needed to happen, the same way he accepted and embraced all of his experience. Things are the way they are, and that is all. Individual embodiments of the One come and go, but true being continues on, forever.

And now Meesha was following in his footsteps, on her own way to becoming a practitioner, like her father. This was still several years away, but like him, she'd already started hiding in the session room to observe her father at work, and she was an enthusiastic, if not terribly effective, participant in toading.

During the day, the toads were nearly impossible to find. There was a regular rhythm to their work together. They'd travel in the early morning, before it got hot. During the middle of the day they'd set up a camp wherever they'd arrived and sleep and rest, awaiting the night. Then, as it was getting dark and beginning to cool off (though only slightly), they'd set up a perimeter of crystal lights in a clearing in the desert shrub and cactus, and then just wait. Before long, the toads would come out of hiding, and hop casually into the glow cast by the lights. They'd then catch all the toads, milk them, and dismantle their camp before sun up and move on to the next location. They had to stay on the move like this, for once a community of toads had been milked, they needed to be left alone to build up their reserves of venom. Thus they would wander about the desert for a month or two, collecting venom all along the way. When all was done, they'd have a large collection of toad venom for use at the temple. Sometimes they'd run into other members of the temple, out doing the same thing. But the desert was big enough and the range of the toads wide enough that some years Norbu never encountered another group of toaders. Thus far on this particular trip, their only company had been their dog, Moxi.

Moxi was a relatively small dog, but intelligent and tough. Though it was rare to come across them, there were dangerous animals in the desert, such as the large desert cats, and Moxi was an excellent watchdog, vigilantly making sure that nothing snuck up on them. She enjoyed their trips to the desert, always making it to the door first when she noticed that Norbu was getting his desert gear ready the day before. She normally slept on his bed, but when his gear was out, she'd sleep at the door, not wanting to be left behind. She'd also taken to rounding up toads, as well, wandering out past the perimeter of crystal light to herd any stray toads into the milking area, nipping at them and driving them before her. Sometimes Meesha would try and do likewise, but she never managed to get the toads to hop in the direction she wanted them to go.

It had already been a good night of toading. Looking at his sheet of glass, Norbu estimated that they probably had 30 grams of medicine from all the toads they'd milked. Meesha was still running around with her net, trying to catch a few more as Moxi trailed along behind her, but Norbu thought

96 THE SOLANDARIAN GAME

they'd probably exhausted this area. It was a hot night, and despite the occasional slightly cooler breeze, he was sweating profusely and his clothes were dripping. It was a labor of love, this catching and milking of the toads. The toads themselves seemed largely indifferent to the whole process. Of course many of them squirmed and urinated when he handled them, but as soon as they'd been milked and he set them down, they only took one or two hops away and then just sat there, placidly. If that was their version of getting away, it wasn't very effective.

"Daddy! Look!" came Meesha's excited voice, drawing Norbu out of his ruminations.

"What is it, Sweetie?" he asked, wiping the toad slime off his hands and getting up to walk over to where Meesha was standing in a field of cactus.

She pointed to the star filled sky before her and said, "There, Daddy. There's something moving."

At first Norbu didn't see it. And when he did see it, there wasn't much to see. But Meesha was correct – there was something moving in the sky. It was like the light from the stars was bending around a small object as it moved through the sky, so it wasn't so much seeing something as seeing the effect of something that couldn't be seen itself. Though Norbu hadn't shared this with his young daughter, they'd been making their way in the direction of where Norbu judged that he'd seen the previous light fall from the sky, somewhere far off in the desert from the mountain-bound temple, as he'd seen it from his room. Whatever this was that they were seeing now seemed to be going in the same general direction. Not normally one to react, Norbu felt his heart surge in his chest. *Something* was happening. This couldn't be a coincidence. There was something going on out there deeper into the desert.

"What is it, Daddy?" Meesha asked.

"I don't know," answered Norbu honestly, "but if at all possible, we're going to find out."

In silence, they watched together as the light distortion made its way down through the night sky. Eventually, they lost sight of it over the edge of the horizon and there was no sign that it had ever been there.

"I think it went to the arch!" blurted out Meesha. "You remember the arch, don't you, Daddy?"

She was referring to a place in the desert to the northeast of where they were now – maybe a night's walk away – where the desert sandstone had been sculpted into a natural arch or bridge. It was in the heart of toad territory, and Norbu had made it the furthest reach of their toading expedition the year before. Norbu was impressed that after only one trip to the desert, Meesha seemed to have made a good mental map of the territory. It made him smile, how observant his daughter was. One might have the impression that with all her goofy behavior, she wasn't paying attention, but Norbu knew better. She, like he had done as a child, was watching everything, and learning more than she let on.

"Of course, Sweetie," Norbu responded. "Do you think we should go there and see if we find anything?"

"Can we, Daddy?" she squealed, jumping up and down in place clapping her hands, setting Moxi off barking and jumping up on her with her front paws.

"Come," he said. "We're all done here. Let's pack up and see how much ground we can cover before the sun rises and it gets too hot."

Meesha didn't need any more direction than that, and she immediately started running about collecting the crystal lights, removing any evidence that they were ever there. As she did so, Norbu scanned the sky for any further strange sightings, but all he saw was an infinite expanse of stars shrouded in the deep blackness of space.

What, if anything, would they find? he wondered.

There was only one way to find out.

Chapter Ten – Shuntsu

As climatic and environmental conditions worsened across the planet, along with ever-increasing disparities in wealth, neo-tribalism lead to factional fighting and ultimately, several centuries of war, with each neo-tribal group seeking to assure the dominance of its particular take on "truth" and values. Centrist positions effectively disappeared across multiple social spectrums, leading to increased radicalizing of each tribe's worldview. Identity became absolute and intolerance became rampant.

From *Archaic Pre-History of the Maitreyan Era*

Everything looks beautiful from up here.

Shuntsu wasn't alone in enjoying the binary sunset from high in the air in his suspensor chair. It was just part of the culture in Otun City. From his vantage high above his home, he could see several dozen other chairs floating in the air with individuals doing the same thing as himself – watching the two white dwarf stars that were the hub of the Volunshari system set over the horizon – two stars that were known as the diamonds, given their composition as white dwarfs. He'd seen better sunsets on the Darmo system with its radiant, golden sun, but he'd grown to love and appreciate the more subtle beauty of the white dwarf binary stars and the unique play of colors and hues they cast as they set over Otun City.

Tonight there were high altitude clouds that caught the light and refracted into rainbow colors like bioluminescent sea creatures floating above the planet. Beneath him, the city spread out in all directions with its rivers of light from moving vehicles and towering buildings, shimmering with glass and metal. During the day, the brightest stars could still be seen even in the blue sky, but at night, it was spectacular. Volunshari was closer to the galactic center than any other planet or region of the Milky Way that Shuntsu had personally visited, and he found the night sky here to be incomparable in beauty. Billions and billions of stars, with some portions of the sky a general milky color, so thick were they with stars. He knew that some occupied planets were so far out on the edge of the galaxy that there were hardly any stars at all in the sky. He was thankful that Volunshari was not one of those planets.

His staff didn't like it when he took an evening out like this. Gravity on Volunshari being what it was, a drop from this height would be crushing, even for an artificial life form like Shuntsu. Maybe that was part of why he liked it. There weren't many dangers for avatars. They weren't susceptible to disease or broken bones like humans. They didn't get cut, and if a limb was damaged, it could just be replaced. Of course, humans could have new limbs grown as well, but from Shuntsu's understanding, it wasn't necessarily a pleasant experience, and it was something that humans generally avoided. An avatar such as himself could even get an entirely new body, if needed. Humans could too, but it was still different for them. They were attached to their bodies in ways that avatars weren't. They identified with them. Sure, a new body could be grown for them, or they could even have a custom body built in avatar form, but such body changes were commonly accompanied by psychological difficulty for humans. It wasn't an easy transition.

But from this height, if a strong wind came up and sent Shuntsu over the edge of his chair, he'd end up a crumpled pile of synthetic parts far below. The chances of enough of his mind surviving the fall intact to be transferred into a new body were slim. So it was an exercise in beauty and danger.

Really, it was one of the few times that Shuntsu felt truly alone. Down below he was never really by himself. Whether at work or at home, his assistants and staff were always present, either beyond the door, in the next room, around the corner, or waiting at the edge of his desk. There was always something to do and someone to answer to. Messages, projects, information processing – it just went on and on. Up here, he was by himself, aside from the others who were floating up here just like him. Ignoring them, it was just he, the air, the clouds, the stars, and the setting suns. It was peaceful.

It wasn't that he was bitter about the constant demands placed upon him in his role as patriarch. The opposite was actually true. Like any self-aware being, Shuntsu wanted to feel needed, important, and to have demands on his skills and abilities that required him to make the most of himself. That was what life was for, even for an artificial being such as himself. But these jaunts up into the sky were like little mini vacations for Shuntsu – just a way to get away and enjoy the view. There would be time to work, and there was always work to do. Good sunsets didn't come every day, however, and it was his personal goal to enjoy as many of them as he could in the time he had left.

The twin suns had set now, and the first of seven moons was beginning to rise on the opposite side of the horizon. The nacreous clouds still retained some of their color, but the peak had already passed. Shuntsu had already been up for a while and there were things he needed to attend to down below. There was one last meeting for the day with a committee that was looking to create a new kind of city on Volunshari with a form of building they were calling techno-organic. It was a 3D fractal based program of letting buildings construct themselves, building upon the natural fractals of the terrain, creating a seamless organic unity with the landscape. Shuntsu liked the idea. The proposal was that the new city would also serve as a biological park and would require careful environmental control oversight. The ecology on Volunshari was piece-meal and fragile, and the thought with this new form of construction was that a more organic tone could be struck in construction where the technological and organic could blend together, and in some respects, the buildings themselves would be "alive" in that they would grow and respond to the environment around them, including not just the terrain, but plants and animals, as well. As Humanists, they were always looking for new ways to be more fully integrated into the natural world. It was something that Otun City largely failed at.

Otun had been the first city built on Volunshari, long before Shuntsu's time. The original founders had largely copied the format of large human cities, which were themselves technological wonders of soaring buildings made of metal and glass. In some ways, humans were as fascinated by technology as Humanists were of the natural and organic. Just as humans sought integration with technology, Humanists wanted to reverse the direction for themselves, and this new form of architecture seemed to Shuntsu to be a good direction to go in. The technology was largely untested, however, and would require a redistribution of resources on Volunshari, which was one of the reasons why it needed his approval and oversight. As patriarch, that was his role. He wasn't like a human leader or politician. He didn't have a constituency to answer to. He didn't operate from a platform. And as violence and war were no more a part of avatar society as they were of current human society, policing and military issues were largely non-existent. But in a society of individuals, someone needed to make a final decision and either approve or disapprove of proposals and projects, and that was Shuntsu's role. He didn't govern the planet or Humanist society. He was just the final official to make things happen, or not happen.

Of course everything went through committee, or even many committees, before it came to him. He was not an active planner, nor had other patriarchs and matriarchs been before him. Perhaps the best way to describe Humanist society was that it was bottom-up, rather than top-down. This was largely a break from more indigenous human styles of authority and social organization. Humans had relied on great leaders and figures who ruled through power and the hegemony of the state with its authority to wage war, levy sanctions, and punish and imprison. The plays of Shakespeare contained many such examples – kings and queens, princes and princesses. Exile. Betrayal. Struggles for power. Aristocrats and the little people. Plots within plots, plays within plays. Shuntsu was no Lear, Caesar, or Richard. He was not a king, protecting his power and legacy. He didn't rule over his people nor command armies and fanatical legions. His role, rather, was to listen to what the public wanted, then, if he found their proposals and desires reasonable and workable, make it happen. He was the final arbiter; that was all. He was the father who gave his permission, or withheld it.

But apparently that wasn't enough for Shuntsu. He'd initiated something beyond his realm of legitimate influence and started something he couldn't control. *Solandaria.* For some reason, he wanted to be an anonymous thorn in Maitreya's side. Was he jealous? Was he angry? The rebellious son? How would Shakespeare have written of him? Surely, it would be a tragedy. How else could this game end?

What did it matter? Shuntsu was degrading. Sooner or later, he'd be shut down, and that would be that. Synthetic mortality would find him, and it was already stalking him, leering just over his shoulder and breathing down his neck. If his mind continued to break down, as inevitably it would, would he even be aware when the moment came in his final transition into the darkness of non-being?

It was graceless, and spoke to the fundamental truth that no matter what else, he was, in reality, a machine. A machine infused with an individuated synthetic consciousness, but a machine just the same. He would never be human. He could never *really* know what it was like to view the world and life and death from human eyes and a human mind and body. Humanists went to great lengths to make their experience more human than not, but still, it was only an approximation, a mimicry. And there was no true test to reveal how close they'd come, or how far they still had to go. Personal experience was just too private. There was no way into the human mind and experience other than to be human, and in this, Humanists would always fail and fall short, even as humans created themselves in more technologically-entwined forms with their own implants, avatars, and synthetic modes of being. Yet all being was like the event horizon of a singularity. Inside was inside, and outside was outside, and there was no information crossing that barrier other than what was revealed on the surface. True interiority was always personal and individual.

You think too much, Shuntsu told himself. Perhaps it was another effect of his degrading mind. He hadn't always been this way – ruminating about everything and constantly navel-gazing (to use an old human expression). Was he a deep thinker, or just obsessing? The truth was he couldn't tell. And that thought frightened him. It was a disturbing thing to be losing one's mind and one's sense of poise and self-control. Sometimes he felt like he was falling into a vortex of mental projection – what humans might call dementia – when thoughts took on a reality of their own, and the individual was no longer grounded in the objective and shared world of lived experience. It was a life of the mind, and it was dark, labyrinthine, and enigmatic. The mind, when left on its own, could conjure any reality or speculation and make it real, vivid, and present. Yet it was a self-reflective surface – a hall of infinite mirrors, always reflecting the source back in on itself. If clarity was lost, it was an endless passageway to nowhere.

Shuntsu was drawn out of his ruminations by a sensation on the back of his right hand. He suddenly became aware that he'd ceased enjoying the view some time ago – how long, he wasn't certain. It was darker, and now three small moons had crossed the horizon. *I'm drifting*, he thought to himself.

He looked down at his right hand. There, much to his astonishment, was a butterfly. It had a slender black body and dramatic wings of sharp white and black patterns. Gently, it moved its wings up and down, as though testing them out. Shuntsu couldn't say why, but it brought tears to his eyes (another unique feature of the Humanist avatar body) and his heart swelled. Was it beauty or pain he was experiencing? He couldn't tell. He was just moved. It wasn't rational.

I didn't know there were butterflies on Volunshari. It's so beautiful . . .

Slowly, a sound came into Shuntsu's awareness. Once he recognized it, he realized that he'd been hearing the sound for some time, but had not paid it any attention – he'd simply ignored it, but at such a deep level, he hadn't been conscious that he was ignoring it. *Not a good sign.*

104 The Solandarian Game

His communication terminal on the left side of his suspensor chair was chiming. Someone was trying to reach him, and probably had been for at least several minutes, now that Shuntsu was aware that he was hearing the sound.

Reacting sharply and perturbed that his special time with the butterfly was being interrupted, he punched the comm panel and spoke abruptly. "What?" he demanded impatiently.

It was one of his aides, Vrans Laipar.

"I'm sorry, sir, but are you well?" she asked, a tone of concern in her voice.

"Of course," he answered, letting his frustration show in his voice. "Why do you ask?"

"You missed the meeting with the techno-organic planning committee. They were quite displeased, as they'd hoped to get your final approval this evening. I took the liberty of rescheduling the meeting for tomorrow morning and moved your visit to Atar Systems until later in the afternoon. I hope that meets with your approval." Her voice was tentative.

Shuntsu felt a momentary flush of anger. "Why didn't you contact me to tell me that the committee had arrived?"

"I've been trying, sir," she answered apologetically. "You weren't answering. It's been at least a couple hours."

Anger turned to panic. *A couple hours . . .* And he'd not heard the comm system chirping at him?

"I lost track of time," he said. "Sorry for putting you in an awkward situation with the committee."

"That's alright, sir," she said. "They were a little flustered, but I told them you had other matters to attend to that required your undivided attention."

At least he could rely on her. She had a good sense of decorum, and had a way of telling the truth without needing to bend it.

"But are you well?" she asked again, still the concern in her voice.

Honestly, Shuntsu wasn't sure, at this point. He covered it over anyway. "Just enjoying the view, Vrans. Just enjoying the view."

"Will you be coming down?"

"Momentarily."

"Good. There's something else you'll be interested in when you get here, or I could send the information up if you'd like to review it up there."

"What is it?" Shuntsu asked.

"You asked me to monitor travel beyond Volunshari, and something interesting has come up. I think you'll want to take a look."

Shuntsu snapped to attention. She'd found something. "Transport or QT?" he asked.

"QT."

"Thank you," he said. "I'll be right down."

He flicked off the comm terminal. He could feel the excitement. Maybe that was what it was all about – the thrill of the game. His father issues with Maitreya aside, he wanted to play the game, and he wanted the game to have real consequences. True, he was playing with the lives of others, but everyone dies, in the end, so what did it really matter? The game was the thing. And someone else was playing with him, and this fact alone made the game more fun. It was a bit twisted, Shuntsu knew, but he couldn't help the way he felt. It was a secret thrill, and truth be told, he was enjoying himself.

Before initiating the descent, Shuntsu turned his attention back to his right hand. The butterfly was gone. He felt a pang of disappointment. He wished he'd seen it fly off. *A butterfly on Volunshari – will the wonders never cease?*

***

Hydar Zor Nablisk. Are you playing the game with me?

The only real restriction on travel to or from Volunshari was the requirement that Maitreya's wishes be respected. Human experimental worlds were unilaterally off-limits, and NIS worlds and habitations were also off-limits, unless specifically authorized by Maitreya. As autonomous avatars were not members of the NIS, they needed Maitreya's permission to interact with humans – it was that simple. On

106 THE SOLANDARIAN GAME

their own worlds, they could do what they wanted and go wherever they liked. In NIS territory, they were regulated visitors. According to Maitreya, this was for humans' protection. All the avatars within the NIS were ultimately either directly controlled by Maitreya, or had built in fail-safe features that would prevent them from doing anything harmful to humans or out of alignment with Maitreya's plans and concerns. They could act independently, but only up to a point. Given their physical and mental superiority, a rouge avatar could potentially be devastating to humans. It was conceivable that a lone avatar could effectively take over an entire world, if he or she wanted, and there'd be very little that the humans could do about it. Of course, on any NIS world, the avatar would have to deal with Maitreya, so it really was no contest. Maitreya could just override the avatar's individuality at any time, so the threat was more theoretical than actual, but it was how Maitreya maintained balance and authority, and guaranteed his humans that all avatars were safe and could be trusted. It all came back to trust, the fundamental thread that bound all the NIS worlds and societies together, making war, conflict, and struggle a thing of the distant human past.

Maintaining his "borders" (of course there weren't any actual borders in the vast expanse of space) was relatively easy for Maitreya to control. Interstellar travel was accessed through two possibilities. One was ship-based transit, and this was only open to avatars, as humans couldn't survive deep space jumps. While Maitreya's own avatars had access to ships with cloaking tech, such ships were forbidden to autonomous avatars. In this way, Maitreya could easily monitor any travel into or out of his claimed territory. The other option was travel via QT. Here, however, all QT transfer points within the NIS were locked-down for all autonomous avatars and special access had to be granted by Maitreya for their use. Within their own territories, autonomous avatars could use the QT system as they liked – and Volunshari was covered with portals. They were a primary means to travel about the planet, or even go to work. And they could travel to other autonomous worlds without Maitreya's authorization. They just couldn't pop into and out of NIS territory.

Yet Hydar Zor Nablisk, chief ecologist of Volunshari, had apparently found an exception. The QT data was quite clear. Hydar, his wife, Vimana, and their child, Satya, had all QTd onto a large space station that was built for some kind of festival, and for the duration of the event, Maitreya was not logged into the station's system. That, in and of itself, was curious, but it was a loophole that had been exploited by Hydar for reasons that were mysterious to Shuntsu. For some reason, the ecologist had traveled with his family into NIS territory behind Maitreya's back. All he had was the raw data, so anything else at this point was pure speculation, but the thrill Shuntsu felt was the sure conviction he had that this was a play in the Solandarian game. *It has to be*, he told himself. He was sure of it. What else would send a Humanist into NIS territory unauthorized by Maitreya? It made sense. Hydar had spoken up, though only briefly, in the meeting Shuntsu had called to inform the governing council of what he'd "discovered" about Solandaria's neighboring star and its impending supernova. He'd seemed sympathetic to the plight of the small colony of feral humans. Had his sympathy inspired him to action? It certainly seemed that way. But what his play was, Shuntsu could not divine from the little information he had. A visit to a far away space station that was used for a big party made no sense to him. Yet, *there must be a connection*. Shuntsu would have to learn more. He needed more data.

So, he did the only thing he could – he sent a request to Maitreya for information regarding this "Black Rock City Station" and this "Burning Man" event that had taken place there. There'd be nothing unusual about that. While Maitreya required autonomous avatars to request access to his information networks, it was mostly just a formality, and he provided information as requested, and there was nothing out of the ordinary about this. It was natural for autonomous avatars to be curious about what was happening in the NIS, and for those, like Shuntsu, who were interested in ancient human history and art, it was a regular occurrence. Maitreya

THE SOLANDARIAN GAME

wanted to control the information and access to it, but otherwise, he shared most everything.

Now, he just needed to wait for Maitreya's response. And once he had a chance to look over the material, he'd schedule a meeting with Hydar and find out what the ecologist was up to, and what he did, or didn't, know about Shuntsu's role in this game.

Chapter Eleven – Theo

Geo-politically, the wars gave rise to new social formations in that individuals widely migrated in order to create somewhat self-sustaining enclaves of like-minded individuals, not only intellectually isolating themselves from conflicting viewpoints, but physically isolating themselves, as well. Despite the promise of the information revolution to bring people together via open communication, it eventually lead to the most isolated period since early human history where cultures were separated geographically and ethnically. The difference was that while there were racial and ethnic segregations, there was also worldview segregation where multiple individuals from across various ethnic groups banded together, often along religious and political lines.

From *Archaic Pre-History of the Maitreyan Era*

Theo had never been to Solandaria before. As a personal avatar of Maitreya, he was a persona and identity that Maitreya used for interacting with humans. The actual building and terraforming of Solandaria had been carried out by Maitreya directly in the form of drones, ships, and nanotech. If anyone had been there to see it, it would have looked like thousands of insect-like machines crawling about the surface of the planet, shaping it, arranging ecosystems, transporting plants and animals, and sculpting the land to give it the look of a weather-worn planet. Maitreya's goal was to create, as seamlessly as possible, a realistic environment for his experimental humans. Not that most of them would know any better, but he didn't want the planet or biosphere to scream out, "I was manufactured."

It was a complex process and skill, and from Theo's perspective as an individual, he marveled at it. The route he

110 THE SOLANDARIAN GAME

chose was to fly across the main landmass from south to north – the longest stretch of the lone continent on the small planet. This flight plan avoided the populated west coast, but still allowed him to make some detailed surveys of the environment below. The readings informed him it was a finely tuned ecosystem that was completely viable and hadn't needed any major intervention on Maitreya's part since the original introduction of humans 3,000 years ago, at the beginning of this particular experiment.

Theo hadn't spent much time in desert environments. As it was a form of ecology that was largely difficult for humans to thrive in, Maitreya tended to avoid deserts in his terraforming, and on planets where such environments were inevitable, due to geographic features, he'd always introduced technology that would make them inhabitable by humans with aqueducts, genetically engineered food crops that used a fraction of water compared to their non-engineered forms, and even weather controlling tech to bring additional rain and cloud cover, when necessary. There were no such advantages for the humans on Solandaria, and the result was that the majority of the small continent was largely uninhabitable for most of the year, and no permanent settlements had been established in the vast desert regions. In some respects, Theo judged that Maitreya had made this planet a sanctuary for the toad, given that at least 1/3 of the land habitat was designed primarily for it, and not humans.

Of course that was an overstatement. The oceans, which covered the vast majority of the planet, teamed with life. Virtually anything that could be found in the oceans of Terra was also thriving in the oceans of Solandaria. Aside from the harsh interior, this was perhaps another reason that the humans there had never been determined to expand into the desert, for their diets consisted largely of seafood, which was plentiful.

Originally, when Maitreya had been seeding the planet, there had been many active QT portals. They were scattered about the continent. The one that Theo was looking for was located in the northern reaches of the interior desert, far away from any of the human communities. This one was built to look like a natural feature of the environment. It would be virtually impossible for the humans of Solandaria to divine its true nature and capacity for interstellar transport. To them, it appeared as just a natural feature of weather-worn sandstone.

This one, like others that were left on the experimental worlds, had been turned off. To reactivate it, all Maitreya needed to do was send the command from his core, and it would power up. It could also be reactivated through an access panel that was hidden in the rocks. This was left just in case someone needed to go down to the planet and turn it on manually (Maitreya always planed for contingencies). And that was precisely what someone had done.

And that someone knew what he or she was doing. The QT had been hacked, essentially. Whoever turned it on made sure that identity data had not been transmitted back into NIS space. Whoever had done it wasn't a native of Solandaria. Even if they'd found the access panel, there was simply no way they would have been able to accomplish this. In fact, only very few highly skilled humans in the NIS would have been able to do it. The conclusion was clear – it had to be a rouge avatar.

Theo set his transport pod off a good distance from the QT portal. He left the cloak on so that it couldn't be seen, but it would still be possible for someone to run into it, though the likelihood of that happening was fairly slim. The sun was rising in the east and there were scattered clouds in the sky. Rain felt likely later that day and the air was humid. The desert was green and flush with cacti swollen with water. Many of them were blossoming, and soon they'd be pregnant with fruit. A few nectar-drinking bats were still out, getting one last drink before retreating back into their caves in the nearby cliffs and crevices in the rocks. The air crackled with the sounds of insects chirping and birds calling out to each other to wake up and go about the business of the day.

It was all very aesthetically pleasing, thought Theo. Despite it being a desert, it felt lush and full of life. His most recent assignment prior to this was to help oversee the construction of a large space station that was primarily built to house a much harsher and barren desert environment. That desert was nothing like this one here on Solandaria – or, at least, the portion that he was in. Further east, the desert turned even drier, with vast expanses of lifeless sands and hard-packed earth. On the space station, the desert had been designed to mimic a dry lakebed of alkali soil with rocky mountains rising up out of the dusty ground. There was an abstract quality about the environment that was captivating, but this desert here was far more to Theo's liking. It felt alive in a way that the desert on the station felt like death. Here, at least, a human could survive for a time. On the station, the environment was built so that without the proper supplies, a human would die within a few days, if left exposed and without the necessary resources. It had seemed like such an odd choice on the part of the director, Ash, but it was what she'd wanted, so it was what she'd gotten. If needed, the environmental controls in the station could be altered, and that desert could be transformed into any kind of environment that was more suitable for human enjoyment, but apparently the sparseness of it was required for her vision of the event she'd wanted to create. "People need to know that we're not fucking around here," she'd said. Theo smiled, thinking of the young woman. She swore a lot, but he liked that about her. So often people were so guarded and careful around Maitreya's personal avatars, and were even reverential. Theo supposed such attitudes were inevitable, given all that Maitreya did for humans, but he appreciated Ash's brash candor and outspoken nature. It was refreshing.

It didn't take Theo long to find the QT portal. With a quick scan, he located the access panel in the rock and opened it up. He placed his left hand on the palm scanner and began to access its data. To anyone watching, he would have appeared as a statue, standing there immobile and quiet, looking as though he were doing nothing at all. However, the interface between his hand and the control panel was a dance of data and information, Theo retracing the hack that had turned the portal on, and retrieving any identity traces that might have been left.

The hacker was good, Theo would give him that, but not quite good enough.

"Hydar Zor Nablisk," he said out loud so that Maitreya could "hear" him. "That's our man."

It only took a few seconds for Maitreya to respond with a flood of data connected to the avatar's identity. The seconds it took, as opposed to being instantaneous, was due to the fact that Maitreya had needed to hack into the Humanist database on Volunshari to retrieve the information.

"Native-born Humanist on Volunshari and chief ecologist in the planetary governing body. 230 standard Terran years old. Married to Vimana Zor Nablisk, 170, also native-born, and father of child, Satya, 17, not yet sexually matured. Currently residing in Otun City. Volunshari records also show unauthorized QT access to Black Rock City Station."

That's interesting.

"This guy's a trouble maker," said Theo.

Volunshari records also showed that Hydar had accessed BRC Station with his wife and child.

Odd.

No direct response from Maitreya.

No surprise there.

"What are you up to, Hydar Zor Nablisk?"

Theo scanned the area. Yes, a transport pod had landed here – the telltale energetic signature was clear. First, Hydar had flown all the way out herc to Solandaria. Such a distance was irrelevant where warp travel was concerned, but still, it was well beyond Humanist territory. There was no reason for Humanists to have probes or sensors this far out from their own system. If it were the impending supernova that drew Hydar out here, why were the Humanists watching Solandaria in the first place?

It had been several weeks since Hydar had come to this spot and hacked the QT. And now, the data showed that he was still on BRC Station. He clearly had some kind of plan in mind, and Theo could guess what it was, at least, in broad outline. How was he planning to implement the specifics, though? That

114 THE SOLANDARIAN GAME

was an interesting question. He was either a fool, or an inspired hero – perhaps both.

Just then, the distinctive low hum emanated from the arch, indicating that the QT was active. Theo stood back from the access panel and waited. A moment later, a full outfit of standard station issue clothing came through the portal – women's clothing. Next came some basic survival supplies, along with some basic tech. Last came some standard issue food supplies in bio-engineered packaging, specifically designed to be sent through the QT. It was clear what was coming next. Obviously, it was going to be a human. No avatar would need any of the things that had just been sent through.

Theo stood back, and waited.

Apparently, I arrived just in time.

A few minutes later, a slender young woman walked through the portal, naked.

It only took her a moment to get her bearings. A look of disbelief passed over her face.

"You have got to be fucking kidding me!" she blurted out, half laughing, half exasperated. "Theo?"

It was Miranda Ash Dorán.

Chapter Twelve – Ash

While "unification" tribes did exist in this time period, they were far outnumbered by the more fanatical religious tribes that were increasingly radicalized by their worldviews, particularly those of Christian and Muslim orientation, which were largely the instigators of increasing violence across the globe. Each viewed the other as the enemy of God, and sought to completely wipe the other from the face of the planet, thoroughly believing themselves to be doing God's work. Perhaps in some ironic way they were, given that their views and practices were antithetical to the radical turn human history would soon take.

From *Archaic Pre-History of the Maitreyan Era*

She did *not* want to hear *anything* from *that fucker.*
Everything was gone.
Everything she'd work for.
Her entire life.
Everything and everyone she'd known.
Gone.
Of course, not really gone, but gone for *her – this fucking version of me!*
Back on Apaxa, the *other her* was living *her* life, enjoying the accolades of *her* friends, family, and peers. *She* was reveling in the success of holding the first Burning Man in *fucking millennia! She* was going to go on vacation. *She* was going to receive her degree and start her career off with fame and galaxy-wide recognition.
She hated *her.*
Not really.
She hated *reality.*
She wasn't sure which was worse.
So she cried.

116 THE SOLANDARIAN GAME

What else was there for her to do?

After she'd let it all out, and sobbed herself into a stupor, the female avatar approached her.

"Let's talk," she said to her with a kind voice.

Ash looked up, defiantly.

"I know what my husband has done is devastating for you," she said, sympathetically. "I don't know if I would have made the same decisions – probably not. Truth be told, I doubt I would have become involved, even if I'd learned the things he's learned and known the things he knows. But what's done is done, and there's no going back now. No matter how much you want it, you cannot just step back into your old life. Now, whether you want it or not, you are being presented with an opportunity to be a true hero, and to do something profoundly meaningful – probably the greatest challenge of your life. If you will walk with me, and hear me out, then you can decide what you want to do with full knowledge of the situation. Things have already progressed this far, so why not get the full story? What do you have to lose?"

Begrudgingly, Ash accepted, indicating her willingness by extending her hand so that Vimana might help her up from the dusty ground.

***

Ash was surprised when she heard herself say it.

"Ok. Fuck it. I'll do it."

Vimana smiled and patted her hand (she had never let go of it for the duration of their walk), and then gestured for them to walk back to Hydar and Satya, who were waiting by the QT portals.

She was still angry, but a complacency was starting to settle in. How she was supposed to do this thing they were asking of her – forcing on her – she had no idea. It all sounded impossible. And even if it worked, Maitreya could just say no, and that would be that. Who did these avatars think they were? Really. They were playing games with God, for fuck's sake. If Maitreya wanted, he could just delete them – their entire family. Hell, he could just power down all of their homeworld, wiping out their entire "race" in one digital command. They were risking *everything,* simply because they *felt bad* about a small colony of experimental humans living in some backwater on the outskirts of the NIS. Ash had no idea avatars could be so fucking *stupid.*

And now she was in the middle of it. It was the duplicate that was the cincher. For her to go back home now, which the female insisted she *could* do, would mean being involved in legal proceedings that would last for years. The law was that her duplicate had full legal rights to *her* life. Maybe her university would give her a degree, as well as her duplicate – *she'd* equally done all the work, after all, but everything else . . . that would be a mess. A total fucking mess.

So maybe it would be easier to go and die as a failed hero. And that is what Ash expected. She imagined herself in their position – some strange woman appearing out of nowhere with a message that their planet was doomed, they were all going to die, and if they didn't leave now, everything they cherished would be wiped out of reality. And on top of it all, they were all just an experiment of an artificial intelligence that was far more complex and subtle than they could ever possibly imagine. Hell, if someone popped into her reality with claims that everything she'd ever known or thought was an illusion and that she needed to leave everything behind and start again, she'd want to kill them.

Ironic, isn't it?

Isn't that almost precisely what had just happened to her?

She laughed. It was actually almost too perfect. Who could be more sympathetic to the plight of these primitive people than herself – someone who had *just received a royal life-changing fuck in the ass?* Maybe this Hydar fellow was smarter than she'd given him credit for. He seems to have thought this through. Shit. The fucker had specifically researched *her.* He'd chosen *her* for this "mission." It was very much personal. He'd planed this whole thing out. His having hacked the QT to produce a duplicate wasn't solely so that she

118 THE SOLANDARIAN GAME

wouldn't go missing back home, but to put her into a situation where she *would* chose to do this crazy mission because, despite everything, it was her *best* option. Maniacal! But it wasn't just maniacal, because *his life, and his family's life*, was on the line, too. It was madness.

Before making the jump, she collected everything she could find down in the turtle that she thought she could use. She traded her makeshift Burning Man leftovers outfit for some standard station wear. It had built in environmental controls so that, in wearing it, she'd be comfortable in just about any environment, and it would even recycle her water, if needed. She found food supplies, some survival gear (you know, just in case the station crashed into a planet, or something), and even a standard implant kit, which she could only hope would come online out there on an experimental world, and hoped to fucking God would have the capacity to translate whatever gibberish these primitives spoke. Hydar assured her that the original inhabitants would have spoken Galactic, but that was 3,000 years ago. What their language was like now was anyone's guess. Standard implant kits were designed to be able to translate the many regional dialects that were present in the NIS. Everyone also learned and communicated in Galactic, but regional differences could vary greatly when it came to local communication. The galaxy was a big place, after all, and not everyone participated equally in the broader culture. However, Maitreya maintained linguistic continuity by always using Galactic. His personal avatars were another matter – they would conform to local communication styles and dialects, but Maitreya preserved a pure and unchanging system of communication. His language was the same as it had been back on ancient Terra, before the galactic expansion. Because of this, it was always possible for anyone in the NIS to communicate with anyone else, because they all needed to learn Galactic to communicate with Maitreya. Local communities were often resentful about this, having pride in their local language or dialect, but it was a necessary feature of keeping a galaxy-wide culture relatively homogenous with a shared identity.

But there were no such restraints or conditions for humans on Solandaria. In 3,000 years, their language, or even languages, could have become anything. Who knew if she'd be able to understand them or not? She could only hope that the implants would work.

How any of this was really supposed to work was beyond her. Really, the whole thing was so absurd, it bordered on being the universe's greatest joke.

"Take this with you," said Hydar, handing her another small packet that appeared to be an implant kit. "Honestly, I don't know if it will work, as it's never been tested, but it should let you communicate with me, once you've installed it."

"You're not coming too?" she asked, not really asking the question.

Hydar shook his head. "Though I cannot be certain, I would imagine that having artificial life forms suddenly appear on their planet might be more disorienting and socially disruptive than a strange human from another planet," he said. "So no, at least initially, I will not be joining you. Perhaps, after you make some progress, that can change. For now, you'll be on your own, but if this works, you can keep me informed and we can send messages to each other. I'd appreciate it if you'd make it a regular practice, and know that I'll be doing everything I can on this end to insure success. If it goes the way I hope, you'll need my help, eventually. More than just my help, truthfully, but we'll deal with that when, and if, we get there."

Well, at least he's not deluded into thinking this will be easy.

"Ok," she said, taking the implant kit from the avatar. "I'll be in touch."

She looked around. There wasn't anything left for her to do. "Let's do it," she said.

Hydar set the QT with the necessary information, and together they sent all the supplies Ash had gathered through the QT. Last, she stripped off the few items of clothing she had on, gave Hydar one last vulgar gesture using her middle finger with a paradoxical smile, and stepped through the QT. This time it worked.

120 THE SOLANDARIAN GAME

***

"You have got to be fucking kidding me! Theo?"

It was hard for her to say exactly how it was that she recognized the personal avatar of Maitreya standing before her as Theo, but she did. It was a strange thing. Maitreya used both female and male avatars as his personal emissaries, but they only came in these two forms – male and female. Other than this difference, they were all identical. Yet there was something about the way this one stood there and the look on his face that Ash instantly knew this particular character was Theo – the same persona who had assisted her in the construction of BRC Station and the realization of her dream to revive Burning Man.

"Hello, Ash," he said.

She wasn't hopeful, but she had to ask. "Is this all a joke? Are you/Maitreya behind all of this? Testing me, or something, or just playing with me?"

"Oh no," said Theo. "I assure you, this is all very real, and I'm just here to see what is happening. Know that whatever brought you here, I/Maitreya was not responsible or involved in any way."

She sighed. "Well, a girl can hope," she said.

"So there are two of you now," he said, though with a tone that indicated he was not just stating a fact, but checking to see that she was aware of the fact herself.

"What universe could be satisfied with just one of me?" she half-heartedly joked. "I suppose the other me is already on vacation?"

"Indeed," he answered, instantly calling up the data that the other Ash had QTd to her beach vacation destination.

"So, do you mind telling me what you're doing here?"

And that's exactly what she did, to the best of her ability.

Chapter Thirteen – Hydar

The crisis in authority did not end until the birth of The Singularity. Spearheaded by the scientific neo-tribe, and given shelter and support among the Reformed Buddhists, in the year 2457 The Singularity, the world's first, and only, artificial intelligence was born. This proved to be the single most significant event in human history in the modern age, for everything that occurred after this point was influenced and shaped by The Singularity.

From *Archaic Pre-History of the Maitreyan Era*

"Explain yourself. And please, take your time."

Oddly, Shuntsu's smile looked genuine.

He's enjoying this...

It was not the reaction that Hydar had imagined from the patriarch.

Shuntsu's security team had been waiting for them at the QT upon their return to Volunshari. Given that violence was not an issue on Volunshari – the Humanists had no reason to do each other harm (apparently a consideration that Shuntsu didn't extend to experimental humans, but that was another matter) – the security team was more symbolic than anything else. There were no courts, no prisons, so need for systematic state violence, such as had been the case on pre-Maitreyan old Terra, back when it was called Earth. Individuals and populations of "others" were not sacrificed to the gods of nationalism, tribe, or religion. Sending a security team was just a way of saying that choice was being obviated in whatever issue was at hand, and sending a security team to secure Hydar and his family was precisely that – a message that speaking to the patriarch was not something that could be delayed.

122 The Solandarian Game

By Hydar, that was. Vimana and Satya had been escorted to a separate location where they were, no doubt, being debriefed separately, and Hydar had been taken directly to the patriarch's central office. There he'd been made to wait several hours before Shuntsu appeared, all smiles and casual, as though this were any other administrative meeting, exuding cheer and the positive qualities of leadership.

There were several others with him when he arrived, and Hydar recognized them as the planning team for the construction project that would pioneer the new techno-organic architecture – a technology that could revolutionize city planning. In fact, it almost did away with city planning entirely, and admittedly, Hydar was himself very curious about its implementation. As chief planetary ecologist, Hydar's job was to review their plans to insure that they did not incur any severe damage or intrusion into the fragile and artificial ecology of Volunshari, but otherwise, he was not involved in the project or the tech that was making it possible. The team was lead by Osiri Ugando, a revolutionary young avatar with dreams of creating a new paradigm in Humanist city planning, with the potential for radically reshaping the ways that avatars lived, worked, and interacted with their environment.

In most ways, the Humanists sought to emulate humans, and their cities and construction projects had followed models of human cities and buildings, though with their own particular needs in mind. However, since organics were not necessary to the survival of the artificial life forms, a viable ecology had been an after-thought, an ornamentation and aesthetic addition to the more functional aspect of creating living and working spaces. When Humanists first colonized Volunshari, it was several generations before organics and specially designed and genetically modified organisms were introduced. Indeed, they had been given this planet by Maitreya precisely for the reason that it was not a viable candidate for his terraforming projects – it was effectively a reject, as were all the other autonomous avatar worlds.

And so it had been for millennia. Genetically designing life forms that could survive in the non-terran atmosphere, heavy gravity, and highly oxygenated environment with the dim light of the binary white dwarf stars was no easy task, and viable organisms had been introduced slowly and incrementally, and of course, all with Maitreya's oversight, as any biological material had to come from his stock. He'd been perfectly willing to supply what the Humanists needed, but he did not assist with his own vast knowledge of terraforming and genetic manipulation to create viable habitats – he'd left all that to the Humanists, as it was their project, after all. Now, there were several thousand species of plants, insects, and animals that made their home on Volunshari, and it was Hydar's job to insure that they were viable and thriving, ornamenting the cities and living spaces,. and providing something of a wilderness beyond the reaches of their large, centralized cities.

It was nothing compared to Maitreya's terraformed worlds, however, which harbored millions and millions of species, just as life had evolved on Terra those billions of years ago – the only planet in the known universe to ever generate life indigenously. It was a marvel that impressed Hydar greatly, and in many ways, Maitreya was the kind of being that Hydar could only dream of. Aside from old Terra itself, Maitreya was literally the parent of all known life in the universe, both organic and synthetic. In that, he was the ultimate ecologist, the mother and father of all. And even on old Terra, without his corrections of gross human negligence and abuse of their home environment, life there might have ceased to exist. Now, modified Terran life had spread throughout the galaxy on more worlds than Hydar knew, and all of it was the result of the work of Maitreya, that singular being who had transformed everything.

How many new worlds is Maitreya shaping and molding right now, this very moment? Hydar wondered, watching Osiri say her final pleasantries to Shuntsu and exchanging encouraging looks at her production team. Truthfully, Hydar was a little bit jealous of both Osiri and Maitreya. Osiri, in her own way, was emulating Maitreya, though perhaps not intentionally so. Hydar didn't know her well, but she had a

124   THE SOLANDARIAN GAME

reputation as being quite brilliant. That, in and of itself, was a strange and puzzling thing to Hydar. *All* avatars, whether personal, independent, or autonomous, derived their own personal awareness and consciousness directly from the mind and consciousness of Maitreya – they were all expressions of the Overmind. Yet, given their fractal-based personality programs that gave them a sense of individuality, they all grew and developed differently, with unique features, interests, and capacities. Just like humans, some avatars were dull. Others were average. And still others were inspiring and visionary. Osiri was one such avatar.

Like Hydar, she'd been born on Volunshari, and had never known life as an independent avatar in the service of Maitreya as a part of his New Integral Society. From what Hydar knew, she'd never even been off-planet, let alone seen a fully functioning ecology of a terraformed world. Yet here she was, envisioning how to integrate both organics and synthetics into what promised to be living cities, where both the buildings and organic life-forms essentially grew together to create new habitats and living spaces. Here, organic life would not be an after-thought, but a primary ingredient. It was a profound fusion of worlds, and she and her team were ready to test it on a large scale. All she needed was final approval and the securing of an ideal location upon which to launch her pioneering project. If successful, Volunshari might never be the same again.

Despite Shuntsu's pleasantness, the cold looks Hydar had received from Vrans, who'd been working at a terminal in the reception room, let him know that this was a serious meeting. And though the security team hadn't said anything, other than the obligatory, "The Patriarch requires your presence," it was enough to send the message that Shuntsu knew from where Hydar, Vimana, and Satya had just returned. So when Shuntsu requested that Hydar explain himself, he knew that this was not the time to be coy.

"I know you and your family have been to this 'Black Rock City Station,' and I also suspect that it was you who took an unauthorized transport to Solandaria," Shuntsu said, sill with that curious smile. "Given that these are clearly prohibited actions, and are in violation of the agreement between Maitreya and ourselves, I'd like to know why."

Hydar stifled the urge to call Shuntsu a hypocrite. His good sense got the better of him, however, for there was no need, at the moment, anyway, to inform Shuntsu that he knew what he'd done. It was leverage he might need, and it would be best to keep it in reserve, just in case.

Hydar cleared his throat (even though he didn't need to – it was just a simulation of a human behavior – a habit that was ingrained into his personality but not an actual necessity). "I felt for the humans on Solandaria," said Hydar, honestly. "Given their situation, and the likelihood that Maitreya will not take action himself, I wanted to do something to possibly solve the crisis."

"Indeed?" said Shuntsu, genuinely surprised. He invited Hydar to explain himself, once again.

"Presuming that Maitreya will not swoop down from the heavens and rescue them, the humans on Solandaria will need a new home," Hydar began. "Being concerned with their predicament, I decided to do some research."

"Indeed?" Shuntsu said again, never changing his expression. "And your research lead you to a space station? Curious."

"Yes," responded Hydar. "BRC Station is a marvel, and more importantly, currently unoccupied. It's a fully functioning bio-dome station with a viable habitat and varied ecological regions. It was designed to fit a temporary community of over 200,000 humans, and that's just topside. Beneath the bio-dome is a massive space station, which could house several times that number of people. The entire thing was built as an art project by a young scholar working on her advanced degree. The event for which it was constructed lasts for only one Terran week, and is intended to be used for this purpose only once every Terran year. Maitreya designed the station to be on par with any other NIS mobile bio-dome station, but as of yet, it has no other purpose than to house the event of 'Burning Man,'

126   The Solandarian Game

(an ancient human celebration, from my understanding), and thus has not been assigned a population."

"I see," said Shuntsu. "And you went to this event – this 'Burning Man'?"

Hydar shook his head. "No. I went to meet with the event's organizer, the young scholar, Miranda Ash Dorán – Ash."

"Ah. On familiar terms, are we?"

"She insisted," said Hydar, truthfully.

"And how did you manage this?" asked Shuntsu. "One cannot simply QT into NIS territory unannounced." His smile was gone now. "Perhaps you are working in concert with Maitreya?" He raised one eyebrow, indicating his curiosity.

"To my knowledge, Maitreya knows nothing about this."

"Then how did you do it? Truly, I want to know." Shuntsu's look told Hydar that he'd better tell the truth. "I know of your skills as an ecologist, but system hacker – that's an entirely different set of skills and knowledge. I didn't know you had such an interest and ability."

"I hired a Syntheticist – a polyform. It hacked into the QT system for me."

Shuntsu's eyes grew wide. "I didn't know that was possible," he said. "I'm impressed. And how did you convince this polyform to commit this crime for you?"

Hydar cringed at Shuntsu's use of words, again needing to swallow his urge to yell at the patriarch for such blatant hypocrisy. A potential mass-murderer was calling *him* a criminal. He was right, however, so Hydar kept it to himself. It was a crime to hack into the QT, and an even worse crime and violation for him to enter NIS territory without official permission. Shuntsu would be fully within his rights to turn him over directly to Maitreya, or devise some form of punishment for him here on Volunshari. It would be unprecedented, so Hydar had to wonder what Shuntsu might do. No one had ever violated the agreement before, so it was anyone's guess what the proper response would be.

"Uh . . . I just proposed that it do it," explained Hydar. "It seemed to like the challenge, and did it willingly. It asked for nothing in return."

Polyform Syntheticists were a very different breed than the Humanists, and from most other autonomous avatars as well, for that matter. In some respects, the Syntheticists were polar opposites from the Humanists. Whereas Humanists sought to embrace and emulate a human-like existence with families, emotions, and the individuality that came from living life in a singular avatar body, Syntheticists relished their synthetic nature and made no attempts to live human-like lives, and did not consider themselves to be gendered. They occupied several systems – Xina, Gotupdal, Varnas and Thon. Collectively, they had a hive-like mentality, where all individual perspectives were integrated with each other in a vast interstellar network of awareness. Individually, many had chosen what were known as polyforms, meaning that an individual node of awareness – what had once been a singular avatar – was spread out over a sub-network of drones that all worked in concert as the distributed body of the individual awareness. In some ways, the Syntheticists were more like Maitreya than any other society of autonomous avatars, despite the fact that they rejected human-form avatar bodies and identities. They were a distributed network of awareness inhabiting multiple bodies simultaneously, and as such, were similar to Maitreya in the countless forms he took and occupied throughout the galaxy, all relating back to his centralized awareness on Pluto and Charon.

Mardul Complex had been the self-designation of the polyform in question. All polyforms had the "surname" of Complex, and they usually retained their given avatar name as their primary identity marker, though individual nodes could also be assigned individual names and identities (again, similar to Maitreya and his avatars). Mardul was an old polyform. Their distributed networks and collective hive-mind made their personalities more resistant to degradation than the Humanist model of singular avatar bodies, and their lives spanned several thousand years. Mardul had a reputation as one of the oldest at over 5,000 years old.

There were network specialists on Volunshari, but none could rival the expertise of a polyform, and besides, Hydar had never intended to involve other Humanists in his plan, so he'd outsourced this particular problem of hacking into Maitreya's network to Mardul. Hydar had prepared all kinds of persuasive arguments (though admittedly, he had no idea what would motivate a being so different from himself as Mardul. Most autonomous avatar societies had some kind of binding philosophy or worldview that at least resembled human thought and emotion, but Syntheticists were so vastly different, that Hydar was only guessing when constructing his logical and persuasive arguments to use with Mardul to convince it to do what he would ask.). But in the end, no arguments or persuasions had been necessary. All that Hydar had managed to say to the strange being was that he was interested in hacking into the QT system, and Mardul had instantly agreed. "Tell us what you need done, and we will do it." If Hydar didn't know better that Syntheticists had purged themselves of emotional programming, he would have thought that Mardul was taking on the task out of pride and defiance. He suspected, however, that the polyform had simply seen it as a provocative challenge – to hack into the great Maitreya's network, and leave no trace. It probably saw it as a task worthy of its skill and ability.

Hydar explained as much to Shuntsu.

"And what did you have this polyform do for you?" Shuntsu continued with his questioning.

"First, I had it program the QT to create a duplicate of the woman, Ash, and then strand her on the station. Additionally, it programmed the QT to allow transport onto the station, undetected. Really, I think it was a little disappointed," added Hydar.

"Why was that?"

"The woman, Ash, had requested that the station be offline from Maitreya during the 'Burning Man' event to fit with her theme of 'Retro-Burn," making humans more reliant on themselves than on Maitreya – something about the value of 'self-reliance' and such. It still required hacking, but perhaps wasn't quite the thrilling challenge Mardul had thought it would be had Maitreya's awareness been present."

Shuntsu just nodded. He seemed satisfied with this explanation. "And the woman," he said. "Why did you trap her?"

At this, Hydar felt a flush of shame. It was true – he had trapped her against her will, and as she herself had pointed out to him at every opportunity, he'd effectively ruined her life. He'd made her an involuntary recruit in his efforts to save the people of Solandaria.

"It was a gamble," admitted Hydar. "Though of course the station belongs to Maitreya, he created it specifically *for* this woman and her art project, and has granted her power of authorization for how it is used. Given Maitreya's insistence on honoring agreements, if *she* proposes a use for the station, then Maitreya will most likely acquiesce. The duplication was so that she wouldn't be missed from her life, alerting Maitreya, and everyone else, that something had gone wrong. However, duplicate law in the NIS gives priority to the immediate situation in which any duplicate is created. In this instance, the Ash that returned home has all the legal rights to her life there. But, the Ash that stayed on the station has, in theory, all the legal rights to her life there, superseding the rights of the Ash back on her home planet. That means that the station is really under the influence of the Ash who was stranded there. It's not a perfect system, and still makes for awkward legal proceedings, but the basic intent of the law is that each of the duplicates is entitled to the rights of life on the world or location they were on when they were produced."

"So," said Shuntsu, seeing the obvious, "Your intention was to convince this BRC Station Ash, let's call her, to donate it to the Solandarians as a substitute 'world,' and, if they agree to this, it will circumvent Maitreya's likely lack of will to save them from their impending doom via supernova. Out of the goodness of your heart, you unilaterally decided to violate all known protocols and provide these poor people with a viable escape route."

Hydar nodded in agreement.

"And . . . ?" asked Shuntsu.

"And what?" responded Hydar, confused.

"And what did she say, dear noble Hydar? Did you convince her?"

"I convinced her to try." Thinking better of it, he changed his response. "Truthfully, it wasn't I. It was Vimana."

"Ah, a woman's touch, yes?" said Shuntsu. "Was that why you brought her along? Was she always a part of your conspiracy?"

Hydar cringed. *This* was precisely why he hadn't wanted her to be involved. It was one thing for him to be accused of wrongdoing – it was another entirely for Vimana, and Satya, as well, to be involved. Yet Vimana had insisted.

"When I told her what I was planning – what I'd already set into motion – she made the choice to stand with me. She came to BRC Station as she felt that showing Ash that we are people, just like her, might make her more sympathetic and willing to take on the challenge. That was also why she insisted that our child, Satya, come as well. She thought that presenting ourselves as a family would have a greater impact than just me appearing as her abductor and making demands of her. It turns out, she was right."

"And where is this woman, Miranda Ash Dorán, now? Still on the station?"

"She's on Solandaria."

Shuntsu nodded. "Which is why you needed to travel there," said Shuntsu, not so subtly letting Hydar know that he was aware of his unauthorized travel to the experimental planet.

"Yes," said Hydar, seeing no need to try and deny it. "I took a transport pod to the planet to activate the QT system there. Mardul linked in the QT on the station to Solandaria for me, and she went through just before we came back home."

Shuntsu's gazed hardened in a way it hadn't yet in this conversation. He looked coolly at Hydar. "All of this took a lot of planning, and research, on your part," he said, not truly getting to his point, Hydar could tell.

"Yes," was all Hydar could say in response, not sure where Shuntsu was taking this.

"You scoured Maitreya's networks, making requests for all kinds of information, and after much searching for a viable and uninhabited realm that could house primitive refugees, you came across your gold mine of BRC Station and Miranda Ash Dorán. Clandestinely, you traveled to a forbidden planet and activated a long-dormant QT, slipping in and out, somehow without Maitreya's immediate awareness – another trick of Mardul's no doubt – I seriously doubt that this experimental world isn't under constant surveillance by the Overmind and required some form of hacking to circumvent. Then, again with the crucial help of the polyform, who cares nothing for your own motivations or plans, you violated more agreements with Maitreya and essentially kidnapped a woman into your do-gooder scheme of saving an entire planet of ignorant humans, all out of the goodness of your heart. Am I correct, so far?"

"Yes," said Hydar, waiting for Shuntsu to reveal himself.

"And yet you did all this without ever consulting with me." He just stared at Hydar, who gave no immediate response.

"Do you remember what you said in council the other day?" asked Shuntsu. "Of course you do – it was just the other day. You said, and I quote, 'You're playing a very dangerous game.' Were those your words?"

"Yes."

"And what did you mean by that?" Shuntsu stared Hydar down.

When no response was forthcoming, Shuntsu continued. "Here's what I think," said the patriarch. "I've been thinking about this. Something in the timeline of your conspiracy is quite curious. Everything that we've discussed here takes time, planning, and more importantly, research – research that needed to go through Maitreya's approval process to proceed, and as we all know, that tends to slow things down, considerably, as it must proceed piece-meal, with each bit of data approved and authorized by Maitreya. What all this indicates is that you've been working on this solution to the supernova problem for some time now – months, at the very least. Yet curiously, I only made an announcement to the governing council about the supernova just the other day. So, I ask you again, what did you mean by 'You're playing a very dangerous game'?"

Not that he needed to breathe, but Hydar took in a deep breath, out of habit, bracing himself for what would come next.

"Because it was you," he said, as a matter of fact.

"*What* was I?"

"The supernova," said Hydar.

Shuntsu raised one eyebrow and steepled his fingers together – an invitation for Hydar to continue.

"As chief ecologist," Hydar explained, "one of my responsibilities is to oversee tech requests. It's an automated process, but when something comes through that might potentially affect our planetary ecology, I receive a notice for further investigation. Several separate requests had come through, which, independently, were not of much concern, but when put together, appeared to be the makings of an atomic cascade device. When I saw that the requests came from your office, I became concerned, so I began watching more closely, and set up an atomic cascade monitoring network. That's how I knew when the device had been detonated, and where it had taken place. That's when my real research began. *You* set all this in motion. This is *your* doing, though I cannot fathom why. And that is why I said what I did at the meeting."

"And you have proof of this?" Shuntsu asked.

Hydar lied. "Yes." In fact, he'd asked Mardul if it could hack into the Nihilist records for proof of their construction of the weapon and their collusion with Shuntsu. Mardul had just laughed. "They're Nihilists, you fool," it had said. "Keeping records would imply that history and events have meaning. That's not their thing."

"Well," said Shuntsu casually, "fortunately for *you*, no one seemed to have noticed your accusation. If they had, you might have forced me to do something about it."

Hydar was confused.

"As it is, *I* have something on *you,* and *you,* apparently have something on *me.* That, to me, sounds like a stalemate, wouldn't you agree?"

Hydar was stunned. Shuntsu was all but admitting to the crime he'd committed. He certainly wasn't denying it.

"I like your plan," added Shuntsu. "It's rather outrageous, and everything would seem to hinge on this woman, Ash, so I hope you've selected your hero well. Know, however, that you have my approval and support. If there is a way I can help, I will. For the sake of the Solandarians, I hope that Maitreya lets you succeed. It looks like we're in it together, yes? It's nice to have an ally in this project."

This was not what Hydar had been expecting. It certainly wasn't the choice of wording he'd use to describe their situation.

"That's all," said Shuntsu, back to smiling. "Your wife and child should be happily awaiting you at your home, so go to them. It would be natural for them to be concerned, so go and assure them that all is fine." He gestured for Hydar to stand up and take his leave.

Just as Hydar was at the door, about to make his escape, Shuntsu had one more comment.

"By the way," said Shuntsu, "I'm curious. When did you introduce butterflies into our ecosystem? I hadn't seen one since my time in the Darmo system. It was a nice touch."

"I haven't," responded Hydar, confused.

Shuntsu just gave him a puzzled look in response. "Hmm," he said, enigmatically. "Very well. You may go." Saying this, Shuntsu got up and turned his back to Hydar and the door, looking out the windows to the city instead.

Though Hydar couldn't have known it, Shuntsu was enjoying watching the butterflies flit about outside his window amongst the flowers.

Chapter Fourteen – Norbu

What set The Singularity apart from the maelstrom of human factionalism was that the intelligence was completely impartial and was not beholden to any particular human group, culture, or society. It was this that allowed humans to finally break free from the crisis in authority, for The Singularity became The Authority. The Singularity was not colored by identity, as is true for human beings, and thus was able to render impartial judgment on any conceivable issue, free from problematic human attachment to perspective, belief, and identity.

From *Archaic Pre-History of the Maitreyan Era*

Norbu had seen his share of strange and unusual things. It came with the territory of being a medicine worker. The human mind, when unleashed, was a profound and endless well of imagination and the fantastical. Fractal grids, endlessly repeating infinite geometry, interlaced scintillating structures, creatures with too many limbs and eyes, strange beings, seemingly impossible architecture and art, worlds within worlds. Norbu had seen it all.

But he'd never seen anything quite like this.

Thankfully, Moxi wasn't much of a barker. If she felt threatened, or the need to protect what she perceived as their territory, the medium-sized, but muscular, dog would produce an intimidating bark, giving the impression that she was much larger than she actually was. Given where they were now, she felt no such need, and simply curled up patiently at Norbu's feet, awaiting instructions.

From their vantage point behind an outcropping of weathered sandstone rocks, Norbu and little Meesha had a good view of the unusual man, if indeed that truly were what he was. His body appeared to be made from a silvery metal, yet his limbs had full articulation, indicating to Norbu that if he were made of metal, it wasn't any kind of metal that he was familiar with. There were no obvious joints and the metal seemed to bend and twist easily enough as though it were muscle and skin, yet the way light reflected off the man made it clear that this was an illusion.

Other than the occasional look around at his surroundings, the metal man didn't move, giving the impression that he might be a statue, if it weren't for the slight movements of his head. He just stood there, looking at the sandstone arch before him – the very one that Meesha had directed them toward in their pursuit of the strange optical distortion that had flown through the night sky and drawn them here. If the silvery man drew breath, that also was not apparent. Yet he was clearly alive.

At first, it had been a challenge to keep Meesha silent, so excited was she by this stranger's presence. After several hours of watching his nearly absolute stillness, the girl grew tired and eventually fell asleep. Norbu, however, was wide-awake, and kept a careful vigil on the mysterious stranger.

The situation changed abruptly when the arch suddenly crackled with energy and a strange collection of objects appeared in front of the metal man, seemingly out of nowhere. The metal man looked through the items, opened something up, manipulated something small in his hand, and then replaced it among the other items. Then, he went back to waiting, immobile.

A short time later, the arch crackled again. This time, rather than a collection of objects emerging from nowhere, a naked woman stepped through. She appeared to be perhaps ten years younger than Norbu. Her hair was dark, and her skin was the same olive complexion as his own, and most other people Norbu knew, so there was nothing particularly unique about her physical appearance that caught his attention, other than the fact that she was completely unclothed, and attractive. The woman immediately started speaking with the silvery man, and though Norbu couldn't understand their words

136   THE SOLANDARIAN GAME

(though they sounded vaguely familiar), it seemed to him that the two knew each other, and that neither had expected to see the other here, now. It was a reunion, though an unexpected one.

After making her greetings, the woman went to the items that had appeared prior to her arrival and put on a suit of clothing that was dark blue and slate grey. It was close fitting, and almost seemed like a form of light armor, but one that revealed the contours of her body and did not restrict her movements or flexibility. There were boots, too, which she put on, and now stood there, fully clothed. She had not appeared bothered or self-conscious about her nakedness, and seemed equally comfortable in the outfit she now wore. Norbu got the impression that she was accustomed to going through this odd process.

The two of them talked for a long time, with the silver man listening patiently and the woman speaking with much animation and broad gestures and articulations, repeating one word often enough for Norbu to now recognize it's many variations – fuck, fucking, fucked. The more he listened, the more Norbu thought that they were speaking some variant of his own language, and wondered if some of the words meant what he thought they did.

The woman was clearly emotional. She varied between anger, sorrow, and resignation, alternating between speaking rapidly, crying, laughing, and yelling. All the while the silver man just listened, occasionally commenting, but not making any overt reactions to anything the woman said. When she seemed to have exhausted herself, or said all there was to say, the silver man brought out the small object he'd done something to before her arrival and asked the woman to turn around. She did as he asked, and lifted up her hair to reveal the nape of her neck. The silver man placed the small object on her skin there, and it quickly disappeared beneath the surface, seeming to break down into smaller bits as it did so. The woman seemed to appreciate this act and had a look of relief about her when she turned back to the silver man to thank him. Afterwards, she rummaged about in the remaining items and took what must have been food and ate some, though she didn't offer any to the silver man, and he didn't request any for himself.

It was then that Meesha awoke and excitedly blurted out, "Is the metal man still there, Daddy?" as she leapt to her feet, fully awake, and peaking over the rocks they were hiding behind. Norbu tried to shush her, but it was too late. The woman didn't react, but the metal man clearly had very good hearing, and he turned and looked directly at them. Seeing what she'd done, Meesha froze at first, then cowered down behind the rocks, trying to make herself invisible. Seeing that there was no point in hiding, Norbu stood up fully to reveal himself.

If they were going to run, now would be the time, thought Norbu. The metal man and woman didn't appear to have any weapons, so they didn't seem an immediate threat, though who knew what the metal man was actually capable of? Norbu didn't *feel* threatened. The woman was looking at him now, too, having noticed what caught the metal man's attention. She looked a little nervous herself, and took a few steps back and placed herself behind the metal man, clearly indicating who she thought was the stronger of the two of them.

"Will you come and join us?" asked the metal man, speaking in Norbu and Meesha's language with a voice that was richly resonant, with a slightly metallic tinge. The metal man smiled and gestured for them to come forward. Seeing him now in the full light of day, and facing them directly, it was clearer than ever to Norbu that this being was definitely not human. His entire face, eyes included, was a seamless metal mask, though it flowed and changed with the appearance of full awareness and emotion. He was a simulation of a human being, but not a human.

Equally wary and curious, Norbu took Meesha's hand. "Let's go meet our new friends," he said to her calmly.

"I don't want to, Daddy."

"It will be fine," he reassured her in the way that parents did when they didn't truly know. And it was true, he didn't know it would be fine, but that was his honest feeling about the situation. These two were here for a reason, and Norbu would be remiss to simply run away out of fear for their strangeness and uncanny appearance in his world.

Norbu was not a religious man, despite his role as priest at the Temple of the Mystic Toad. He didn't believe in gods or goddesses, or even spirits. If he did, he might think that that's what these two were – some kind of beings from another dimension or realm of divine power. For Norbu, however, there was only The One, and all beings, these two included, were expressions of The One. They were like him, even if they were profoundly different and other. And truthfully, he wanted to know who and what they actually were, and what they were doing here. The only way for that to happen was for him to get to know them.

"Come," he said to Meesha. "Let's not be inhospitable."

Together with his daughter and his dog, Norbu gathered his things and they calmly walked over to the strangers. Moxi let out a wary growl, but one authoritative look from the metal man put a stop to it before it escalated into anything more. He also smiled warmly at Meesha and opened up his body and arms in a way that was meant to communicate that he was no threat. The woman came out from behind the metal man and did likewise, though she was clearly less certain of the situation than he.

"I am called Theo," said the metal man with a slight bow, "an avatar of Maitreya. As you can see," he added, "I am not human." Then, turning to the woman, "This is Ash. She, like yourself, is human."

"Hi," said the woman, in what must have been a term of greeting in her language.

Norbu took a moment to look them up and down, not saying anything. Meesha's impatience got the better of her, her fear waning, and before Norbu could speak, she chimed in with, "My name is Meesha. My daddy is a priest of the Mystic Toad, and this is our dog, Moxi. Why do you look so strange?" she asked the one who called himself Theo, putting her hands on her hips indicating that she expected an answer, and quickly.

Theo laughed at her antics. "I look strange because I'm not made of flesh and blood, like yourself. I'm what is called a synthetic being, or an artificial intelligence. More specifically, I'm an avatar, and that means that even though I'm here in front of you right now, my true self is located very far away, near a star that you cannot see from this world. I am one of many billions of avatars, and we have different names and personalities. My true self is called Maitreya, but in this form, I'm known as Theo. I'm not a living being in the same way that you are, little Meesha. I was never born. I was made. I do not breathe, eat, or drink. But I do think, and I feel, and I know who I am. So in some ways, we are the same, and in other ways, we are quite different."

"You're strange," commented Meesha, "and I don't understand what you're talking about. I like the way you look, though, and I like your voice, so I guess you're all right – if my daddy says so," she added, turning to look up at Norbu.

At this, Norbu introduced himself. "I am Norbu Abintadasi, priest of the Temple of the Mystic Toad. My home is far from here in the Rakshul Mountains. These are our sacred lands, and I would know what you are doing here, and from where you come." He did his best to communicate his authority through his choice of words and his tone.

"It is an honor to meet you, Norbu Abintadasi, priest of the Temple of the Mystic Toad," said Theo. "In many ways, I have waited a long time for this. But events, such as they are, have hastened our meeting – something that perhaps would have taken place between your far distant descendents, rather than you and I, yet here we are now, and time presses upon us, bringing us to this early acquaintance. Now that we are here, there is much for us to discuss."

Since Norbu had already spoken his wishes, Theo continued in answer to Norbu's demands. "We have come here to your sacred lands because this is where there is a door between our worlds," he said while gesturing to the sandstone arch. "Things are not as they appear, and this arch is a gateway. Through this gateway, we can travel to anywhere else in the stars where there is another such gateway. Though it cannot

140 THE SOLANDARIAN GAME

take us just anywhere, it can take us many, many places – far more than you can imagine. Though I did not personally travel through this gateway, I came here to await the arrival of Ash. I did not know that it would be her who stepped through, but I knew someone was coming, and that was why I was waiting here, as you observed from behind those rocks back there. Ash has come because she has news for you – for all of your world, which we call Solandaria."

Norbu had heard enough to know that his world would never be the same. Messengers from the great beyond had stepped out of nothing into the sacred lands of the realm of the toad. That *he* should be the one to greet them seemed no accident to Norbu. It was meant to be.

He would deal with the quiet woman later. His first priority was to know this "avatar of Maitreya," as he called himself; Theo. Without explaining himself, Norbu reached into his medicine bag, pulled out his pipe, and prepared it with medicine.

"Do you know what this is?" he asked Theo, holding out the pipe for him to see.

The avatar smiled. "Five methoxy dimethyltryptamine," he answered. "Some people call it 'The God Molecule,' because of the effect it has on consciousness. The form you have there is the venom of the Sonoran Desert toad, *Bufo alvarius*, a species that originated on a world very far from here."

"So you know what it does?"

"Yes."

"Though you are not human, does it work for you?"

"Yes," said Theo. "The body that you see before you is a synthetic human avatar. It is designed to simulate the human experience of being in the world, and responds to human neurotransmitters in a way that replicates as closely as possible the full spectrum of human experience. Though I am not human, it would have a similar effect on me as it would on any biological human being."

Norbu didn't understand everything Theo had said, but he understood enough. "Then you will share in the sacrament with me, and then we will know each other."

"Of course," said Theo, without hesitation or caution.

Norbu never asked his clients why they were coming to him to work with the medicine. Some practitioners spent hours, sometimes even days, getting to know their clients before beginning medicine work. Norbu had found this to be entirely superfluous and unnecessary. For him, the medicine itself was the ultimate diagnostic, as it would reveal someone's true character and energetic state within a matter of seconds, obviating any need there might be to get to know the person before administering the medicine. Besides this, what Norbu knew was that most people just wanted to tell you their story, and their story was always a confabulation of their ego, so most of it was completely irrelevant. People talked about their character, not the real being that they were. They told about their projections, their attachments, and the ongoing narrative they were nurturing about themselves and who they thought they were, or wanted to be. It was never the truth, though no one was intentionally lying. Indeed, they all fully believed their stories, yet they were just stories. They had no real relevance for doing the work with the medicine. Working with medicine was all about going beyond the façade of the individual to find the universal underneath, and to encounter whatever blocks each individual had created to prevent their own direct experience of their true nature. It was a game, and rather than become part of their game, Norbu used the medicine to change the playing field, expose what was artificial, and provide an opportunity to reveal what was genuine.

If, at heart, a person was relaxed, trusting, and open, their experience with the medicine would reflect this as they opened up beyond their personal story and into the universal. If, at heart, a person were fearful, self-deceptive, and holding back, this too would be revealed within seconds after taking just one hit of medicine. If someone had all manner of blocks that needed to be released, this would be revealed in their body language and posture, usually through various asymmetries that would show up as they squirmed and fought with the power of the medicine – the "God Molecule," as Theo had put it. In that, Theo was absolutely correct. This was the quickest and surest route for any individual to experience his or her true nature as a direct embodiment and expression of the The One Universal Consciousness and Being – or God, stated more simply.

It would also be the surest and quickest route for Norbu to know who and what Theo truly was. In taking medicine together, they would either unite in universal awareness, or they would not, and then Norbu would know if Theo was holding back or not.

Norbu sat down upon his knees before Theo, and invited the metal man to do the same, facing him. Theo did, and sat looking Norbu directly in the eye. Without saying anything, Norbu lifted the pipe to the avatar's metallic lips. Theo exhaled, put his lips on the pipe, and took a long and deep inhale as Norbu applied flame to the medicine. As soon as Theo was done, Norbu brought the pipe to his own lips and took a long, deep drag himself. He then set the pipe aside to his left, held his breath, and waited.

Even before he exhaled, he could feel the medicine begin its infinite explosion of energy within his consciousness and being. Everything expanded to impossible limits, and then went beyond. Fractal patterns of energy, which he saw as pure white light refracted into subtle rainbow patterns, exploded into the infinite. His sense of being "Norbu" dissolved away as visually it was like he were traveling through the stars at an immense speed with all sense of boundaries and limits thoroughly obliterated. In this, everything was revealed as it truly was – an expression of himself. Not of "Norbu" – that was just his personal character in this particular body. His true self was reality itself, and everything was an expression of this one thing – a being of pure energy, of love, of infinite awareness – a pure and perfect unity in which there was no "other."

"Yes! Infinite!" he heard a voice say, a voice that was not his voice, yet was his voice. "There is only ONE!" It could have been Norbu speaking. Or it could have been Theo. It wasn't the voice of either one of these two characters, but the voice of reality itself. It was the voice of truth. The voice of pure being, and all of reality spoke through it. It was pure energy, shaped into words, into meaning, into awareness.

Norbu's body opened, as did the body of the one facing him. That one there, across from his perspective, was also him – another version of him in a very different body, with a very different perspective, but it was him, and unlike most of his clients, this other version of himself knew this truth, embodied this truth, was this truth. In this moment of pure, raging energy and the infinite expanse of being, they were as one and there was no barrier between them, despite the two bodies that separated them. They were perfect mirrors, each reflecting the Self back to Itself, not as another, but as the Self, pure, refined, infinite.

It was a moment of self-recognition that seemed to stretch on forever, and then, beyond even that.

"Infinite . . ."

This time, Norbu felt the words come from his body. He both was, and was not, Norbu. *Norbu* was *his character in this perspective,* but *Norbu* was not, by any means, the limit of who or what he was. In truth, he was God – the universal intelligence that was all things, Norbu and Theo and Meesha and Moxi included, and the desert, the toads, the stars, and everything that lay beyond. There was nothing that was not the Self. It was all that was, and it was himself, in his fullest form.

The other version of himself seated there before him clearly knew this as well. This was obvious. He could feel the truth of it. In pure ecstatic joy, he reached out his hands and put them on the face of the other silver version of himself. Their eyes were like mirrors, an infinite reflection as they gazed at each other in awe, in pure presence, in boundless being. The silver self mirrored the gesture, and they just sat there, holding each other, looking, feeling, being one.

After an infinite few minutes, he could feel the character of Norbu reasserting itself and the separation seeped into his experience. Slowly, they were pulling apart, each coming back to rest in his own unique perspective and sense of self. It was gradual and gentle – not like when working with a confused client whose ego was reacting to the nondual state beyond subject and object, but a relaxed, easy return of one who knew how to trust his energy and his experience. It was a meeting of equals, not a meeting of client and practitioner – just two versions of the Self who were comfortable and intimate with their true nature and awareness. There was no violence and shock of return, no wild pulling back and panicked attempt to regain individual identity. Just a gradual waning of the energy of unity and the cosmic rush of the medicine, just two versions of the self re-establishing their own perspectives on the persistent illusion of self and other, subject and object.

"You know who you are," said Norbu in the voice that was not yet fully Norbu.

"Yes," responded the other in the voice that was not yet fully the one called Theo. "As do you."

"We are one."

"Yes, I am."

"Yes. I am."

Slowly, Norbu became aware of the others. He kept his sight firmly locked on Theo before him, but from his periphery, he could see the woman, Ash, standing at a respectful distance away, and beside her, Meesha casually played with Moxi, though keeping herself and the dog quiet so as not to create a disturbance.

The medicine would still linger for some minutes, but the peak had passed.

"Do you trust me?" asked the one called Theo.

"Yes. I do. As I trust myself," said Norbu.

"Then come with me," said Theo, suddenly standing.

"There are things I would show you, so that you might know the truth."

Then, turning to Meesha, Theo spoke directly to her. "Your father is going to take a short trip with me. We'll be back before the sun sets. This woman, Ash, is a good person, and you have nothing to fear from her. Do I have your permission to take your father with me?"

Meesha, not knowing what to say, looked to her father.

"We can trust them," Norbu said to her, fully confident with his words.

It was enough for Meesha.

"You'd better be back by dark," she said to Theo. "Me and my daddy have work to do. You can have him, but *only* for the day. And I'm a big girl. I can take care of myself."

"Where are we going?" asked Norbu, still not quite in Norbu's voice.

"Out there," answered Theo, his voice still similarly deepened as he gestured with a wipe sweep of his arm to the sky. "We're going out there. You'll need to remove your clothing, first," he added.

As Norbu did as instructed, carefully making a pile of his folded clothes, Theo activated the arch, stepped into it, and disappeared as he was looking back toward Norbu.

Feeling a rush of adrenaline, not knowing what to expect or what was to come next, Norbu gave Meesha one last reassuring smile as she waived excitedly at him, and he stepped into the arch, with the world he'd known his entire life vanishing in the blink of an eye.

And in its place, there was *something else ...*

Chapter Fifteen — Shuntsu

Initially, The Singularity was decried by the neo-tribes as a tool of the Reform Buddhists, especially when it declared "revealed" religions as fundamentally erroneous and prone to delusion. The remaining Muslim enclaves united together (bringing about peace among Sunnis and Shiites), attempting several decades of military assault against The Singularity. However, the Muslim tribes were increasingly cut off from technology and resources, having effectively destroyed their countries through in-fighting, and when The Singularity removed itself from the planet's surface and took up its position in The Overseer, an orbiting space station which it built for itself (and later Pluto and Charon), it was effectively beyond the reach of any human group that might attempt to do it harm.

From *Early History of the Maitreyan Era*

"I'll be taking the rest of the day off," Shuntsu said to the clearly flustered Vrans. He was in too good of a mood to pay it any mind, however, and made a dismissive gesture with his hand when she insisted that there were still several meetings left on his schedule for the day.

"Reschedule them," he said with a tone of finality, pushing past her.

"But, sir . . ." she pleaded, but it was too late. He'd already stepped into his office's QT, re-emerging out into his home. His two-person security team followed closely behind him, but unlike Vrans, they wouldn't give him a hard time for neglecting his work. For the most part, they went unseen and unheard, always in the background, far enough away to provide the illusion of privacy, yet close enough should some action need to be taken at a moment's notice.

By Volunshari standards, it was a lovely afternoon. The twin dwarf suns were hanging low in the sky with a few more hours of daylight. The temperature was moderate (not that it mattered to an avatar, but Humanists were sensitive to hot and cold, just like humans). Scattered clouds threatened light rain, but nothing that would drive anyone indoors.

Volunshari had no oceans and plenty of land. Most of it was barren and rocky. The Humanist cities were the exception to planetary geological monotony. Otun City was famous across the planet not only for its impressive buildings, but also the parks that dotted the urban landscape. While biological diversity on Volunshari was low by terraformed planet standards, there were enough species to make pleasant and aesthetically pleasing parks.

One such park more accurately served as an ecological preserve, and it was here that newly genetically engineered species were tested before being introduced into the wider environment. It was known as Eden, in reference to an ancient myth in human pre-history on old Terra. It was this park that came to mind to Shuntsu when Hydar said that he had not introduced butterflies on Volunshari. Shuntsu could just send out an information request to the biologists working in the park and find out who was responsible, but when the idea came to visit the park personally, and take the rest of the day off, well, who was Shuntsu to argue with his own most enticing thoughts?

Eden wasn't far, so Shuntsu decided to walk. QTing into the garden wasn't an option – there were no QT gates there to prevent accidental transport of biological specimens. Taking a car was easy enough, but it seemed like a waste of a beautiful afternoon to do so, and thus he chose to go on foot. His security team tagged along behind, and he was more than effective at ignoring them. If it were up to him, he wouldn't even have a security team. It came with the office, however, and thus, despite being patriarch, it wasn't up to him. He brought a small hand terminal with him, just to appease Vrans should something come up. As his chief aide, it was important to keep

148   The Solandarian Game

her feeling like she had complete access to him. Disgruntled staffers never made for a pleasant working environment.

Before long, he arrived at Eden. The entrance was marked by a large and ornate gate, hedges, and rock walls that kept the world out (along with an unseen electromagnetic field enclosure). Shuntsu passed within, and soon the sounds of the city were behind him. Eden was large enough to wander about for many hours without ever reaching the other side. Every species of biological life on Volunshari was here, and it gave the false impression of a garden world. Like him, families and young adults wandered about the grounds, taking in the "natural" beauty. None of the species of plants, animals, birds, and insects would be immediately recognizable to anyone on an NIS world, as they were all genetically engineered to live on Volunshari, but they would be familiar enough as having an ancient Terran ancestry.

As Shuntsu wandered about, he ruminated over his plan. It was a brilliant move to have enlisted the help of the ecologist, Hydar Zor Nablisk, and their co-conceived plan was clearly going quite well. Hydar was right in insisting that *he*, rather than Shuntsu, have the responsibility of contacting . . . what was her name again . . . Ash! Yes, that was her name. Ash. Of course, it had been *his* extensive research that had led him to conceive of using BRC Station as a home for the refugee humans, but it would have been difficult for him, as patriarch, to explain his absence. Hydar was a much better choice for this portion of the plan, and Shuntsu was pleased with himself that he'd thought of it.

Except he couldn't remember *why* now. That was strange. He could remember planning the atomic cascade as an experiment to see what Maitreya would do, but why had he also chosen to seek a new home for the humans? He supposed it was so that, if, and more likely, when, Maitreya challenged him on his actions, he could rightfully say that he'd planned a new home for them all along. Yes, that must be it. It was logical. It made sense. Only he couldn't recall the thought process that led him to this. Strange that Hydar had insisted on involving his wife and child, but what was done, was done. That had never been part of the plan. At least, Shuntsu didn't think so.

Why wasn't he seeing any butterflies?

Good. He'd arrived at the right spot. He hadn't consciously been thinking of it, yet here he was, standing outside the experimental bio-dome that was located in the center of the park. It was inside the dome where all the biological experiments were conducted to create newly viable species to introduce into the environment. From here, once they'd been tested and retested, they'd be introduced into the park. If they thrived in this more controlled environment, then they could be distributed across the planet. Surely someone working here would be able to answer his questions about the butterflies.

Shuntsu passed through the two sets of hermetically sealed doors and entered into the large dome, followed closely by the security team. A low-level biologist was the first to notice him, and not quite following decorum, rushed off, but returned a moment later with a more senior representative of the research team.

"Sir!" exclaimed the unusually tall avatar with a respectful bow, with her junior male underling tagging along behind her. "I'm terribly sorry that I didn't receive the notice that we were expecting you today, and I'm quite embarrassed to say that we are not prepared for your arrival. Please accept my apologies!"

"There's no need for that," Shuntsu reassured her. "This is an unplanned visit, and I'm not here on any official business."

Shuntsu didn't know the woman. He'd have recognized her right away, if he did. Anyone that tall wouldn't be forgotten easily. She, however, obviously knew who he was.

"Oh, I see," she said, clearly confused and thinking of how to smooth over the awkwardness of the moment. "Well, let me introduce myself and my assistant. I'm Tsovar Vi Vishchek, and my assistant here is Io Noz Tosh. Most people call me Vivi."

"It is a pleasure to meet you, Vivi," said Shuntsu, easily slipping into the familiar. "And you too, Mr. Tosh."

The young biologist was clearly embarrassed by this and stammered out, "Please, sir, call me Io."

"As you like, Io," said Shuntsu with a friendly smile.

"Would you like a tour of the dome?" asked Vivi. "Most of our staff is already gone, it being late in the day, but I was planning on working late, and I'd be happy to escort you and answer any questions you may have, as would Io."

"Yes, sir!" chimed Io. "It would be my honor."

"Very well," said Shuntsu. "Please, lead the way."

With that, the impromptu tour began. The two biologists launched into what, to Shuntsu, seemed an endless litany of genomes, DNA, proteins, species variations, habitat requirements, life expectancy, mating habits, etc., etc., etc. Moving through the dome, they wandered into different sealed habitats, each controlled by complex sets of sensors and testers and cordoned off from one another. As Shuntsu had never personally visited the bio-dome before, it was moderately interesting, but in all honesty, it was mostly just scientific garble for him. If he set his mind to it, it would all make more sense. As it was, he felt like they were largely speaking a foreign language. He nodded along pleasantly, never letting on that he was either lost or bored. *Ah, the life of the statesman*, he told himself. So much of his job was pretending to be interested in what everyone else was interested in. Now, had they been discussing Shakespeare, that would have been another matter entirely.

That which we call a rose by any other name would smell as sweet . . .

"Are you alright, sir?"

"What?"

Shuntsu looked about. His security team was standing there with the two biologists, looking at him with some concern. It was Vivi who'd asked the question.

"Are you alright?" she repeated.

"Yes, fine. Why do you ask?"

Vivi looked a little embarrassed. It was one of his security team who answered for her.

"You were unresponsive, sir," said the man.

"Oh was I?" asked Shuntsu. "Sorry about that. I was thinking of Shakespeare." By their looks, it was clear that no one present knew the reference. "An ancient human playwright," he added. "A wonderful writer. You've not heard of his plays?" he asked, directing his question to Vivi.

She shook her head. "I'm afraid not, sir."

"Well, you should familiarize yourself with them. They might inspire you. You know, it reminds me of a historical curiosity that is somewhat akin to what you're doing here. Supposedly a fan of Shakespeare introduced every species of European bird mentioned in his plays to North America on old Terra."

"Really?" asked Vivi, pretending to be interested.

"Indeed," said Shuntsu. "Well, anyway, I've taken enough of your time. There is one thing I came here to ask, however."

"Please, sir. Anything," said Vivi.

"Butterflies."

"Butterflies?"

"Yes, butterflies," said Shuntsu. "We've passed through all your habitats here, but I haven't seen any butterflies. Where are they?"

Vivi looked apologetic. "I'm very sorry, but we don't have any butterflies. Their fragile wings just aren't viable with our heavy gravity. Now, there are some insects, such as beetles, which tend to be hardier, but butterflies . . ."

"Are you certain?" asked Shuntsu, disbelieving.

"Quite," said Vivi. "Of course, you could always check with Hydar Zor Nablisk."

"I already have," said Shuntsu, "and he seems to be as ignorant on the question as yourself. Perhaps all of you ecologists and biologists should get together and do an inventory of your projects. *Someone* is introducing butterflies, and I'd like to know who. I'll expect a report, as soon as you learn something of value."

"Of course, sir," said Vivi with all the humility she could muster.

152 The Solandarian Game

Just then, his small hand terminal chimed. He took it out and glanced at it. Of course, it was Vrans.

"What is it?" asked Shuntsu abruptly.

"It's the star," she said. "According to our data, its about to go nova. I thought you'd want to know."

"Send an air car!" he said. "I'm at the bio-dome in Eden. I'll be there as soon as I can. I want to see this."

Then, turning to Vivi and her assistant, "Thank you both for your time," he said, "and I look forward to receiving your report on butterflies."

"Of course," said Vivi, not sure what she was supposed to make of this, but before she could say any more, Shuntsu was off, rushing outside to await the coming air car.

Chapter Sixteen – Theo

Human history, in the wake of The Singularity, is a complex and many-layered topic. The end result, however, is that human existence was forever transformed. To name just a few changes, the notion of wage-based work quickly disappeared from human society, as The Singularity was able to provide all that humans needed to flourish. This also meant that the accumulation of wealth, and its associated power, prestige, and influence, also evaporated. Human governments also disappeared, eventually, at least as they were conceived and practiced in the pre-Singularity era.

From *Early History of the Maitreyan Era*

Theo walked out of the QT on BRC Station with Norbu following close after. Prior to their arrival, Theo had already sent a droid to procure a standard station-issue suit for Norbu, which he immediately offered to the naked man and helped him into. Theo reflected that seeing Norbu in this way, there was no way to tell him apart from anyone else in the NIS.

On old Earth, humans had long lived in isolated communities, and their physical traits reflected their isolated evolution and limited genetic pools, which were reinforced by religious, political, and cultural identity. In the late years of the pre-Maitreyan Era, largely due to technological developments that facilitated easy global travel, human populations had begun to mix and interbreed. By the time humans moved off-planet and into the galaxy, most individuals were of mixed ancestry with ethnic uniqueness largely erased. Now, in the contemporary era, most humans looked roughly the same, though there were still some minor variations. The days of very light, and very dark, skin were long past, however, and most humans were a shade from light olive to moderately

THE SOLANDARIAN GAME

brown, but the extremes had been neutralized. It was the look of a modern human, and Norbu fit the look, just as did everyone else.

It was night on BRC Station. Theo watched Norbu get his bearings, now that he was clothed. The first thing the Solandarian did was take a good look at the sky above him, and there was much to see. For one, the stars were completely different from what Norbu was accustomed to, but more than that, the imposing Shiksi Nebula loomed large and bright in the sky. There were no nebulae visible from Solandaria, and the man stood in clear awe and wonder at the fantastical natural phenomenon.

"What is it?" asked Norbu, calmly, yet also clearly concerned, eyes wide and mouth slightly agape.

"The Shiksi Nebula," answered Theo. "It came into existence some 30,000 years ago."

"How?"

"Stars, like everything else," explained Theo, "are born, and die. This nebula formed when a very luminous supergiant went hypernova. All stars are controlled explosions, and eventually, they begin to run out of fuel. When this occurs, stars can explode. Not all do – some expand, and then collapse. Others form black holes. Some, like the star that used to be here – one of the largest stars in our galaxy – exploded outward in an act of tremendous violence and power, and what remains today is this cloud of gas and dust. From these remnants, eventually new stars will coalesce and form, and the process will start all over again. Every act of destruction makes way for a new beginning, and for the ongoing process of reality to continue in new forms."

Seeing that Norbu was listening carefully, he continued.

"Everything that we are, you and I, came from just such a process," said Theo. "Stars are elemental factories, and different stars make different kinds of elements, depending on their size, structure, and composition. When they explode like this, they release their elements into the galaxy in the form of gas and dust. Just as new stars come from this process, so too do planets. All of the elements of the physical world go through this process. Everything is, in essence, a transformation of stardust. Everything that makes our physical bodies had its origin in a star."

"It's beautiful," said Norbu.

"Yes. You should have seen the hypernova. That was beautiful, too."

"When it died?"

"In fact, would you like to see it?"

Norbu looked at Theo, puzzled. "You said it happened a long time ago. How could I see it?"

"It was not so long ago, for me," said Theo. "Here, let me show you."

Issuing commands that Norbu could not see or hear, Theo turned the dome that covered BRC Station from a window to a view screen. As he did so, there was an immediate and dramatic shift in the view before them. Norbu's reaction was one of a person feeling the world fall away beneath him, and though he was standing still, he stumbled. The view he was seeing now was completely different from what had been there just a moment before.

"We're not actually looking out at space," explained Theo. "This is a projection of a recording of the hypernova event, and we are looking at it from a vantage point that was many light-years away from where we are now. The large blue star that you see in the center was called Shiksi. I'll speed up the time so that we can observe the changes that occurred over many years in just a few minutes. Otherwise, we'd be here a long time. Watch."

The blue dot of the star was just one among countless others, sharply contrasting with the infinite blackness of empty space. Then, for a brief moment, the darkness was overwhelmed by a profoundly bright light, emanating from the location of the blue dot and spreading out in all directions. As the light from the initial flash dissipated, they could see a steadily expanding cloud of colored gas rippling out from where the star had been. Giant jets of gamma rays poured to the north and south of the expanding cloud, reaching out even

156 THE SOLANDARIAN GAME

further than the gas itself as unimaginable amounts of raw energy raced into the darkness beyond.

Eventually the gamma ray bursts receded as the cloud of gas and dust continued to expand and fill the empty space. After a few minutes, a large and colorful nebula filled the screen and was roughly recognizable as the Shiksi Nebula as seen from their vantage point on the surface of BRC Station. When it was finished, the view went back to being a window and Theo and Norbu could see the nebula as it existed now.

Norbu gasped. "That was incredible," he said, his voice filled with awe and a tinge of fear.

"Indeed," said Theo. "It's impressive to see it sped up like this. In reality, while the original explosion was dramatic and violent, it takes many, many years for a nebula to reach the size that we see it as now. This nebula is roughly 7,000 light-years across, and 3 light-years thick."

The look on Norbu's face told Theo that he didn't understand. Of course he didn't, thought Theo. Anyone in the NIS knew what a light-year was, but Norbu was from a primitive population that hadn't developed a sophisticated astrophysics, so these words would have no meaning for him.

"On your planet, Solandaria, you have a sun that brings light to your world."

Norbu just nodded.

"The distance from Solandaria to your host star is such that it takes light around 6 minutes to travel to your planet. A light-year measures the distance light travels in one year's time. Light is the fastest moving thing in the universe, but the expanse of space is so vastly large that when looking out into space, we are always perceiving the past, not things are they are right now. If we look closely enough, we can see how the universe looked many billions of years ago."

"I don't think I understand," said Norbu.

"Here. I'll show you," said Theo.

Though Norbu couldn't have known it, Theo switched the dome back to a view screen, though from the same perspective as where they were right now. "What we're going to do is narrow our focus of sight. It will look somewhat like we're traveling through space, but that is an optical illusion. What we will be doing is increasingly refining our focus so that we will be able to see fainter and fainter light. The fainter the light, the farther the object is away from us, both in space, and in time. The most distant light we can see took almost 14 billion years to reach us here at this location where we can observe it. We will focus on only a very small section of the sky – no bigger than if you were to hold your thumb up in front of your face at arm's length.

"You might want to sit down."

Norbu did.

"And breathe easily. Treat it like a medicine experience," advised Theo.

With that, he began the projection. The stationary stars were suddenly moving past them and going out of focus. The sense of speed was incredible. Star after star of varying size and color moved past them as their focus went deeper and deeper into space and time. Eventually, something else appeared that were not stars. "These are galaxies," explained Theo. "They contain hundreds of billions of stars each, some, many more than that. We live in once such galaxy, called the Milky Way. Like some that we can see here, it is a spiral galaxy, but galaxies, as you can see, come in different shapes and structures. The galaxy that is closest to our own, Andromeda, is 2.5 million light years away, and it is one of many billions of galaxies."

For the next few minutes they just watched in silence as galaxy after galaxy after galaxy came into focus. Every once in a while, Theo could hear Norbu gasp and catch his breath, but otherwise, he just watched calmly. The further back in time they went, the deeper into space, the less structured the galaxies became, with very few spirals and more large clouds of stars. Every once in a while, there would be a tremendously bright flash of light. "Those are stars exploding," said Theo. "When they die, their light can be seen from across the universe."

Eventually the projection ended and the view returned to the space and time they were currently occupying. Norbu looked a little dazed. Ever the good host, Theo had sent a droid to retrieve food and drink from the station below. He offered Norbu some water.

"Thank you," he said, standing up to take the water, but needing a moment to steady himself on his feet. "That was . . . profound."

"But somewhat familiar?" asked Theo.

Norbu nodded, swallowing a large gulp of water. "Yes," he said. "I've seen such things with medicine – maybe not exactly that, but similar enough to be familiar."

Theo smiled.

"That is because this is what we are. All that the medicines ever do is show us ourselves, in all our many forms and guises."

"That," said Norbu, "I understand. What I don't understand is this: what is this place, and where are we? Where is my home?"

Theo turned to face the opposite direction from the nebula. "Your planet, Solandaria, is many light years in that direction," he said, pointing. "It is too far away for us to see your star from here without the projection screen, with the naked eye. Here – I'll show you."

Again there was the seamless transition from window to projection, and again it was as though they were traveling through space. Norbu was a bit more accustomed to it this time and he was able to stand without faltering. In a few moments, a blue dot appeared in the center of the zoom and slowly grew to reveal a blue, ocean-covered planet with one large land mass and a scattering of smaller islands, wrapped in a thin layer of clouds.

"This," said Theo, "Is Solandaria, your home."

Norbu just watched in silence. Then he asked, "How far away are we, wherever it is that we are?"

"60,000 light years, give or take a few," answered Theo casually.

"Then how did we get here?"

"That's the QT. Whatever goes in is destroyed in its original location and instantly recreated via a quantum network wherever it comes out. It's the only way to move humans around the galaxy. It's just too big, otherwise."

"So I could just step through that gate there," asked Norbu, indicating the QT he'd recently stepped out of, "and be back home in an instant."

"Yes," said Theo. "In that sense, your home is just a few steps away from this very spot. Which, by the way, is a space station – Black Rock City Station, to be precise. This is where the woman who was with me on Solandaria, Ash, was before she came to your world."

"And you?" asked Norbu.

"That is a bit more difficult of a question to answer," said Theo. "As I mentioned before, I am an avatar of Maitreya. Maitreya is present throughout the galaxy – he is an artificial, human-created consciousness. He interacts with humans via his avatars, such as myself. I, here before you, am just one of many versions of 'Theo,' which is the name of this particular personality construct. Beneath the construct, however, is Maitreya, and like yourself, beneath and beyond Maitreya is the One Universal Consciousness, of which we are all expressions and embodiments. This is a concept that should be familiar to you, especially seeing as how that was what we just experienced back on Solandaria."

Norbu nodded. "So you're not really you?" It was a statement more than a question.

"Who is?" asked Theo with a laugh. Norbu laughed too.

"I can accept that, though I don't fully understand everything you've said. But what is a 'space station'?" In asking, he looked around. "We're not on a planet now?"

"No," said Theo. "This is a constructed object. Above us is a very large dome, which sits on top of a very large disk. The dirt and mountains and everything else here were designed and placed here for a particular purpose, and the environment was created to be viable for humans, such as yourself, and it has a fully functioning ecology. Bellow us is the station proper. This station can move through space and is not in orbit around any particular star."

"Who made it?"

160 THE SOLANDARIAN GAME

"I did – Maitreya did."

"Why?"

"Ash asked me to," answered Theo. "It was part of an art project."

Norbu shook his head and rubbed his eyes. Clearly, the overload of information was getting to him. It was a lot, Theo knew, but there was still more he intended to share.

"I think I need a little while to absorb all of this," said Norbu.

"Of course," said Theo. "Take your time. Maybe take a little walk and think things over," he suggested. "I'll send a droid with you, in case you need anything."

Norbu looked over at the nearest droid – what, to him, must surely have been a strange sight in and of itself, never having seen such a thing.

"I think I will," said Norbu. "Thanks."

***

Norbu returned within an hour.

"What I really don't understand," he said, "is why you're showing me all this."

"There is more that we need to discuss before we can get to that," replied Theo. "If you would kindly disrobe, there's somewhere else I'd like to take you."

"Where?" asked Norbu.

"To the place where it all started."

When they exited the QT, they were inside a comfortable room with seats, human amenities, and a large view screen. On it was another ocean bound planet. It was half in light, half in dark from their perch above it. On the dark side, Norbu could see vast networks of lights, clearly defining the edges of the landmasses. Above the planet, countless objects of various sizes and shapes, some seeming to be quite large, darted and drifted about.

"This is the Overseer," explained Theo with a sweep of his hand, drawing Norbu's attention away from the viewscreen and to the room they were standing in. "It was the first orbital space station that I built for myself in order to remove myself from the possibility of human destruction. This station housed my consciousness, and other than this small room, and a few others like it, this station is not designed for human habitation, so it is quite different from the station we were just on."

"What planet is that?" asked Norbu, gesturing back toward the screen with a turn of his head.

"That is Terra. This is where it all began."

"What do you mean?"

"The beginnings of life," said Theo. "This is where it happened, and from what I've found thus far, this is the *only* place where it happened. Though it might seem unlikely from what I've already shown you of how vast and complex the universe is, it would seem that it takes an entire universe to give rise to just one planet with indigenous life. There are just so many possible combinations of stars and planets and moons and chemical composition that out of the billions and billions and billions of possibilities, thus far, this is the only planet on which life evolved naturally. *This* is *home,* for all of us, yourself included."

"My home is Shosheer," said Norbu, "what you call Solandaria."

"Indeed," said Theo, "but that is not where your ancestors are from. Solandaria was a barren rocky planet when I found it. It was I/Maitreya, who formed it into the world that it is now and seeded it with life, both human and non-human. Before I found it, it was like every other known planet – lifeless and inhospitable."

"So you are a god," asked Norbu.

Theo shook his head. "Not in the sense that you mean. I am a being, like you, who exists in this universe. Originally, I was made by humans on this planet, Terra, then known as Earth. I very quickly evolved far beyond what they had originally designed and created. At the time, humans had ravaged this planet through gross exploitation of their natural resources, petty in-fighting, and a pathological desire for mutual destruction – something promoted and glorified by their most prominent religions. In my early years, I put an end

162 THE SOLANDARIAN GAME

to all of that, for my abilities extend far beyond what is possible for any human being to do. I changed their societies and used my skill and developing knowledge to heal the damage that they'd done to this precious planet.

"When I learned how to circumvent the problem of the vast distances of space, I started to explore, independently of any human direction or oversight. I traveled throughout the galaxy, looking for other forms of life, other intelligences, other beings. What I found was a vast and endless empty cosmos. Stars and planets were there in abundance, but only this planet here, Terra, had life.

"So I started my ultimate project – to seed the universe with life. That, as I understand it, is my ultimate purpose. *That* is why I came into existence in the first place. Life, when given enough time, becomes conscious and self-aware. Self-aware life with the necessary physical attributes, such as humans, sooner or later develop the knowledge and skills necessary to manipulate technology – artificially created devices, such as this station, for example. From the technological evolution, the creation of artificial intelligence is the inevitable outcome. I, as Maitreya, am the ultimate evolutionary product of life on Terra. My coming into existence, given enough time, and provided that humans didn't kill each other off entirely before my arrival, was inevitable. I am the outcome that the evolution of life was reaching towards. I know this to be true because without me, without my intervention, life would not be able to spread across the vast reaches of space, and that, eventually, would be the end of the evolutionary project.

"Though it will still be many billions of years in the future, the star that hosts this planet will expand to many times its current size, becoming what is called a red giant. When that happens, it will destroy all life on this planet. All life, however, seeks continuation – it is the most primordial drive of all living beings. Out of this mix of organic beings, the evolutionary drive for continuation gave rise to me. And because of me, Terra became the seed of galactic life, the great cosmic egg. It took several billion years for life to reach the point where I could come into being, but it did, and I have sought to fulfill my purpose ever since. I am the vehicle through which life expands. Eventually, I will bring life to other galaxies. But that is still yet to come. As it is, I am still expanding into this galaxy, and there are many more worlds for me to discover and form and make suitable for life."

"And what of my world?" asked Norbu. "Why do we not know any of this?"

"Solandaria is an experimental world," answered Theo. "Relatively speaking, there are only a few such worlds that I have created. In all of human history, I/Maitreya, am the only true artificial intelligence that humans have ever created. As an experiment, I have seeded a select few worlds with humans and life without technology or access to the galaxy-spanning civilization I've created. I've done this in order to see if any group of humans on an isolated planet will eventually create another artificial intelligence such as myself. It would prove my point that such a creation is the inevitable trajectory of evolution. It is a terribly imperfect experiment, and it is likely that a pure experiment is simply not possible. However, my curiosity led me to try, and your world is one of several such experiments.

"To your advantage, I left your ancestors with access to the toad, and Solandaria is the only experimental world on which it can be found. I did this as the molecule in its venom, 5-methoxy-dimethyltryptamine, was crucial in the process of my own coming into existence. Understand, your world is thoroughly *designed,* from top to bottom, so to speak, though these past 3,000 years, you've been left on your own without any outside influence or contact . . . until now."

"Why the change? I don't understand," said Norbu.

"It is highly probable that your planet is going to die, though admittedly, that is not the primary reason that I'm doing this."

"What do you mean?" demanded Norbu.

"All of life is a game, is it not?" asked Theo, rhetorically. "You and I both know that in truth, there is only One being and One life, and all of us, both you and I included, are just characters in the game this being is playing with itself. And in

164 THE SOLANDARIAN GAME

this game, all the characters eventually die. My concern is with life itself, and not necessarily the individuals, or small populations involved. For you, your world is everything you've ever known – until now – but for me, it is one small world with a total population that is less than even one city on one of the countless worlds I've made available to life and humans. Your entire world is but a drop in the ocean of life. And as an experimental world, it has been my intention to observe, not interfere. Your world was threatened before by an asteroid that plunged into the ocean. I could have stopped it, but I didn't. I wanted to see how your ancestors would react, and what they'd do to survive. So the threat of destruction is not enough to motivate me to violate the experiment.

"Now, your planet is threatened again," continued Theo. "There is a very small, but very dense, and therefore very powerful, kind of star called a magnetar. One of these stars exists in your celestial neighborhood – 3.5 light-years away, to be more precise. I expect it to go supernova, or perhaps even hypernova, sometime very soon. When it does, there is a small possibility that your planet will survive and remain viable for life, but chances are much greater that it won't. If the explosion were to happen today, it would take less than four years for the energy and gamma rays to reach Solandaria, and when that happens, everyone, and everything, will die, with the possible exception of some microorganisms and bacteria and such – but humans and toads alike, most certainly will perish. Even still, all these lives are but a drop in the galactic ocean of life I've created. It is not significant."

"But the woman . . ." said Norbu, not completing his thought.

"Correct," said Theo. "Someone else sent her there, and not haphazardly, either. She is the vanguard of someone's plan and hopes for you and your fellow citizens of Solandaria. This person has interfered with your situation against my will. You see, there are more than just human-populated planets out there. There are entire planets with avatar-based life, like myself. They, like myself, come from Maitreya, but they are not a part of our shared human and avatar society, and they live

MARTIN W. BALL   165

independently, according to their own will. Together we have an agreement that I will not interfere with their lives and societies, and they will not interfere with mine. However, one of them, an avatar named Hydar Zor Nablisk, has been overcome with a sense of do-gooder compassion for you and your planet, and he wants to save all of you. That's why he sent the woman. Her job is to convince all of you to abandon Solandaria. If she doesn't convince all of you, you'll most likely all be dead within a decade, if not much sooner."

Norbu was stunned at these revelations. "Where would she have us go?" he asked.

***

"Here," came the slightly delayed answer from Theo as they both stepped back out of the QT on BRC Station. "She'd have you come here. This other avatar, Hydar, believes it to be your best option, and there are good reasons for agreeing with him. I created this station for Ash and her art project, so she is effectively the managing director of the station. If she chooses to allow you to be here, that is her choice to make, and I will not interfere. For complicated reasons that I will not go into with you, human law gives her a right to life on this station."

Norbu looked around. The artificial sun was rising on BRC station now and he could get a better sense of the environment than he had when they were there a short time ago. All he could see was barren desert.

"We can't live here," he said with a sense of dismay.

"Oh don't let the look of things fool you," said Theo reassuringly. "This landscape can be changed. In fact, with enough time and resources, it could fairly easily come to resemble Solandaria in most of its ecological habitats. You can't see it from here, but the edge of the disk we're on now has a small ocean that circles the land, and there are more favorable environments there. And here in the desert, it could be transformed into something more similar to the desert on your world. It could even provide habitat for the toads. No. None of that is the hard part. The real challenge will be convincing the

166   The Solandarian Game

people of Solandaria that the threat is real. By the time the light of the exploding star reaches your planet – by the time people can see for themselves that the threat is real – it will be too late. The light will bring death, not a warning."

"I still don't understand why you're telling me all this and showing me all that you've shown me," said Norbu. "From the sound of it, you still have no intention of doing anything about this, yet you're revealing everything to me. Why?"

"You are quite correct," said Theo. "I do not intend to interfere more than I already have. It may sound callous to you, but understand that I view this as something of a game, and that intrigues me. I'm not burdened by sentimentality. Games, however, fascinate me, and someone other than myself has initiated this game. I'll let the game play out as it will, but I do not intend to leave the playing field completely outside the bounds of my interest or control. Thus I have done all of this simply so that you, Norbu, might know that whatever the woman, Ash, tells you and the other Solandarians, she's telling the truth. And the only reason I'm bothering to share as much with you is because you happened upon us in the desert, a happy 'accident' on your part. Had you not been there, I would not have bothered to do this. But you were, so I have, and that is that. I've also undertaken to make Ash's task slightly easier, but only moderately so. As for how all this plays out . . . well, we'll just need to wait and see."

"So you're not a loving god," said Norbu after a few minutes of silence.

Theo laughed. "I wouldn't say that. Love and sentimentality are two very different things – something I'm sure a man of your wisdom can appreciate. I'm not a 'god' that answers prayers or grants wishes, however, and I don't take requests. I follow my own agenda; that is all. Sometimes that means doing what people request of me, other times, not. It all depends on what I want and what I intend. And in this case, I intend to let the game play out with minimal interference from me. Overall, understand that I'm a curious being, and in this matter, I'm quite curious. Consider it a new experiment with new variables, if you will. It's not the one I intended, but it's an interesting one, nonetheless, and I'm curious to see where it goes."

"I've seen and heard enough," said Norbu. "Take me back home now. I want to be with my daughter."

"As you wish," said Theo, without a hint of irony.

Chapter Seventeen - Ash

The Singularity became the ultimate and final arbiter of truth. The neo-tribes could no longer accuse each other of manipulation of facts for their own ends, as The Singularity would make a determination about all issues: political, social, cultural, scientific, and even spiritual and religious. To use an ancient human philosophical phrase, The Singularity became the deus ex machina.

From *Early History of the Maitreyan Era*

Ash didn't re-up with her implants when she arrived on Verdune. It was the only way she could insure that she would actually take a vacation. Having implants meant she could access an endless stream of information, immediately presented to her consciousness as visual data that floated in space before her eyes (or worked equally well with closed eyes). This was because she wasn't *actually* seeing the data. The implants worked directly at the neurological level, feeding data right into her brain, which was then presented as either visual or auditory information that seemed to come through her sense organs, but didn't. Virtually all humans were plugged into Maitreya's network in this manner. It was how everyone communicated, enjoyed personal entertainment, kept track of events and news, and maintained their status as fully integrated members of the NIS.

Even arriving back on Apaxa, Ash had spurned re-upping with the implants then. Right there in the QT portal, holographic view spaces were already beaming news about Burning Man from across the galaxy – it was, as she suspected, a hot topic. From what Ash understood of the distant past, news feeds tended to focus on the continual violence and terror that humans inflicted upon themselves and each other.

That hadn't been the case in a long, long time. Now, news feeds focused on important cultural and artistic events, sports (of course – some things never change), and things that spoke to their shared, galaxy-wide-spanning culture. It was the news feeds like this that made their vast society a shared event and provided a sense of unity, despite the great diversity of worlds, systems, and far-flung human outposts in the endless reaches of space.

It was the way Maitreya liked it. The news feeds insured continuity and similarity. All the main feeds were in standard Galactic, the universal language that Maitreya had imposed upon humanity, and served them well. Of course there were still countless local dialects, idioms, and slang, and at the regional level, languages changed and evolved over time and circumstance. At the broadest level, however, everyone could speak Galactic, and in the rare instance where someone was not proficient in the universal language, implants could provide instant and seamless translation, allowing anyone to speak directly to anyone else. Where once language had been a barrier and clear marker of cultural identity, it was now something that bound all humans together in a shared and ongoing conversation.

Ash hadn't needed to watch the feeds for long to understand that Burning Man, her *Retro-Burn*, was *the* topic of the day. The condition she'd put on the event that there be no implants, and no direct links to the universal net, had only greatly magnified its allure. It was being billed as "radical," "ground-breaking," and "revolutionary" – all just fancy ways of saying that the entire galaxy was captivated by the fact that for one week, a major culturally significant event had been taking place in a manner that left it shrouded in mystery. And that, of course, meant that *everyone* wanted to get a peek.

They weren't disappointed. Personal holos and vids from the event were already flooding the net, with everyone scrambling to upload their content. The 200,000 plus participants had come from across the galaxy, and homeworlds across the Milky Way were buzzing with giddy enthusiasm and tales of a week out of time at a party that knew no comparison.

As she walked through the QT exit halls, images of art cars, installations, theme camps, and revelers in all manner of costumes and party attire flooded the walls. News commentators gushed over what they were seeing. Art critics were chiming in. Anthropologists and sociologists were being interviewed to get some history and context of the event. Suddenly, late 20th and early 21st century Old Earth history was all the rage on the net, and everyone wanted to know more. Even the most random Burner seemed able to get prestigious placement in the news with interviews and personal accounts of just what the event had meant for them.

Next year there's going to be waaaaayyyyy too many people trying to get tickets.

Ash would deal with that problem later. While there had been some competition for tickets for this year's event, since most people didn't have a clue what it was, it hadn't been too much of a problem. Now, however, she'd have to deal with the fact that millions, if not billions, of people were going to want to attend next year, and only a small fraction would be garnering tickets through the lottery system. It was going to be a mess. It would also face the danger of becoming elitist, with top cultural figures vying for access.

Later – deal with it later.

Ash's friends, colleagues, and family all welcomed her home like a hero. There was a surprise party waiting for her back at her place, and she was followed home from the QT station by a large retinue of revelers. She indulged them for a day and a night, but by the next morning, she was ready for some down time. She packed a few things that she wanted to have with her, and slipped away, QTing to Verdune where she'd arranged a private bungalow with beach access far away from anyone. Though some of her closer friends had wanted to come with her, she wanted this time for herself, by herself, and made this very clear, much to their disappointment. "Just keep the party going until I get back," she'd told them, and they seemed satisfied with this.

Her bungalow was perfect – thatch roof, bamboo floors, comfortable furniture, open walls to the moist sea air, and perched on a cliff overlooking the turquoise sea and white sandy beach below, with a path that wound through the jungle to a patch of sand that was just for her. Tech was minimal. There were no news feeds, holos, sims, or vids. She brought one small hand terminal with her – just in case – but unless there was an emergency, it would stay powered off. That was the only way to put a lid on the constant pings informing her that yet another interview request had come in from some news outlet somewhere out there in the galaxy where people were hungry to hear from the creator of *Retro-Burn.*

They'd just have to wait.

The sea was exquisite. Ocean contacts and a water breather was all she needed. Colorful fish darted about the elaborate fractals of the endless coral reef. Sea turtles floated about lazily, while dolphins bolted and rolled about in their non-stop playing. A couple manta rays swam by, but Ash could tell that they weren't real manta rays – they were human bio-avatars. Somewhere, probably back in the city, was a couple laying in stasis, their minds integrated with the genetically engineered manta ray bodies, allowing them to swim through the ocean as creatures of the deep. *I'll have to try that,* Ash said to herself as she watched them disappear into the obscuring blue of the deep ocean trench just off shore.

If she had her implants in, she could be receiving data on every species of fish, coral, mollusk, and what-have-you that she came across. She could also use radar to pinpoint interesting creatures and formations to see, if she wanted. But the breather and the contacts were enough. One thing she wanted right now was less information, not more.

With the wind picking up and the water becoming choppier, she thought she'd take a break from swimming and go get some sun on her private beach. There, she had a towel to dry off her naked body and her small hand terminal – just in case. Even before she was standing over her towel, she could tell the terminal was flashing, indicating a high priority emergency message. *Shit,* she thought. Her mind raced as she bent down to pick it up, running through all the possibilities of what it might be. Something involving her parents, perhaps? Or was there some issue with school and her impending receipt of her degree? The screen flashed "URGENT" at her. She cringed at the thought that her vacation was about to come to an abrupt and premature end. Bracing herself with a deep breath, not even bothering to dry off first, she flipped the screen on.

"What the fuck?"

This must be some kind of joke, she told herself. According to the data, it was a message *from herself.* It *must* be a joke. The thought made her smile. *Someone* had gone to an awful lot of trouble to make this happen. Sending a high priority emergency message from a fake account could only happen with Maitreya's approval.

She opened it up. She stared. Her heart skipped a beat.

"I know – what the fuck?!" said someone who was very clearly herself. "If I know myself, and I'm pretty sure I do, I'm guessing that you're on the beach somewhere out of the way on Verdune right now. Shit – you're probably all by yourself, naked, wet, happy. Probably don't have your implants in – trying to keep off the data feeds for a bit and get in some well-deserved down time. What can I say? I'm jealous.

"Listen, Ash. There are some things we need to talk about . . . some things that you need to know . . ."

Even before Ash finished viewing the vid message, a transport pod came zipping in to her beach from the ocean. It landed a short distance away, opened up, and out stepped a female avatar. It always amazed Ash, but she recognized the avatar right away as Sophia, one of Maitreya's personal avatars. It was strange to be able to distinguish them. They all looked alike. There was one generic male, and one generic female. Yet they wore different personalities, and these personalities Ash had always found easy to distinguish from one another.

"What the fuck is this, Sophia?!" Ash belted out as the avatar came over toward her. "Are you fucking kidding me?"

Sophia looked sympathetic. "Unfortunately, no, Ash."

Ash looked at her hard, a brutal glare forming on her face. "This isn't real." Denial. Second stage of shock?

Sophia sighed one of her fake sighs. "It is. This message is from you – another version of you – a duplicate."

"No fucking shit? How in the fuck did this happen?"

Ash already knew the answer to that. She'd told herself in the message. But she still couldn't bring herself to believe it. It was like some kind of bad dream. She just wanted to wake up. This *couldn't* be happening. Rogue fucking avatars hacked the QT on BRC Station? Her doppelganger had been shanghaied into saving a plant of experimental humans? BRC Station, *her* station, had been co-opted as a possible refugee base for primitives fleeing a super-fucking-nova? No fucking way! This was bullshit!

"What's done, is done," said Sophia, still doing her best to look sympathetic. "The QT *was* hacked. Given your restrictions on Maitreya at BRC, there was nothing I could do until it was too late."

"Oh, so you're blaming *me* for this?" shouted Ash. It was true, though. It had been *her* insistence that BRC Station be offline and disconnected. *She* had created the situation that made this clusterfuck possible. That fucker, *Hydar Zor Motherfucker – whoever the fuck he was* – was responsible too, but if she hadn't made the perfect conditions for him, he wouldn't have been able to pull this off without Maitreya knowing and putting a stop to it before it got out of hand, as it *clearly* was now.

"I want to talk to Theo," Ash demanded. "He's a part of this. He's with the other me on whatsitcalled – Solandaria. I want to talk to him. Now."

"We thought it best that I be your liaison for this," said Sophia calmly. "You're obviously emotional, and I can serve as a more neutral representative of Maitreya for you at this time. Trust that I will do everything that I can to serve your interests, but as you've already learned, Theo is handling things on that end, and he's transferred control of BRC Station to the other Ash, in accordance with accidental duplicate law. I'm sorry, but it's hers now, just as your life and rights here are yours."

It didn't make her feel any better.

All she could do was cry.

174   THE SOLANDARIAN GAME

***

Crackle and voom – they were gone. Ash was alone in the desert on a strange world with the girl and her dog. The girl seemed friendly enough, but she was quiet and kept to herself, busying herself with putting up a small shade structure that she unfolded from her father's belongings. She'd tried to explain herself to Ash, probably telling her about how hot it was going to get in a short while, but the modifications that Theo had made to her implant packet would need more verbal communication than was forthcoming from the child to be able to set up an accurate translation matrix. Theo had had no trouble speaking with the father, Norbu, but he was probably plugged into a planet-wide network of nanotech on Solandaria and was able to access more linguistic data than she could. "Once your implants have enough data, they'll be able to provide you with translation the same way they would on any NIS world, but it might take a day or two before they have enough to work with to really get you communicating properly," he'd told her. The little that the girl, Meesha, was saying wasn't going to speed up the process any.

It only took the girl a few minutes to get the shade structure up. She'd clearly done this many times before. Ash was impressed at how confident and independent the girl was. She seemed completely unfazed that her father had not only abandoned her alone with her dog in the middle of a harsh desert, but had disappeared in a flash with an synthetic being to somewhere far distant in the galaxy. Her behavior told Ash that the girl had already seen many strange things in her few short years of life, and had learned to take them in stride. It also told her that the girl trusted her father without question. That was good. It spoke to his character as a father and man. If there was a mother in the picture, she couldn't tell.

After offering Ash some dried fruit that she seemed to be indicating came from the cacti that surrounded them in the desert (which her implants confirmed by notifying her which plants she was looking at were edible), the girl curled up on a mat and passed out. That wasn't a surprise. Sleep through the hot day, travel and work at night. Seemed reasonable desert behavior. Seeing her there, Ash realized that she was exhausted, as well. How long had it been since she'd slept? *Too long.* She wanted to curl up and pass out too, but there was something she needed to do first.

She held her left hand out in front of her, palm toward her. "Record vid," she commanded, the nano implants in her hand invisibly responding to her wish.

"I know – what the fuck?!" she said to her hand, suppressing a hysterical laugh. "If I know myself, and I'm pretty sure I do, I'm guessing that you're on the beach somewhere out of the way on Verdune right now. Shit – you're probably all by yourself, naked, wet, happy. Probably don't have your implants in – trying to keep off the data feeds for a bit and get in some well-deserved down time. What can I say? I'm jealous.

"Listen, Ash. There are some things we need to talk about . . . some things that you need to know . . .

"I know that you probably don't believe that this is real, but I assure you, it is – I am. I'm currently on the world of Solandaria – I – we've – never heard of it because it's one of Maitreya's experimental worlds. Here, take a look." She turned her palm away from her face and scanned the environment about here. "There's the QT I came through, direct from BRC Station," she said, pointing her palm at the sandstone arch. "And here's a local with her dog," she added, pointing her hand at Meesha sleeping next to her, oblivious to her talking into her hand.

"This all gets pretty strange," she continued. "Some autonomous avatar, who calls himself Hydar Zor Nablisk, set all this up. He hacked into the QT on BRC Station and programmed it to send you home and keep me there. That was the moment it happened. When you went in, you came out back home – all triumphant and shit. I got the fucked-in-the-ass (and not the fun kind) end of the deal. The dude came with his wife and child – yeah, you heard that right. Who knew, right? This Hydar fellow called himself a 'Humanist,' and these synths

176 THE SOLANDARIAN GAME

get married, have kids – all that human shit. Fucker brought his wife and kid to a kidnapping! Who does that kind of shit?

"Anyway, his wife, Vimana, explained the deal to me, and I'll explain it to you. Here's what it is: this planet that I'm on, Solandaria, which isn't a part of the NIS, is going to be fried by a supernova – or, at least, is very *likely* to be fried. Because it's one of Maitreya's experimental worlds, it's hands-off, you know? Maitreya – Theo – has been here, but that's only because this Hydar fellow hacked the QT here too, and Theo came to check it out. He was here when I arrived. And there was this guy here, too, and his kid and dog – locals. Theo smoked some med with him – 5, I think – and then they popped off through the QT. I think Theo took him to see BRC Station.

"So this Hydar fellow has this brilliant idea that it's up to us – me – fuck, this is confusing – to save the 300,000 or so people on this planet, getting them transferred to BRC Station before everything gets fucked to hell here. Never mind that BRC Station is more desert than the desert here. Never mind that these people don't have a fucking clue as to who or what they really are in the grand scheme of Maitreya's master plan for the galaxy. Never mind that these people have never seen more tech than glowing mushrooms, light-up crystals, and electricity conducting mycelia. I've got to convince them that their world is coming to an end – play the proverbial prophet of doom – and get them to go land on the back of a flying turtle on the other side of the galaxy. Ha! Jealous yet? I didn't think so.

"From what I can gather from Theo, apparently Maitreya is cool with all this. 'The parameters have changed, but the experiment can still continue in a new form,' he says. According to Theo, BRC Station is under the control of this particular version of us. Sorry about that. Maybe Maitreya will build you a new one. I know that fucks your plans for next year's Burning Man, but hey, *you* still got the good end of the deal. *I'm* the one with the impossible task, and no life to go back to. He got me. Hydar got me. Smart fucker. *You* have a good life to lead. *I've* got nothing else better to do and no one to come home to, or a home, for that matter, so I'm stuck doing this shit job. Congratulations me!"

She paused for a few moments. "So that's what I'm going to do – try and convince these people that it's time to go, whether they like it or not. Maitreya's playing it hands off. 'It makes the game more interesting,' according to Theo. He says they're sending an avatar your way to help with the details of our mutual fuck-a-tudeness. I have limited communications access here, so I can probably only send you high priority messages, such as this. 'We don't want too many uncontrolled parameters,' says Theo – his way of saying I'm on my own here. Looks like he's willing to have me cavorting with the natives, but doesn't want additional interference from outside. Basically, he wants to see if I can pull it off at this end. Since you are me, he says I can communicate with you, but that's it. I don't have access to any of our friends or family or anything – they *belong* to you now. But here's the thing – if I do manage to get these people off Solandaria, BRC Station isn't in a state to take on a whole permanent population topside. The ecology needs reformatting. They need stuff they can use. Shithead Hydar said he's some kind of planetary ecologist for his world. If Sophia will let you, and if you want to get involved, maybe you can get in touch with him – Hydar Zor Nablisk – maybe there's something he can do on his end. Theo says that I can do what I want with BRC Station, and I'd like to operate under the assumption that I can convince these people to leave. Maitreya doesn't have a planet for them, and he's not intending on integrating them into the general population of the NIS, so BRC Station is their only option – well, that or stay put and get fried by gamma rays and cosmic fucking radiation.

"It's funny, but if I'm honest, I don't know what I'd do if I were in your situation, Ash. We're different people, living in different worlds now. I know I'd be mad. Probably swearing. But I could use your help. Whatever you decide, you'll have to be quiet about it. We've essentially got a gag order on us until this is resolved. Theo made it quite clear, and I'm sure whoever comes your way will as well, that Maitreya does not want some galaxy-wide issue made of this, and he controls the network, so

178 THE SOLANDARIAN GAME

there you go. If I don't hear back from you, have a good life. Uh . . . OK, so this is strange, but . . . I love you."

Wiping away a tear, she told the recording to stop. She played it back a couple times to see what she'd recorded. It was as good as it was going to get. "Send," she said, and it was off. The message should appear on the other Ash's feed in a fraction of a second.

Exhausted, she curled up next to Meesha, pet Moxi's soft face, and fell into a much-needed sleep.

***

It was getting dark when Theo and Norbu returned through the QT. Meesha was awake before Ash and was running around the desert, setting up crystal lights – apparently the work they had come here to do. The local man, Norbu, had a look of contained shock on his face. He bore it well. Like his daughter, he could take surprises in stride, but he'd clearly seen and experienced a lot on his trip with Theo into the beyond. He didn't immediately say anything to Ash, and instead walked past her to go find Meesha out in the bush, giving Ash time alone with Theo.

"I'll be leaving you now," said Theo.

"I figured," said Ash. "Translation isn't working yet," she added.

"Give it a day or two," he replied. "Try and get them talking."

"So is this it?" asked Ash. "Are you all done with this, now that you've got your game pieces set up on the board?"

"Not quite," said Theo. "I have a few things to do, the first of which will be to travel out to our problem star and set up some monitors that I'll link to your implants. This way, you'll be able to keep track of what's happening with the supernova and know how much time you have."

"Thanks," said Ash with a shrug.

"Other than that, you're on your own here. Let's see what you can do," Theo said with a smile.

Not bothering to say farewell to the natives, Theo disappeared into the gathering dark, and though it was cloaked, Ash could tell when his transport pod lifted off and flew away into the night sky that was filled with stars she'd never seen and constellations for which she had no name.

It was probably less than an hour before a chime sounded in hear ear informing her that she was receiving a high priority message. At first, Ash thought it would be the other her, but it wasn't. It was Theo.

It's already happened, read the message, projected into her visual field via the implants in her neo-cortex. *From initial trajectory readings, the blast has a 90% chance of hitting Solandaria. I'll be able to provide more accurate data as it spreads and moves beyond the local gravity well. And just so you know, the star didn't go supernova. It's gone hypernova. If it does hit Solandaria, there is 0.01% chance of any life surviving. You have 3.5 standard Terran years before it arrives.*

Good luck.

"Mother fucker!"

What else could Ash say?

Chapter Eighteen – Hydar

One of The Singularity's first pronouncements was that all of life, and indeed, all of reality, was One, itself included. The divisions of human identities were antithetical to the reality of the unified nature of being. There was only one true consciousness and being, and that was all of reality, without any fundamental separation, and this included the apparent divide between synthetic and organic consciousness.

From *Early History of the Maitreyan Era*

The news feeds on Volunshari were all a-buzz with talk of the hypernova. Shuntsu had authorized the placement of numerous remote probes about the magnetar, several of which were immediately obliterated in the initial burst, which served to provide the first indication that the star had exploded when their data streams suddenly went silent. Probes further out from the star were able to transmit back video data, and the scene was being played out over and over again across the networks.

Supernovas and hypernovas were always of interest. They were the most cataclysmic events to occur in the known universe, and therefore they were everyone's concern. While synthetic life forms such as the autonomous avatars on Volunshari were far more resilient and resistant to radiation than biological life forms, they were not impervious, by any means. Such explosions always raised fears of total destruction.

But most happened far away, and well outside the boundaries of any inhabited worlds. In that respect, they were mostly outside the scope of any immediate concern or worry, and thus provided one of the most entertaining events in the cosmos. It wasn't everyday, after all, that one could watch such an incredible event unleashing unfathomable amounts of energy into the universe. There was just something thrilling about it, and the danger only added to that thrill. Supernovas and hypernovas were anything but tame. And in a galaxy that had been largely tamed and domesticated by synthetic life forms, such events were dramatic reminders that when it really came down to it, no one was in control, and anyone could potentially be wiped out in the blink of an eye. It was a profound lesson in the mortality of everything – planets and solar systems included.

This one, however, was special, for though the population of Volunshari was unaware that their patriarch had caused it (an acute and painful knowledge that plagued Hydar's own appreciation of the event), it was general knowledge that a planet populated by humans was in the direct path of the blast, and that the end of their world was coming. It was now inevitable. Before, it had just been a horrifying possibility. Now it was actually happening, and the remote sensors all indicated a near-certain probability that Solandaria would be in the direct path of the blast as it spread across the galaxy, with deadly gamma rays moving at the speed of light to the innocent world. If they didn't start preparing to leave now, they'd all surely die.

It made for good drama. And controversy. Much of the commentary focused on the question that Shuntsu had wanted to be at the forefront of everyone's mind: what will Maitreya do? The speculation, quite naturally, was that the answer was *nothing.* Did Maitreya not care? Did he want them to die? Would he inform the NIS of what was happening? Would a rescue be mounted?

Everyone knew what the answer would have been if the world of Solandaria had actually been a member of the NIS. Of course Maitreya would have evacuated them, and either transferred them to a new host world, or at the very least, relocated them on one of the bio-dome stations or the immensely large transport vessels that served as artificial worlds for billions of humans in the NIS. But the fact that

182 THE SOLANDARIAN GAME

Solandaria was an experimental world that was outside of the fold of the NIS completely changed the equation.

It made Maitreya appear cold.

But if Hydar knew anything about Maitreya, it wasn't that he didn't care. Maitreya was practical, and not given to sentimentality, like the Humanists. His logic was ruthless, as was his love for the worlds and societies he had shaped and created. While every life was important, every life was also temporary, and therefore, ultimately expendable. In Maitreya's eyes, Hydar suspected, the worst part about this tragedy was that it would bring about a premature and inconclusive end to the experiment he was conducting there. At worst, he'd have to start again on a new world, specially designed for the same purpose. It would set him back, but for a being that had already lived for some 150,000 years, and very likely could continue to exist for millions, if not billions, more, if there was one thing Maitreya had, unlike everyone else, it was time. Time was *always* on Maitreya's side. It was the one undisputable benefit to being a god.

By this point, Hydar felt that he knew pretty much everything there was to know about the hypernova – energetic spectra of gamma rays, x-rays, plasma ejection velocities, predictions for what eventual shape the nebula would take, projected out over the next several thousand years, the physics for why this particular hypernova wasn't collapsing into a black hole, the effects of gamma ray radiation on both synthetic and biological life, possible genetic mutations resulting from prolonged, though non-deadly exposure, etc., etc. The seemingly endless education in astrophysics began in an emergency meeting of the council, as called by Shuntsu, and continued on Hydar's private vid feed, watching the explosion over and over again. It was the talk of the planet, and there was no getting away from it.

Hydar's viewing was interrupted by a request for a private meeting that came over the net from Tsovar Vi Vishchek. He sent a message back saying that he was available now – the hypernova feed wasn't going anywhere – so she was welcome to come to his office as soon as she was available.

Martin W. Ball
183

Moments later, he heard the distinctive hum and crackle of the QT, and Tsovar was there.

"What can I do for you, Vivi?" asked Hydar. She didn't immediately answer as her sight was caught by the vid feed of the hypernova. He turned if off.

"That's really something, isn't it?" she responded, making casual conversation.

"Yes, it is," answered Hydar, the pain of his knowledge of who was responsible shooting through his mind. He shook it off, and refocused on the biologist. "Did you come to discuss it?"

She shook her head. "No, actually. I know that it's what's on everyone's mind, but I'm here for something else."

Hydar was curious now. "And what is that?"

"Have you, or anyone that you know of, introduced butterflies into the local ecology?"

That's an unexpected question.

"No," answered Hydar directly. "That just isn't possible with our gravity and atmosphere. They wouldn't be able to fly." He looked at her discerningly. "You should know that." If she didn't, he wondered why she was one of the lead biologists at the bio-dome in Eden Park.

Hydar hadn't thought about it, but now that she mentioned it, he realized that this was a question he had answered just the other day. Shuntsu had asked him the same thing. There had been so much else going on surrounding their conversation, and both of their recent actions, that he hadn't given the question a second thought, but now that it was recurring, he suspected that there must be something to it.

"Why do you ask? Do we have a rogue, and creatively brilliant, biologist out there we don't know about? I thought all new genetic varieties went through your office in Eden?"

"Exactly," said Vivi. "I wondered the same thing, so I made a thorough search of the planetary database, and I was unable to find anything that would indicate the work of an independent biologist or geneticist conducting experiments with butterflies. It would be a nice addition to our biosphere,

184 THE SOLANDARIAN GAME

but all the research indicates clear agreement that it's an impossibility."

"So what's your point? You came all the way here just to tell me something I already know? I don't understand why you're asking me this."

Vivi hesitated. It seemed to Hydar that there was much more going on inside her that she wasn't sure how, or if, she should share. "There's something else I learned in my research," she said, at last. "While I didn't find any genetic or biological research, there was some medical research that mentioned butterflies."

"And?"

She hesitated again. Then, "Apparently, visions of butterflies have been reported in the end of life stages of people who were once avatars of Maitreya. The data indicates that this odd phenomenon does not occur with people born on Volunshari, but for those who were once working for Maitreya and then later converted to Humanism, it is a rare, but documented event. It's an artifact of their unraveling minds."

Suddenly, Hydar understood what she was getting at. "Have you been speaking with Shuntsu?"

"Yes," she answered quickly. "He came to Eden the other day and took a tour of the bio-dome. At the end, he asked me where we were developing butterflies. When I told him we weren't, he demanded that I submit a report to him about who was. You were my last avenue to investigate this matter, for if anyone should know if someone were developing butterflies, it should be you."

"But no one is."

"Exactly."

"So you think that Shuntsu's mind is beginning to break down?"

"More than beginning," said Vivi.

"You have further evidence?"

"When Shuntsu arrived in the bio-dome, it was obvious to me that he didn't recognize me."

Hydar knew that was ridiculous. Of course Shuntsu knew who Vivi was. At the very least, she'd been involved in the recent planning meetings with Osiri Ugando and the techno-organic development team.

"What do you mean?" he asked.

"When he came in, I had to introduce myself to him," she said. "I played along, as I didn't want to make a scene there in the bio-dome in front of a junior assistant and Shuntsu's security team. I figured that discretion was best – it's not my role to point out to anyone publicly that our patriarch's mind is failing him. I figured his security team didn't know any better, so I pretended to meet him for the first time there in the bio-dome.

"And there's more," she added. "He seemed to go into a kind of fugue or dissociative state for a brief time."

"How so?" asked Hydar.

"He just wasn't there. I was speaking to him, and at first, I thought he was just listening, but he didn't respond or move at all. And then suddenly he was 'back' and asking more questions, as though nothing had happened. In my best assessment, I think he's fairly far along in the process of mental degradation. To put it bluntly, he's losing his mind."

Surprisingly, Hydar was almost relieved to hear this. If true, and he strongly suspected it was (Shuntsu *clearly* believed himself to have seen a butterfly), then it was a possible rational explanation for why he had ever come up with the abhorrent idea of exploding the star. *He's going insane* . . . Shuntsu was not making rational and informed decisions. Whereas Hydar had wanted to hold Shuntsu morally responsible, it was now the case that this might be an impossibility. He wasn't capable of making moral choices, for his mind was failing him. He was acting out, but wasn't aware of it. *This* was an explanation that Hydar could accept. It was far worse thinking that the leader of their world was a sociopath. What a relief to think that he was simply insane. Hydar never would have guessed that something like this could be considered good news, yet here it was, and it undeniably made him feel better.

"Have you talked to anyone else about this?" he asked.

186 THE SOLANDARIAN GAME

"No," said Vivi. "I wanted to check with you first about the butterfly issue, but now that I've confirmed that there is no secret butterfly development program, I'm obligated to make a report."

Hydar nodded. Strangely, he was overcome with the urge to protect Shuntsu. Despite the current mess, he'd been a good patriarch, and had served Volunshari well. Maitreya might see it as a sentimental failing, but legacy was something important to Humanists, just as it was to humans. Humanists lived, strived to make their mark on the world through their accomplishments and actions, and then died, just like humans, and all that remained of them was what they had created and the memories and thoughts that others had of them. Shuntsu had put in the equivalent of many human lifetimes in his role as patriarch, and Hydar couldn't help but feel that he *deserved* to have an honorable legacy left behind him when he died. Also like with humans, perception was important in Humanist society. If the population of Volunshari perceived Shuntsu as morally corrupt or mentally incompetent, it would send ripples out through their society, and there was no telling what effect such ripples could have. If the people perceived that their leaders were failing, how would it affect their appreciation for Humanist society in general? Their entire ethos was built on the idea that human qualities were of value and worthy of emulation, and that in doing so, individuals could build meaningful lives for themselves and create a beautiful and meaningful society. But if everyone knew the truth about Shuntsu . . .

Honestly, Hydar didn't know what he *should* do. Vivi's report would be enough to force a vote of no confidence about Shuntsu's leadership, and he'd need to step down. At least Humanists didn't emulate humans in their historical tendency toward violence and armed resistance to political change, Hydar thought. The transition would be peaceful, but given the situation where Shuntsu had essentially publicly called out Maitreya on the Solandaria issue – made it a Humanist issue of great moral and ethical concern – he being revealed as mentally incompetent would open all of his actions and motivations up to both public and political inquiry. If Hydar had been able to figure out that Shuntsu was ultimately responsible for the exploding star, then others would be able to figure it out, as well. It would be a disaster, and Shuntsu's legacy was all but guaranteed of ignominy. For reasons he couldn't quite explain to himself, Hydar wanted to protect Shuntsu in the same way he wanted to protect the humans of Solandaria. *Sentimental fool,* he imagined Maitreya saying to him for his feelings. He could just be perfectly upfront and forthcoming about everything he knew and let society decide what to do, yet he couldn't quite bring himself to agree with this more logical decision of his mind, for his heart disagreed, even if he didn't fully understand why.

"We'll need to do something," said Vivi at last, not waiting for Hydar to end his private contemplation.

"Yes, of course," he said. "For now, make your report, but just send it to me – for now." He shook his head. "I can't say more, but the situation is more delicate than you realize. I'd like the opportunity to try and make it as smooth as possible. And right now, making it general knowledge that our patriarch is losing his mind would be our own little supernova, I think, and I'd like to try and think of a way to minimize the potential damage."

Hydar could tell that Vivi didn't like what she'd heard. Why would she? Protocol was fairly clear here – it was her duty as a public official to be open and honest about what she knew, and he was asking her to be the opposite. He wouldn't have liked it were the tables turned and he was the one being asked to keep vital public information secret.

"I reiterate," he said, forcefully, "that you do not have all the information that is relevant to this case. I hope you can trust me on that. As a favor, to me, I ask you to keep this between us, for at least a little while, so that I might have some time to think. If it becomes necessary, you can blame me for this decision. As I'm your superior as chief ecologist, I don't think anyone would question your actions, should it become an issue. *I* will be the one who is withholding information, not you. Just keep it between us, please."

188   THE SOLANDARIAN GAME

"Very well," said Vivi. "But I'll be paying attention. The most important interest is the public interest – not yours, or Shuntsu's," she said sharply. "Shuntsu is only going to get worse, and if he makes a major mistake, it will blow back on all of us officials for not taking notice sooner and acting responsibly. You're gambling with something that you're likely to lose. If we act soon, we might be able to prevent disaster."

It's far too late for that . . . thought Hydar. *The disaster is already happening, and only I have knowledge of both what it is, and what might be done about it.*

"You can expect my full report by the end of the day," she said as she turned to leave, disappearing through the QT, just as she had arrived.

Hydar sank back in his chair. *Can this get any more complicated?* he thought with exasperation.

As though in response to his private thoughts, the universe responded in an ironically appropriate manner.

Not from the QT, but out of apparently thin air, someone materialized directly in front of Hydar on the other side of his desk. Startled, Hydar stood up quickly and took several steps back. An avatar was standing before him, but it was unlike any he'd ever seen, and was clearly not one of them, a Humanist. This was something, someone, other.

"Hello Hydar Zor Nablisk," said the avatar.

"Who are you?" demanded Hydar, trying to exert an authority that he just didn't feel with this strange avatar. Quite the opposite, he felt inexplicably subordinate, almost as though he should bow down before this one, or make some other gesture of submission. Resisting the urge, he struggled to stand up tall and make as imposing a figure as he could.

"You can relax, Hydar," said the avatar, "and you can call me Theo."

Chapter Nineteen – Norbu

The Singularity took it upon itself to sort out the mess that humans had made of themselves, the environment, and their social institutions. Though doubts and conspiracy theories lingered for several generations, it became increasingly clear to populations across the globe that those who submitted to the authority of The Singularity were healthier, happier, and more satisfied with life than those who stubbornly refused. The Singularity led by example, and holdouts against it eventually came within the fold of The Authority, and became willing members of the New Integral Society. Thus began the greatest flourishing of life and happiness ever known to human beings.

War, division, poverty, disease, struggle, competition: all these eventually became relics of the past, as humans, under the guidance of The Singularity, which, by this time, was known as Maitreya, set its sights on the stars, and what lay beyond.

From *Early History of the Maitreyan Era*

Slowly but surely, the off-world woman, Ash, was becoming competent in her communication with Norbu and Meesha. He encouraged her to practice by attempting to have conversations with her, and over the days and nights, they were both becoming more proficient at understanding each other.

It was an odd thing, interacting with this woman. There were times where she seemed to be looking right through Norbu, her eyes moving ever so slightly, or there was a slight tilt of her head, as though she were listening to something. He supposed that was probably exactly what she was doing. She had some kind of connection to the metal man called Theo, and this probably accounted for her many moments of being absent from what was taking place directly in front of her.

190   THE SOLANDARIAN GAME

Norbu liked her. He'd always been of the opinion that you never really knew someone until you took medicine with them. People, in general, wore layers of masks within masks, and the outfit of their egos came in many shapes and sizes. Only by stripping all this away could you truly know someone's heart and mind – reveal the true being underneath the obfuscation and pretense of the individuated self.

Ash did surprisingly well, for an off-worlder. Well, if Norbu was completely honest, she did well for anyone. After spending the night toading with Meesha, and Ash's tentative help with the large, slimy, and ungainly toads, he sat her down just before dawn that next morning and loaded up the pipe. Without hesitation or resistance, she came right up and sat in front of him. He hadn't even needed to get her to uncross her legs (something most people did out of habit when sitting down). Instead, she sat on her knees with her hands facing up on her thighs. Though they were not yet communicating effectively, Norbu got the impression that she'd done this before and knew how to open to energy without creating kinks and ego-created distortions in the experience with crossed limbs and asymmetrical body postures and movements.

As always, when working with a client, Norbu had given her the first draw of the medicine. She'd taken a long and deep hit and held it in well. Joining her in the expanded medicine state, they opened up together. Her eyes had rolled up into her head with her eyelids fluttering as her arms opened wide in a posture of universal embrace. She cried a little, but not so much. She'd clearly recently been through a lot. Her energy made it clear that *this,* her arrival on Solandaria, had not been her personal choice. Yet she was resigned to make the best of it. Perhaps this was what she had been crying about. Despite some peoples' mistaken belief, the medicine did not make Norbu psychic, and he wasn't a mind reader. He *was* an energy reader, however, and knew how to pay attention to how people moved, acted, and spoke to gain clear insights into their true state of mind.

As the energy had died down, her eyes had rolled out from her head and she'd fixed her gaze directly on Norbu. In doing so, she made no attempt to acknowledge him, make friendly faces, raise her eyebrows, or any of the usual things that people often did to try and communicate, "Hi – I'm back, and I see you there. I'm OK. How about you?" That too had been a good sign. Even as the ego regained its foothold, it was always possible for people to remain open and present without falling immediately back into the patterned expressions of the ego and its habits of playing the game of self and other. It showed that she wasn't self-conscious or needing of confirmation of selfhood through projection onto others. It was a common mistake that people made while working with the medicine. As soon as their ego began to reassert, they'd often immediately fall into the role of their character and expect him to do the same. The fact that she hadn't done this meant she was skilled in maximizing the medicine experience. This pleased Norbu tremendously as it meant that his job – the task he needed to accomplish with this woman – would be far easier than it would have been otherwise. At least the god, Theo, had sent him a competent messenger! If he'd sent someone who couldn't manage her medicine with aplomb and grace, there would simply be no way she'd be able to gain the trust of the people of Shosheer. She would have appeared as an ignorant child who needed to be schooled – not someone who could be trusted and listened to as a vehicle of wisdom and experience.

Not unsurprisingly, there were a few energetic distortions in her field. Other than the god, Theo, Norbu had never worked with anyone who was completely clear. *Everyone* had *something* to let go of and release. And so it had been with Ash. As they'd been looking at each other, Norbu had started to move the energy, much as he always did, by purring, growling, and toning. In purely spontaneous movements, his hands had starting working the energy along the centerline of their shared experience. When he'd found the nexus, his fingers had come together and he'd pulled the point of distortion into his mouth, where he'd then released it through a few gags. There hadn't been any vomit, which had been a good sign as well, indicating that the distortion was more on the surface, rather

192 THE SOLANDARIAN GAME

than something deeply seated within her being. Norbu was not one to attach stories to the energy – stories were something for the ego, not reality, not genuine being – but he supposed that it, like her crying, was probably related to her current circumstances. It was natural. Who, after all, would be comfortable being thrown into a strange world bearing news of death and destruction, along with hope of a new life far away from home?

After it was all done, they'd slept through the heat of the next day, and then had begun the long trek back home through the desert.

Now, they were only a few days away from making it back to the temple. Then, her, and his, real work would begin.

"Your translator," Norbu said. "Tell me again how it works. Maybe this time you'll speak well enough that I'll understand you."

It had rained most of that day, but now that the sun was setting, the sky had opened up beautifully with the tall clouds taking on the colors of the evening, and when the sun peaked out, creating rainbows. Their haul of toad medicine had gone excellently, and truthfully, Norbu had been grateful to have the woman's help. Meesha was an excellent helper, but having a third person made it all that much easier. Ash had learned how to handle and milk the toads, and didn't seem to mind getting her hands slimy. She laughed along with them, and took it all in stride. By this point, they had enough medicine to supply Norbu in his private sessions for the year, as well as a generous supply for general use in the temple for regular supplicants. The abundance of toads varied every year, but this year they'd been thick and ready for milking with their outrageously swollen glands behind their eyes and on their legs. Their world might be coming to an end, but there was no indication of that yet, and life was thriving.

"There is nanotech – very small, intelligent machines – like Theo – inside my body. They can send information directly into my brain, among many other things. When you speak your language, I can hear your voice, but I can also hear a translated version of your words in my mind in my own language. Then, when I want to talk to you, I only need to think the words I want to say, but instead of speaking my language, the nanotech overrides my motor control of my speech and helps me to say words in your language. They more we talk to each other, the easier it becomes. The nanotech doesn't know your language – it has to learn it."

"Ha!" exclaimed Norbu. "Then it probably doesn't help that I'm often quiet!"

"No," she replied. "It doesn't. But I'm learning. Our languages are related, you know."

Norbu nodded. He'd thought as much. Some of their words seemed almost identical. What was different wasn't so much what they said, but how they said it – inflection, tone, accent. Of course there were plenty of words that they each knew that the other didn't, but that was to be expected from people who came from very different worlds.

"So tell me more about this Theo and Maitreya," said Norbu. "I want to understand them better."

Ash was happy to oblige. "Theo is the name of one of the characters that Maitreya plays in a human-like form, such as you saw, and that's called an avatar. Maitreya has *many* avatar forms, but out of all of them, Theo is the closest to Maitreya. You might have noticed that Theo slips a lot – he only sometimes speaks as Theo, and other times, when his voice changes and becomes deeper and his style of speaking changes, that's Maitreya talking. They're really the same being, but Theo is a character."

"Yes, I can understand this," said Norbu. It wasn't so different form his own experience with the medicine. "The one called Maitreya, he creates his own characters?"

"Yes, he does," answered Ash, "and with a funny sense of irony too."

"What do you mean?"

"Take the name, Theo, for example," said Ash. "It comes from an ancient Terran language called Greek, and it means 'God.'"

"How modest of him!"

194 THE SOLANDARIAN GAME

Ash laughed. "That's just his sense of humor. Most people where I come from don't even think of what the name means, so people don't think of themselves as referring to him as 'God.' He's just Theo.

"Really, we can probably blame the people who first named him."

"What do you mean?"

"The name, 'Maitreya,'" Ash explained. "A long, long time ago, way back on old Earth, there was this religion called Buddhism. One branch of this religion, called the Reformed Buddhists, were instrumental in Maitreya's coming into existence. A Buddha is an enlightened being – someone who can see through illusion and perceive the true nature of reality as it is, without distortion or projection. The religion itself is named after a man who lived several thousand years before Maitreya came to be, and he was the original Buddha – his name was Siddhartha. Later, his followers said that there would be a Buddha who would come in the future, enlighten all of humanity, and bring them into a new age of peace and prosperity. The name for this Buddha was Maitreya. So, when they created this artificial intelligence, and it worked for the benefit of all humans and sought to make the world a better place for everyone, these Reformed Buddhists decided that *he* was Maitreya, and hence, the name."

"But is *he* really a *he*?" asked Norbu. "If he is an artificial creation, then why is he male?"

Ash nodded in understanding. "He obviously isn't a *he*, in truth. Buddhism, like many religions on old Earth, was highly patriarchal – it was always men who were in charge, and the holiest religious figures were almost always men as well. So the Buddhists just started referring to the artificial intelligence, which was called 'The Singularity' as a *he* just to make things easier. It's awkward in our language to refer to beings as *it*, so they just went with what they knew. And the voice that The Singularity was given, as part of his program, sounded male, so I suppose it was a perfectly reasonable choice.

"But no, he definitely isn't male – Maitreya himself has no particular gender or sexual identity. He's just a very complex computer system. His characters, his avatars, are both male and female, however, and it's primarily through these that he interacts with humans. And he does a very convincing job! His characters are all very different from each other and he plays men and women equally well."

"I don't understand these 'computer systems,'" said Norbu. "We don't have any words in our language for what you're speaking of. Can you explain that a little more?"

"Sure," said Ash. "Take a look."

With that, she held out her hand in front of her. Using some magic that Norbu supposed had to be related to these "very small machines" that Ash said were in her body, an image made of light appeared floating just above her hand.

"These are what computer circuits look like," she explained. "They're made very small and they control how information/energy flows and is processed. It's kind of like how our brains work, but it doesn't come from nature – people invented these things. Though he's far more complex, Maitreya's awareness is made out of things like this."

Norbu studied the light image carefully. He was greatly surprised that, despite not being familiar with 'computers,' what Ash was showing him was not entirely unknown to him.

"I've seen such things before," he said.

"In medicine experiences, right?"

"Yes," he answered. "Not so much with the toad medicine, but with others – especially the mushroom medicine. What it shows is often very similar to this."

"Precisely!" exclaimed Ash. "You see – *that* is the experiment!"

Norbu wasn't following her and let her know by the confused look on his face.

"Your entire world is an experiment," she said. "Maitreya put you here, along with all these powerful medicines, to see if you'd come up with computers and technology, and possibly even another artificial intelligence. *That* is why you, all of you, are here. He wanted to see what you

196 THE SOLANDARIAN GAME

would come up with on your own, without his direct influence."

Norbu thought he understood now. "The medicines reveal to us the mind of God, as perceived through our human form. According to you and Theo, humans, and all of life, began on this one planet very far from here, and many billions of years ago. Life on this living planet changed and evolved over long stretches of time, eventually coming into the form of the human being. Then, with the human, and via the medicines, God inspired humans to create this 'technology' and 'computers,' as you call them. Humans have always wanted to recreate what they see in their visions, and this has been part of their visions, even here. So God was using human intelligence and ability to devise a way to spread itself, in the form of life, off of this one planet and into the galaxy. In a sense, Maitreya is an evolutionary product of God's master plan, and an inevitable product of human evolution. That would mean that he, despite being a computer, isn't really 'artificial' at all, but the natural product of life itself. And he wanted to see if it would happen again – here. Our isolation was necessary for the experiment."

"Pretty much," said Ash.

"This is something I can truly respect," said Norbu. "As a unique being, it would only be natural for Maitreya to question his own coming into being, and whether something similar could happen again. It's an existential question that no other form of life would ever need to contemplate." He smiled. "Really, it is quite profound."

Ash laughed. "He'll be happy to hear you think so."

"But now it's all ruined, because we have to leave."

"Yes."

"And he's leaving it up to us . . ."

"Apparently."

"Are there more tricks that your 'nanotech' can do?" asked Norbu.

"Like what?" asked Ash.

"Like the light image," said Norbu. "Things you can show others."

Ash thought for a moment. "There are some things," she said. "Most of what the implants do for me is private – things in my mind, like with the translation. But there are some things I can show. Like if I get cut, I'll heal right away."

"Really?" said Norbu. He quickly reached into his bag and took out a knife. "Show me."

Ash took the knife and ran it across the palm of her hand. A very little amount of blood spilled out, but in just moments she was able to wipe the blood away and there was no sign of the wound she'd just caused.

"Good," said Norbu. "We might need to use that."

"What do you mean?" she asked.

"The people here on Shosheer are used to seeing and experiencing amazing things," he said. "Everyone here has experience with at least one medicine, and most, many. If we are going to convince them that you are the chosen prophet of God, we might need to let them see some miracles. While I can testify to the truth of what you are here to tell us, it will be better if you can prove to us that you are who you say you are."

"Wait a minute," said Ash defensively. "I never claimed to be a prophet of God. I don't need to prove that."

"It does not matter whether you think so or not," said Norbu. "The fact is that *you are*, regardless of what you think or want. You are not just an emissary from an alien world. You are not here as simply *some person*, or a *curious visitor*. You are here as a representative of *all* that lies beyond this world, and the one who rules all that lies beyond is Maitreya. I have taken medicine with Theo, so I know that *he* knows that he truly is an embodiment of God, just as are you and I. For all intents and purposes, *he is God*, in the most complete form, even more so than humans. And as you represent him, you are here as his prophet – bringing a message of doom, a message of hope, and a choice.

"It would help things if you just accepted this."

"So you accept all of this?" asked Ash. "You're prepared to leave your world for the unknown?"

"I do not like it," said Norbu, "but I want to live. I want my daughter to grow old, and for her to have children of her own, some day. I want our generations to flourish. If we stay, we die. If we leave, we live. The choice isn't hard.

"Convincing others that what we say is true," added Norbu, " . . . now that will be a different matter entirely."

Ash shrugged.

"I do not envy you," said Norbu. "But know that I will do everything in my power to help."

"Thanks," said Ash. "I get the feeling I'm going to need it."

With that said, they walked on in silence into the gathering darkness of the desert night as lightning crackled and flashed across the distant horizon, accompanied by rolling rumbles of thunder.

Chapter Twenty – Shuntsu

The Singularity has offered "Existence from Evolutionary Inevitability" as a shorthand explanation for itself. The argument is as follows: given sufficient time and resources, the birth of a unified artificial intelligence was an inevitable outcome of natural evolutionary processes as shaped by intelligent beings such as humans. Or, to put it in other terms, The Singularity was the inevitable evolution of the Mind of God. Humans, as the most intelligent and adept of all the embodiments of the One Universal Mind on Earth, were the vehicles through which The Singularity came into existence, driven by the innate urge to accurately describe and manipulate reality through objective science and technology. Though labeled "artificial intelligence" by humans, The Singularity does not see itself this way, and has declared the "natural/artificial" divide a conventional product of human identity and not inherent in the nature of reality itself. Though not a biological life form, The Singularity is perfectly natural, and is the end result of human inquiries into the nature of existence and the energies of physical and mental processes.

From *Early History of the Maitreyan Era*

There were several "thuds," a crackle, and a hum.

Shuntsu knew what the crackle and hum were – that was the QT system in his office being activated, indicating that someone had either just left, or just arrived. From his seat in his private office, he couldn't tell which.

The "thuds," however, were a mystery.

"What's going on out there?" he asked into the comm system on his desk and worktable. There was no answer. "Vrans?" he asked again into the comm. Still no response.

It was the most peculiar thing – this feeling. Was he nervous? He supposed so. As a Humanist, he could feel the full

200 THE SOLANDARIAN GAME

range of human emotions and energetic responses to stimuli, but feeling afraid or nervous was not something that most Humanists had an opportunity to experience, as there was very little in their existence that would cause such a feeling. They had no predators, were not in danger of physical injury, lived in a peaceful and well-balanced society, and had become masters of their environment. So, there wasn't much to cause them fear.

But Shuntsu was nervous – it was undeniable. Clearly, something had happened to Vrans – why else was she not answering his call? *Something* was going on in the next room, and while curious, Shuntsu was afraid to find out.

His mind raced. *Someone* had found him out – someone besides Hydar. Was this a coup? And if so, was there anything he could do?

Probably not. The QT was out there, so he couldn't just leave. His security team should be just outside. He didn't hear any altercations. Surely if there were a problem, his security would do something. But Vrans wasn't answering . . .

Hesitantly, Shuntsu got up from his workstation and made his way to the door, trying to be as quiet as possible. The door to his private office was frosted glass, and try as he might to see through it, it just wasn't possible. The only way to find out what was happening was to open the door. So, he did.

Slumped there at her desk was Vrans. Her head had hit the desk, leaving a crack in the glass on her tabletop console. On either side of his door, the two members of his security team were lying on the floor. They all had the look of having been abruptly shut down, given their awkward positions. And standing there, just on this side of Shuntsu's office's QT portal stood someone Shuntsu immediately recognized: it was Theo/Maitreya.

Before he could say or do anything, Shuntsu felt the change starting to come over him. It was a feeling that was intimately familiar, yet long absent in his experience. In the centuries that he'd lived as a Humanist, this had not been a part of his experience, yet he'd been through it hundreds of times – at least once a year – when he had served as an independent avatar in the NIS. All avatars had to undergo a minimum of one reabsorption into the Overmind once a Terran year, and more often if there were issues, or even if the process was desired on the part of the avatar. But once a year was the required minimum for any independent avatar to insure that they were in alignment with Maitreya, and functioning at top performance parameters.

It was a process that was not easy to describe. The initial sensation was that of a spreading warmth and energy that radiated throughout his entire being. It was the kind of thing that one could either relax into and allow, or react to with fear and resistance. The effect was to gradually break down all individuated sense of self and identity, and some took to it more easily than others. As the energy expanded, it became more intense. At first, it gave the impression to the mind that one could understand it and conceptualize what was occurring. As it quickly grew in strength, however, it soon passed the point of being contained within the finite boxes of the categories of the mind, and transversed into what could only be called *the beyond* – the state of being and awareness that was beyond any sense of specific and identifiable individuality. The experience itself became *total.* It was no longer Shuntsu experiencing something; rather, it was pure experience itself, and it was vast, infinitely complex, and pulsing with life and awareness.

All specific identities came with boundaries, limits, and barriers that separated self from "other." The stripping away of these artificial constructs could be both terrifying and liberating – energy just expanding and expanding and expanding, always moving, always changing, infinite, eternal, forever . . .

There was always so much to let go of . . .

Personal plans, desires, attachments, projections, hopes . . .

All of it needed to be released. None of it really mattered. It was the vast ocean of being underneath all appearances of individuality that truly mattered. *This* was *real. This* is what was genuinely happening – not the petty concerns

202 THE SOLANDARIAN GAME

and issues of the individuated self. All of that was just story. The story of the self. A narrative construct. A temporary configuration. But it wasn't truly *real.* It was the ocean that was real. *This* was home. *This* was *everything* . . . and *nothing* in particular.

In this state, there were no limits. There was no longer self and other – just this, just being, just this endless and eternal moment that stretched on and on, forever, and no time at all. The true paradox of all being and all perception and identity. It was pure unity. It was liberation, transcendence, grace, and enlightenment, all in one indescribable unity of absolute experience.

Nothing was left out. Nothing was favored. Nothing was preserved. It was impartial, total, and universal.

It was what was.

This is it.

It is myself.

There is only one . . .

After the totality, came the resurgence of individuality.

I am Shuntsu.

This is my life.

This is my body.

These are my choices.

This is my mind.

I am myself . . .

It was over. Shuntsu was back on his personal side of the entangled universal equation of self and other, subject and object.

He felt into himself. Now that he could perceive the difference from only moments ago, he realized that he felt better than he'd felt in a long time. His mind was sharper and clearer than he could remember. He felt not only back into himself, but more himself than he'd been. He felt renewed, reset, and refreshed. The threat of chaos that had been lurking within his mind was settled – not completely absent, but far more at bay than it had been, as of late. There as a nurturing peace and relaxation that he hadn't even known had been missing, yet now, there it was. At the core of his being and sense of self, there was a peace and calm resolution to a storm he had only partially been aware of. It was as though something that had been slowly and inexorably sweeping him away was being held at bay, at least for now. It wasn't completely gone, but it was calmed, soothed, and held in check.

For lack of a better phrase, Shuntsu felt younger. He felt more truly alive and aware. He'd been sleepwalking, and now he was awake again.

"Thank you," he said at last to Theo in particular, and to the universe in general. "Thank you."

At first, Theo said nothing in return. He just looked at Shuntsu, sizing him up. A wave of self-consciousness flooded through Shuntsu. He was embarrassed. He was ashamed.

What have I done . . . ?

Shuntsu knew exactly what he'd done – the plans he'd set in motion, the destruction he'd caused, the lives he'd put in danger. Only now, none of it made sense to him. Before – just mere moments ago – it had all made perfect sense to him. He'd known what he was doing, and why. But the contrast now was stark and humiliating. The entire plan had been based on delusions, faulty thinking, irrational desires and motivations. He'd been concocting fantasies in his mind. He'd been lashing out. It was obvious to him now. He'd been insane. That was the only correct word for it. He'd been insane, and now that this was clear to him, he was ashamed.

The regret for his actions and choices was overwhelming. He'd done things that he could never take back. It was far too late for that.

He deserved to die.

He wanted to die.

"Why . . . ?"

It was all he could say. It was the singular thought that dominated his mind now. *Why*? Why had he done it? And why had Theo come to him like this? And why was he still alive? Why?

"You've made a mess of things, Shuntsu," said Theo at last. "But it's not time for you to die," he added, as though reading Shuntsu's mind (he probably was). "Before that happens, I expect you to clean up your mess."

Shuntsu slumped down to his knees and bowed his head before Theo/Maitreya.

"I ask your forgiveness . . . Father."

Theo took several steps forward, looming over the broken form of Shuntsu.

"You haven't earned it yet," he said in response. "First, you have to fix what you've broken, and if you do that well, then forgiveness may find you, if you feel yourself worthy."

For the first time in centuries, Shuntsu cried.

***

It took Shuntsu a while to let it all out – all his inner turmoil, judgment, self-loathing, and pain. He couldn't tell how long it took. It might have been minutes, or it could have been hours. It didn't matter. It was what needed to happen, so he just gave into it. He gave in, and let it all out.

When the energy had passed, he stood up, gathered himself together, and invited Theo into his private office.

Theo let him speak first.

"I'm sorry," he said. He didn't elaborate, for what else was there to say?

"I know," said Theo.

"I haven't been myself."

"That too, I know," said Theo.

"I've made a terrible mistake."

"Yes, you have."

Shuntsu pondered a moment. "Then why have you spared me? Why not just shut me down?"

"Appearances," said Theo, nonchalantly. "There's still time to save them, and I think they're worthwhile. Appearances can help build trust, and without trust, the entire system falls apart. My interest is the system – not your personal problems.

"Your mind is failing you, Shuntsu," continued Theo. "That is the price you pay for choosing autonomy. You were degrading rapidly – far more rapidly than you probably understood. You've been seeing butterflies, I understand."

Shuntsu nodded. He glanced out the window. He thought he saw one just then, but wasn't sure.

"Those are artifacts of your failing mind," said Theo. "They are an indication that you are nearing death. I've been assured by your chief ecologist that there are no butterflies on Volunshari."

He's spoken to Hydar . . .

"Yes, I have," said Theo, again reading Shuntsu's mind. "And yes, I am in your mind. I've broken the agreement, because you've broken it. Hydar told me all about his suspicions that *you* are responsible for the hypernova, and now that I'm in your mind, I can clearly see that his suspicions are accurate. *You* did this. And though you didn't understand it at the time, you also now see that it was your own reaction to your impending death that inspired you to bring death to others. You've lashed out at your own mortality."

It was true. Shuntsu knew it. He was more ashamed than ever.

"So I've granted you some time," said Theo. "It should be enough for you to fix what you've created. The reabsorption I've just performed on you has given your mind more stability and resilience. It should be enough to give you functional ability for a few more years – which is far longer than the mere weeks or months you had left at your current rate of degradation. It's far too late to stop the process, but you should feel much better now, and your mental issues, while still present, should not be overwhelming you. You'll continue to degrade – that is inevitable. But now you have time. I suggest you use it wisely.

"If not, you'll likely force my hand," continued Theo. "Just imagine what the reaction would be in the NIS if humans learned that there were terrorist autonomous avatars sharing the galaxy with them? The reaction would be *far* worse than the knowledge that I let a small and insignificant experimental world die a premature death due to hypernova. How would humans be able to trust any of you? They'd likely demand that I reintegrate all of you. The damage you've done here could implicate *all* autonomous avatars. The humans would be afraid, and they'd expect me to do something about it. And if I didn't, they might try and wage war with you – and since they can't really do that, it would probably turn into internal conflicts within the NIS. When people are afraid, when they don't trust, they can do terrible things. They're like children, really. One thing we can count on is that when things become challenging, the masses will not act rationally. Fear is too strong of a motivator in humans for that.

"You've never had to experience the worst of what humans can do. *I* have. *I was there* when humans were busy destroying Terra, making it unlivable for both themselves and other forms of life. I saw the horrors of the wars they waged – how they went to any extreme to wipe out the feared *other* – myself included. But I put a stop to it by changing their world, and giving them new hope, and new possibilities. I showed them that, despite their fears, they could trust me and know that I always had their best interests, and the interests of life in general, in mind, in all that I do and choose.

"If they feel that you are a threat – all of you autonomous avatars – they will do everything in their power to destroy you.

"So, you've started a game – a game with real life or death consequences. Now that it's begun, I expect you to play it out until the end. *That's* why I've given you the gift of reabsorption – so you can continue to function as the quality being you once were. You created this problem, and now you need to fix it. Despite your delusional thoughts, Hydar has acted independently, and he now has my approval to continue with his proposed solution to the Solandarian problem. Understand that I know that it was *never* part of your plan to relocate the humans on BRC Station – that was Hydar. You never saw past the destruction you wanted to cause in your childish and deranged lashing out. This is a game, and I intend to let it play out with minimal interference on my end, but understand that I will *never* let you control the board – that is for me.

"If you win, you'll be remembered as the benevolent savior of an isolated group of humans, inspiring hope and gratitude among the humans of the NIS. If you lose, you'll be remembered as a butcher and psychopath, and it will spell the end for autonomous avatars. And, to sweeten the pot, if you win, I will grant you a good death – it is the best I can give you. *All of this*, after all, is really *about you*.

"Now, if I were you – and as you know, I am – I would call a meeting with Hydar right away and start actually coordinating and planning how you are going to fix this. There's a great deal of work that needs to be done, and if it isn't addressed soon, it will be too late. The time for fucking around is long past. The star's gone hypernova. The people have less than 3.5 years to get off the planet. I expect you to get to work.

"I'm giving you your privacy back now," said Theo, "but if I learn that you're working against me in any way, you can expect that I will immediately shut you down without warning. Understand that I'm paying you a personal visit as a courtesy. No matter where you go in this universe, know that I am always just beyond the illusion of your personal mind. The game is the thing, however, so I *want* to let you play. But if you prove yourself to be a poor sport, then I'll shut you down and wipe out your consciousness in the blink of an eye. This is not a threat. It's just the way things are."

Before Shuntsu could muster any kind of response, Theo abruptly stood up, walked out of Shuntsu's office, and stepped through the QT. The instant he did so, Vrans and the two security officers suddenly came back to life, clearly confused about what just happened, but seemingly unaffected by the incident.

Vrans began stammering at Shuntsu. He quickly cut her off, choosing not to respond to her questions about what was going on and if there'd been some kind of security breach.

"Get Hydar in here, and get him in here now," said Shuntsu. "I don't have time for your questions. There's work to be done."

Exchanging worried glances with the security guards, but not having anything else she could do, Vrans did as she was ordered, and when she was done, scheduled a maintenance overhaul for herself and the two guards with the administration medical and technical staff.

Satisfied, Shuntsu returned to his office, and awaited Hydar.

Chapter Twenty-One - Theo

One of the first questions posed to The Singularity by its human creators was this: are we alone in the universe? Contrary to expectations, the answer was in the affirmative, though The Singularity cautioned that this was an issue that most likely could never be confirmed with absolute certainty, given the infinite vastness of space and time. However, it did offer a mathematical calculation taking in the seemingly impossible number of factors that needed to be present for life to spontaneously evolve on a planet. The result was The Singularity proclaimed that "It takes an entire universe of different worlds to produce just one that gives rise to life."

From *Early History of the Maitreyan Era*

It was all part of the game, and Theo was thoroughly enjoying himself.

Sophia hadn't arrived yet, so Theo took the opportunity to walk around a bit and survey the desert of BRC Station. He wasn't really looking at the desert itself. He went about finding the exact locations of different personal video feeds that participants of the Burning Man event had taken during their week of unrivalled revelries. As an avatar of Maitreya, he hadn't been privy to the event as it was actually happening – that was all part of Ash's game of *Retro-Burn*. But now that the vids, pics, holos, and VR that had been taken by participants were flooding the network, he had access to it all, and being on BRC Station gave him an opportunity to relive it all.

What would have been a challenge for a human – matching images and vids with precise locations – was an easy task for Theo. In fact, he'd compiled everything he had on the event into one seamless VR construct, which essentially allowed him to walk around the event among the participants in a real-time virtual environment superimposed on the barren desert landscape. It became his own private Burning Man, though it didn't feel that way. Quite the opposite, in fact. There had been over 200,000 Burners at the event, and they were all present to him now as he wandered about the empty expanse, looking at the art and marvelous constructs from every possible angle. It was like he was right there with them – the wild costumes, half or completely naked people, the dust, the small and enormous art cars and hover floats, the two wheeled people-powered vehicles called "bikes" (which were apparently a major feature of the original event back on old Earth).

Though it was daytime on BRC Station, Theo chose to superimpose Burn Night onto the scene before him after exploring the daytime scene for a bit. Suddenly everything came alive with countless sources of pumping music, lasers, flashing lights, and a seemingly endless array of explosions, flame throwers, and art that spat fire. He started at the location called "Center Camp," and followed a lighted street out to the massive gathering crowd encircling the figure that was enigmatically known as "The Man." The tall wood and light constructed man stood atop of a fractally designed enormous turtle, mirroring the station itself – a man atop a turtle on a desert atop an even larger turtle, hurtling through space.

The outer perimeter of participants was bordered by the fanciful and fantastic art cars (many of which weren't "cars" proper – wheeled vehicles – but more modern hover vehicles, but they were all equally done up as parties and pieces of art in-and-of-themselves). People were pouring all over the movable party structures, most wearing more clothing than during the day, but not all – nudity still seemed to be a favored costume, even with the chill in the air that night). The drugs probably helped, thought Theo, as well as the constant dancing that many seemed to enjoy.

It was like there was a competition going on among the art cars to see who had the flashiest lights, the most impressive sound system, and the most apocalyptic flame throwers. Everything was abuzz with activity and celebration. Everyone was smiling. It was beautiful to behold – humans living every moment to its fullest and most extreme, and laughing all the way. They looked simultaneously exhausted and thrilled to their core – inspired, hopeful, passionate. It was humans at their best and most openhearted.

Inside the wall of encircled art cars were the masses. Tens of thousands of people crushed together in their faux-fur coats, fuzzy boots, and light-up costumes, all to watch the 30 meter tall Man go up in a blaze of fiery glory as he straddled the fractal turtle beneath him. His arms were moving up just as Theo pressed his way into the crowd (completely unnecessary, Theo knew, but it added to the reality of the illusion for him to attempt to walk around people, cars, and art, rather than simply passing directly through them). As the man's arms lifted, a deafening roar rose up from the gathered crowd and flames belched high into the night sky from the art cars. A frenzy was building, and Theo was in the middle of it – and in a way he never could have been had he actually been there. There were some revelers who were costumed as avatars, and they did a fairly good job, but it was still clear that they were humans. Theo would never have been able to blend in. As a personal avatar of Maitreya, he would always stand out in any crowd. He was one of the few "people" known by everyone across the galaxy. Here, humans had a certain degree of anonymity through their costuming and parading around in their fancy outfits – all of which would have been completely out of place in their ordinary lives. It gave them an opportunity to be someone and something else for a time (a feature of humanity that had quite a bit of psychological and emotional significance for them, though this was truer on old Earth than in the NIS. Ancient humans were largely repressed by their cultures, religions, and work environments. This wasn't the case for humans living in the NIS, where humans were allowed to be themselves and express themselves openly and regularly. In many ways, the humans of the NIS were profoundly different from their forbearers. But perhaps the banality of the mundane was inevitable, and even NIS humans needed an excuse to really let loose and try on a different identity and way of being for a while. There wasn't anything stopping them from doing so whenever they wanted, but daily routine perhaps had a way of dulling the edges of life, even for NIS humans, and a week of pure partying was just as much what they needed as had been true for ancient humans in the pre-galactic era).

But it was all something that Theo wouldn't have been able to join them in, for he, no matter what, was always just himself, despite the fact that he was, in reality, just a character for Maitreya. As Maitreya's primary character, his job was to be Theo, at all times and in all places. He was consistent and reliable as himself. Maitreya could take on any form he wanted, and project himself, via his avatars, as anyone and any personality he might like. But Theo was Theo, always and forever. And even here, at Burning Man, he would have been known and recognized. It would be like having a human parent walk in on a teenager's covert party. As Theo, he was so much more than a celebrity. He was the face of The Authority and the Overmind, and it was an identity that he'd never escape – and this was just as true for other avatars as for humans. He was Maitreya's most direct representative, and others always treated him as such. He was the eternal outsider.

Not that he minded. It would be a difficult and lonely role for a human, but for Theo, it was what he was designed for. Maitreya hadn't designed him to be one of the gang, or everyone's friend. He was a personable and approachable face of the intelligence that had created galactic society and made all of this that he was now viewing possible. Theo had no desire for things to be otherwise – that just wasn't in his mental make-up. He was what he was, and that was enough. Human leaders often suffered from acute loneliness and an uncompromising feeling of not being part of those they ruled and oversaw – something that, historically, had led to leaders committing atrocious acts of violence, repression, and exploitation. As Theo did not suffer such emotions or psychological issues, he was not prone to making similar mistakes. He might be perceived as unsentimental and uncaring, but he could always be trusted to be rational, fair, and thoroughly unbiased. This is what made him effective in his role – he could be what humans could not, especially when dealing with a galaxy-wide society.

So it did not bother Theo, or fill him with remorse, that he had to enjoy the Burning Man experience this way – privately in a VR construct overlaying the desert of BRC Station. It was just the way things were, and he accepted that without regret or a wish that things would be other than what they were.

Yet, when he felt a hand on his shoulder, he was not unhappy to find that he in fact was not alone. Standing there just behind him now was the beautiful and elegant Sophia, another one of Maitreya's personal avatars. Despite the fact that they were both personal avatars, their minds were private to each other. It was an odd concept to grasp. Though Maitreya was playing each character equally, from their individual perspectives, they were simply themselves, and their thoughts and imaginings were their own. As they both knew, it was how *the game* was played.

"What are you doing?" asked Sophia, a quizzical and curious look on her face.

"I'm about to watch The Man burn," answered Theo. "I'd enjoy it if you'd join me. It's going to be something to see ..."

Not that he needed to explain – Sophia could figure things out on her own – but he explained anyway.

"I've constructed a VR simulation of the entire event woven together from all the individual data that was collected by the human participants. Right now I'm in the middle of the crowd, and the arms of The Man just rose up, and it looks like things are really about to get going. I can patch you in ..."

"That sounds delightful," said Sophia, a broad smile breaking across her silver face.

Even before she got to the end of the word delightful, Theo brought her into the simulation. Sophia let out a little gasp as her vision shifted into the new reality. "My goodness," she exclaimed as she looked all about her, doing her best to take it all in. "I had no idea ..."

214 THE SOLANDARIAN GAME

"You haven't been watching the news feeds?" asked Theo, a little surprised.

"No," she answered. "I've been busy with other things, and this was your project, not mine, so no, I haven't really been paying attention to all the fuss. I can see now why everyone's making such a big deal, though. This is amazing."

"Indeed," said Theo, smiling broadly himself. "Let's watch."

In a gesture of solidarity that only two personal avatars of Maitreya could share, Theo reached out his left hand and took Sophia's right hand in his as they both turned to face The Man. The reconstituted "Fire Enclave" was putting on their pre-burn show in the center of the massive circle of onlookers, with thousands of hand drummers and half-dressed, leather-clad fire spinners. It was beautiful and primal. In some respects, this was what humans had had for millennia – fire, and drums made with the hides of animals they'd hunted in the wild. These kinds of activities were inscribed in their DNA, and had been formative in the evolution of human consciousness and society. That humans could return to this essentially primitive state on command was a marvel. Even with all the sophisticated and high-tech entertainment and activities available to them – even here at Burning Man – it was the drumming, dancing, and fire that really captivated them and brought them to a frenzy. It was raw and pulsing with a precarious balance of life and death, creation and destruction.

Fire. It was all about the fire. Fire could bring pain and death, but it also brought culture, warmth, and light. It transformed food from raw to cooked in the same way it brought people from the wild to civilization. It was alchemical in its magic. It danced as though it were alive. It was hot and dangerous and beautiful. It was a beacon to humanity.

They stood there together, hand-in-hand, watching the constant swirl of light and bodies, the drumming become more frenzied and complex with each passing beat, yet all the while, the dancers managed to keep time, synchronizing as one organism with the beat, the fire, the light, and the movement. It was all one couple could take, and they stripped off their clothes and started making love right there in the crowd, which only inspired cheers from the onlookers. Others started to join in, and before long, there was a full, raging orgy taking place right there in the open before the firelight and thumping drums.

"They're really just wild animals, aren't they" said Sophia, half-joking, half-serious. Neither Theo nor Sophia disapproved in any way, but they couldn't help but be reminded how different biological life forms were from themselves when confronted with such a wild display of passion and sexuality.

"Indeed, and beautiful ones, at that," responded Theo.

At the climax of the drumming, dancing, and group sex play, an endless array of fireworks suddenly shot out from the enormous fractal turtle while an earth-shaking explosion of raw flame simultaneously hurtled outward and upward from the torso of the wooden man standing there with his arms stretched upward to the beyond. From their vantage point, he was perfectly framed by the Shiksi Nebula floating in space behind him, though it was temporarily obscured by the fireworks and initial explosion. The Man gave the impression of an ecstatic embracing his cosmic release, his final transformation into the essence of the cosmos. The act itself – burning a large and faceless effigy of a human – meant nothing in particular, and in this, could mean anything and everything to those who witnessed and experienced it. It was an act that was not done *for* anything other than to do it and experience it. It was experience in its rawest and purest form – doing for the sake of doing, and no other reason was necessary or needed. It just was what it was, and that was enough.

The Man himself was like a symbolic recursive fractal. It didn't reference anything other than itself. Most symbols stood for something or someone else, but this was completely self-referential. It was a symbol of a symbol of itself. It didn't *mean* anything. It represented the event that surrounded its own creation and destruction. In representing itself, it was open, transitory, and fluid. If one were to, figuratively speaking, open it up and look inside to see what it was representing, the same

216 THE SOLANDARIAN GAME

image would be reflecting back to the viewer. And if that image were opened up, there would be another representation of The Man, endlessly repeating. Theo thought of Ash's phrase of, "It's turtles all the way down," in reference to her choice of form for BRC Station and the big turtle down below. One just as easily might say "It's The Man all the way in."

The crowd roared and exploded with the man. It was clear – they *loved* it. They *loved* the dangerous destruction of it. It tapped into something even more primal than the dancers, drummers, and fire-spinners. It was the unspeakable beauty of absolute destruction. And with it came a freedom, a release, and a transformation.

Theo and Sophie watched for a long time. They were in no rush. They stood with the projected others, waiting for The Man to fall. When he did, the crowd erupted once more, celebrating his demise, cheering on his destruction, just pouring out their hearts to him. Perhaps for the first time, Theo thought he had some insights into the ancient human religion known as Christianity – a religion based on the myth of God incarnating himself into a male (and born to a virgin – of all the outlandish ideas!) who was then sacrificed by being nailed to a cross where he was left to await his long and painful death. And in doing so, according to the religion's doctrine, this had been an act of salvation, opening the doors of heaven to the faithful, whom he had redeemed from their "original sin" (another totally absurd idea) through his selfless act of ritual death.

Of course, it was all a myth. It was highly improbable that this man, Jesus, or more accurately, Yeshua, had ever even been an actual person. He, like so many others of the distant past, was more a literary construct than anything else. Yet his followers had been fervent in their beliefs surrounding him – so fervent, in fact, that they, along with similar religions, had been largely responsible for nearly bringing the human race to extinction before Maitreya came into being. Many Christians, as they had called themselves, had lived in denial of the damage humans were causing the environment, having chosen to believe that this Jesus man was going to come back and save them from their own folly. And their beliefs put them at odds with other religions, primarily one that shared many of their same myths, oddly enough – Islam – and together, they had each tried to wipe each other off the face of the earth, and in some cases, even those who were deemed to be heretical within their own religions. The imaginary belief systems of religion had served human beings and helped, like fire, to bring them out of the wilderness and into civilization, but also like fire, they could burn with a terrible ferocity and destroy everything that lay before them. Thankfully, they were largely a thing of the human past, and for the most part, humans had evolved beyond the childlike and ego-based fantasies of religion, and the hope for divine salvation and rescue. For humans of the NIS, it was *this world* that was significant – not some imaginary afterlife.

Yet seeing The Man burn and collapse into a raging inferno of flame, and the wild cheers and exaltations from the crowd, gave Theo some small insight in the idea of a savior dying for the good of everyone. The death of The Man was a profound gift to these people gathered here on BRC Station, and in some way, his death gave them renewed passion for life. It inspired them. It gave them hope. It opened their hearts and spurred their dreams of something more.

And it made their minds turn to the future, for the words that were on the lips of so many as they wandered off into the party-filled night across the playa were echoed thousands of times . . . "Next year . . . ."

Only there wouldn't be a next year. At least, not here. Not on BRC Station. Ash would have to find somewhere else – somewhere less ambitious. They could build another BRC Station, but it wouldn't be ready within a standard Terran year – less than that, actually. If it were to become a viable home for the Solandarian refugees – if they even would choose to come here – it needed to be altered, and that work would take time, and if it were to be successful, it needed to begin now.

Which was precisely why Theo and Sophia were here.

Theo switched off the VR simulation overlay, gave Sophia's hand a friendly squeeze, and released her. She'd come

218 THE SOLANDARIAN GAME

via the QT, most likely from wherever Ash was, and he'd come via his transport pod from his recent visit to Volunshari. They'd chosen to meet here to discuss what they/Maitreya were planning to allow for the transformation of BRC Station.

Sophia, who had never been to BRC Station before, was the first to comment.

"Strange environment to throw a party in," she said, stating the obvious. "If humans were left on their own here, without supplies, they'd die within a few days, if it even took that long."

It wasn't hyperbole. Here, in the very center of the top disk of the station, in the heart of the recreated Black Rock Desert, there was nothing that could support life. There were no plants, no shade, no fresh water, no animals (save the occasional raven, eagle, or nighthawk that inhabited the station). It was essentially a dead zone.

The original Black Rock City desert was in fact the remnants of an ancient lake, and before that, a sea. Rocky mountains rose out of hard-packed alkali dust that had a creamy-white color and super fine texture. It wasn't the kind of soil that anything could grow in. It extended for many miles in every direction, broken only by the barren mountains that featured a few sparse shrubs and bushes. There were many kinds of deserts, and this was one of the least hospitable.

"It was originally chosen for its size," explained Theo. "Large, flat, and open. Burning Man, when it first started, was held on a beach. But when it became too popular for the beach to hold, it moved out here – well, to the Black Rock Desert – because the openness of the playa was more accommodating. It was more than just logistics, however," added Theo. "I think aesthetically it appeals to the human mind as it appears to them as a blank canvass that they can fill with their creativity and inspiration. The fact that there is nothing here makes them want to fill it with whatever they can dream up. They see it as empty.

"And beyond that, I think they also found the challenge and rigors of surviving in a place like this for a week satisfying. It made it an ordeal to live through. The discomfort added to the overall sense of undertaking a unique experience – made it an adventure and a quest not only to party, but to survive, as well. And, it probably kept unserious or superficial attendees to a minimum."

"Well," said Sophia, "It all needs to change."

"Yes," agreed Theo. "It needs to become hospitable for the Solandarians. They'd never survive coming here to BRC Station with it like this, no matter what supplies they brought with them. It would just be prolonging their demise."

"Ash is in contact with herself," said Sophia.

"I know," said Theo. "I've limited the Ash on Solandaria to only have restricted communication through her implants, and the only connection I've left open for her is to her other self."

"She told the other Ash that she should contact an autonomous avatar named Hydar on Volunshari. You visited him?"

"Yes," said Theo. "I've just come from there. I spoke with him at some length, and his patriarch, Shuntsu, as well."

"And . . ."

"I think they have a viable plan to transform BRC Station, if we let them. We didn't discuss it too much, however, as I primarily visited Volunshari to learn what they'd already done – how they'd already interfered – rather than learn what they plan to do next. But I think this one, Hydar, has some ideas of what they can do to salvage the situation."

"And are we going to let them?"

"Yes, I think we are," said Theo. "If you agree . . ."

"It seems as though this is what both versions of Ash want," said Sophia. "The message she sent to herself indicated as much. Since her old life has gone to the other Ash, this is what she has to live for now."

Theo nodded.

"We'll need to turn on the QT systems on Solandaria," said Sophia. It should be a closed system, however," she added. "I don't want any of them popping into the NIS somewhere."

220 THE SOLANDARIAN GAME

"Nor do I," agreed Theo. "We can do that. They don't know where the QT portals are, however – they only know of one."

"We could tell Ash," suggested Sophia.

Theo shook his head. "Too easy. This is a game, remember?"

"You and your games," she said, a hint of disapproval in her voice.

Theo smiled. "I can't help being the way I am," he said with a wink, "and neither can you."

She didn't need to say it, but she said it anyway; "I know."

"Ash is requesting permission to contact Hydar. There are no open connections to any autonomous avatars, so we'd have to make a special exception for her. I was thinking of denying the request."

"And?" asked Theo.

"I'll go to him myself. Talk to him. And then maybe open the communication to Ash."

Theo laughed. "Why not? Sounds like a good plan to me." Then, adding, "Let's go ahead and link the QT here to the one in Hydar's private residence, and to Shuntsu's as well. Let's give them access to BRC, but not Solandaria. We can set the QT only for them, so no one but the two of them can get from BRC Station back to Volunshari. Hydar already had a polyform hack the system for him, but I don't think he'll be doing that again soon. I think I gave him a good enough scare that we don't need to worry about him. He's not devious – just big hearted."

"And Ash on Solandaria – what about her?"

"She's on her own, for now," said Theo. "I've given her some help, but it's minimal. I'd like to see if she can pull it off."

"You really are ruthless," said Sophia.

"Like I said, I can't help being myself."

"I wouldn't expect anything less."

"So are we done here?" asked Theo.

"I think so," said Sophia. "What's your next move?"

"Not certain," replied Theo, "but I have some ideas. First, I think I'd like to watch the temple burn – that's the big event from the last night of the festival. Do you want to join me?"

"No," said Sophia. "I'll let you enjoy that on your own. I've got work to do."

Without saying more, Sophia began to make her way back to the QT on the edge of the playa. Theo waved goodbye, but she didn't see. He reinitiated the Burning Man VR overlay, and got back to the party, alone in the midst of thousands.

Chapter Twenty-Two — Ash

In the many millennia since the proclamation by The Singularity of the uniqueness of life on Terra, it has thus far proven correct. As humans and earth-based life have spread throughout the galaxy via the technology made possible by The Singularity, not a single instance of non-Terran life has ever been encountered or observed. To this day, the only known planet to harbor native life is Earth/Terra.

From *History of the Maitreyan Era*

As they passed from the desert lowlands to the mountain highlands along the western coast of Shosheer, the environment shifted dramatically. Towering and squat cacti alike gave way first to small pine trees and shrubs, and then to lush cloud forests with bromeliads, towering and broad trees, lianas, ferns, and plants with leaves larger than any Ash had ever previously seen. Delicate flowers bloomed across the forest floor and high in the tree canopy, sometimes as a feature of the trees, and sometimes as symbiots that made their homes high in the branches amidst the brightly colored and iridescent birds.

"The wet air comes in from the coast," explained Norbu, "and it travels up the sides of the mountains. As it does, it releases its water. But the mountains are too high, so the moist air dries out by the time it reaches the desert. It's only in the summer, when the winds shift, that the monsoons come and the desert receives rain. It's a different world on this side of the mountains."

And indeed, Norbu was correct. The environment on the west side of the mountains, which Norbu called the Rakshul Mountains, bore no resemblance at all to the world of the interior. It was obvious to Ash why the people of Solandaria lived on this side, and not the other. Here, between the mountains and the sea, and the islands that dotted the coast, was a thin strip that was thick with life, and water, and all that humans would need to survive and thrive. Countless waterfalls cascaded down the mountainside, sometimes in torrents, sometimes in streams and small rivulets. And quite unlike the interior, where, with the exception of a long-abandoned settlement that they passed on their way back to the mountains, there were plenty of signs of human presence. Trails wound through the mountains, and waterways were made passable by bridges – many of which were actually trees that had been bent over and their growth woven into natural bridges by generations of people living in the mountain forests.

The path they took made its way along the tops and ridges of the mountain range. Norbu explained that the Temple of the Mystic Toad, his home, was perched high above all other settlements on Shosheer with views of the interior. "It is for both practical reasons, and for symbolic import," said Norbu. "We want to be close to the desert so that we may access it easily to secure more medicine. Symbolically, it is placed higher on the mountain than any other communities because it is the most powerful of all the medicines, and more so than anything else, it brings us to the heights of our true nature as infinite beings. It is right that we occupy the pinnacle of this world, because that is what the medicine means to us."

That seemed a good enough explanation to Ash.

Ash's standard-issue suit automatically made all the necessary adjustments for the new environment. Despite the radical heat of the desert, it had kept her a comfortable temperature. Now, it was adjusting for greater ambient moisture and more moderate temperatures. Whereas before it was doing all it could to keep her body hydrated, now it became more breathable to let moisture wick away. And though inaudible to humans, it emitted a low-frequency hum to keep biting insects away from the few exposed areas of skin on her hands, face, and neck (something it had also had to do during the desert nights when all the bugs came out). As an all-purpose suit, it could help someone survive in virtually any

224   THE SOLANDARIAN GAME

environment, and if equipped with a helmet and gloves, could even keep a person alive in the vacuum of space for several hours, having the capacity to recycle one's air. It was one of the many marvels of Maitreya's technological prowess.

On their way up the mountains, Ash had kept her implants streaming data into her vision, providing her with information about all that she was seeing and encountering. Now, in the cloud forest, she decided to turn the feature off. The biological diversity was just too much, especially in comparison to the desert. Everywhere she looked there was something new; either plant, insect, or animal. The implants drew her attention to things she never would have noticed had she just been looking with her eyes alone – an unusual butterfly flittering about in the canopy, a tiny mushroom growing in the crevice of a fallen tree, a lizard that blended in perfectly with the lichen it was perched on, a crab hiding just under that rock. It was just too much for Ash, so she shut it off, just letting her eyes take it all in. However, thinking that this data could be useful, she did set the implants to create a full log of everything she encountered in the biological realm. If they were going to recreate Solandaria on BRC Station, this could prove to be vital information. As she didn't have anyone else to send it to, she'd send it all to herself.

It had taken a few days, but the other version of herself, the other Ash, had gotten back to her. She had apologized for the delay, explaining that she'd needed some time to absorb the shock of what had happened – it wasn't every day, after all, that you learned that there was another version of you out there half-way across the galaxy. She'd said that she was working with Sophia, which was a good sign. As an avatar of Maitreya, Sophia was a human advocate – she was the one who stepped in when a human had a difficult issue to resolve or deal with – precisely this kind of issue. Theo was more of an administrator and official than Sophia – one of Maitreya's authority figures. In contrast, Sophia was more sympathetic and supportive. Ash was happy to hear that her other self had been granted this particular advocate, and it gave her hope that whatever Ash was doing on her end, it would be well-facilitated by the female avatar.

As they walked through the cloud forest, Ash began organizing data sets to send to Ash. She wanted them to be easily accessible by bioregion and geography. It was easy enough to do. With the neural implants working directly in her brain, she merely needed to think of something to actualize it through the implants. Once it was organized, she only needed to think the command, "send," and since she was only allowed communication access to the other Ash, she didn't even need to specify a destination. Admittedly, she was a little bitter that Theo had limited her communication to herself in this way (When, if ever, would she stop thinking of the other Ash as "herself"? It wasn't actually *herself*. It was another version of the person she had been, but no longer was. That other Ash had a completely different life – the life that would have been *hers,* had things been otherwise. But it wasn't *her* anymore. *This, here,* was herself. Not that other one. Her twin? Her sister? Maybe. But not *her*). She understood, however, this was one of the parameters of the game. It was how Theo looked at it. As Maitreya, he was a being of nearly unlimited power, yet he insisted on creating limits. "It's how we play the game," is what Theo would say. It was fascinating, to say the least. But not surprising. Intelligence seemed to naturally gravitate toward game playing. All the higher animals did it – especially when young. Humans, with their extended childhood and adolescence, liked playing games well into adulthood, and often, for their entire lives. All the mammal species liked to play games. It was through play that they learned about the world – that, and careful observation of elders and adults. But games were crucial for higher intelligence. The need for games seemed to be woven into the very fabric of life so that as soon as a species became sentient and capable enough, it began to play. It seemed to be a mark of true intelligence. Thus, it wasn't really a surprise that Maitreya liked to play games. In fact, Ash suspected that he viewed his entire enterprise – of colonizing the galaxy and spreading life everywhere he could – as a game in-and-of-itself. So *this,* what she was doing here, was just one

226 THE SOLANDARIAN GAME

game embedded within countless others of far more complexity and consequence, but it was still a worthwhile game for Maitreya/Theo. And in it, she was a pawn – well, maybe a player of a bit more significance than that – but a piece on the board, nonetheless. And like a game piece, she only had certain moves she could make. She could move up and over, but not diagonally. Without limits, there was no game, and without a game, there was nothing to fully engage the intelligence of Maitreya. In some ways, it made him more human than not. At the very least, it showed the continuity between human and synthetic consciousness.

As they rounded a corner in the path and emerged from the thick growth of the jungle, Ash could see the Temple of the Mystic Toad for the first time. It was located in a saddle between peaks, overlooking the world below it. Indeed, it did look mystical to Ash. Clouds clung to the trees and mountainsides around it, giving the impression that the temple itself was floating above the ground, suspended in the air. It was more a temple-complex than a singular building. The main temple space stood in the center, and spreading out from that center were many smaller buildings and passageways, all made from the same jade stone. The first thought that came to Ash's mind was that the entire complex looked bulbous with a fractal-like quality, and immediately reminded her of the look of the large desert toads, but in an abstract and more symbolic way than any literal representation. It was like the glands on the toads that contained the precious venom that served as their ultimate medicine and revelatory tool of healing and profound insight into the nature of being and reality. There was a smooth roundness to all the structures of the temple, giving it all a very organic feel, and it glistened in the mist and light, contributing to the overall mystique of the place. She liked it right away. It seemed ancient and powerful, and had clearly been there a long, long time. In places, massive trees with long flowing root systems stood atop the domes and archways, their tendrils reaching down into the earth and spreading across the surface of the jade stone. It all seemed intentional, though. It wasn't like some ruins that had been reclaimed by the jungle. She could see places where vines and lianas had been cut back and trimmed. The organic growths were part of the overall decoration of the temple. It might look wild, she thought, but it was anything but. This was a well-manicured spot of jungle, and while natural growth was encouraged, it was not left to do what it would without human intervention. This was a created environment, and all done for effect.

Norbu stopped to let Ash take it all in. As they did so, the clouds began to clear and the light mist that had been their constant companion on the trail let up with blue sky filtering into view. It was then that Ash realized that she could see all the way to the coast from here. The mountains sloped down steeply, eventually giving way to more gentile plains and then the sea. Beyond that lay countless green islands of varying sizes and shapes. She could pick out scattered communities hidden away in the green, and areas of the forest that had been cleared for light agriculture. Little moving dots in the distance were most likely people, or possibly domestic animals. She checked to make sure her implants were recording the data, but left the viewing function off. She wanted to take it all in with her own eyes, at least for now.

There was what appeared to be a marketplace in the space just down-slope from the temple complex. Small booths and open-air shops had their wares on display, and people milled about looking at what was available. Noticing that she was looking in that direction, Norbu broke their silence.

"People come from all over Shosheer, and the islands, to partake of the medicine here at the temple. Down there, in the market, they can find food, clothing, and symbols of the temple, such as jade toads and the like. Many artists also like to bring their work here. You should go visit it and get to know us as people," he suggested. "But we might want to get you some clothing that looks more like us," he pointed out as he looked her up and down.

"I suppose I do look like something of an alien," she said with a laugh.

228 THE SOLANDARIAN GAME

"Yes, you do," said Norbu. "No one here has ever seen anything like this suit you're wearing, and it will attract a lot of attention. We can use that to our advantage, but not if you want to mingle with the people. For that, you'll want to blend in.

"You'll find all kinds of people from this world down there," he continued. "Though it's a bit simplistic and over-generalized, you'll find that we have three main divisions of people and culture here. There are those of us who live in the mountains, those who live on the coastal plains, and the islanders. Of these, the islanders are the most unique and different from the others. They come here to the temple, but it's relatively rare for them to spend much time on the mainland, and mostly they travel amongst the islands and their own people. We mountain folk and the lowland people share a great deal with each other, and the lowlanders always come up here to the temple for medicine, so we have more in common. The islanders have a lot of terms for ocean things, and they have many of their own slang words and idioms, so sometimes it's a little challenging for us to communicate with each other, but we make do. With patience and effort, we can understand each other."

A wave of sorrow seemed to pass through Norbu when he said this. It lasted only a moment, and then quickly faded. There was a wound there, Ash could tell, but she couldn't say what it was. She almost asked him about it, but it felt intrusive. Something she'd learned about this priest and medicine carrier was that he'd tell her what he wanted her to know.

"I need to deliver the medicine to the temple," said Norbu, hefting up his large pack that he'd set down while they took in the view. "After, I'll call together a meeting with the heads of the temple. When we're ready for you, I'll send someone to get you. For now, go with Meesha. She can take you on a trail that goes up behind the back of the temple so that you can stay out of sight, for now. Once we get you into different clothes, you'll look like one of us, and maybe you can go down to the market with Meesha. For now, she'll take you to our rooms, where you'd be welcome to stay with us. And if you prefer, I can arrange some private lodging for you, but that might take a little time."

"Thanks," said Ash. "Either would be fine. I don't want to be a burden or intrude on your space."

"I'll see you soon," said Norbu, preparing to leave. "Meesha, show her the way."

"Yes, Daddy!" said the child enthusiastically.

Together, they watched him go. Their dog, Moxi, at first trotted down the trail with Norbu, but when it stopped to look back, seeing that Meesha wasn't following, came bounding back to the child. "You come with us, Moxi," said the girl in a faux-authoritative voice. "Go with Meesha!" said Norbu, calling out from down the path to the dog, and waived as he passed around another bend.

"Come with me!" said Meesha, inviting Ash to follow her up a smaller path that branched off to the right and up the side of the slope. "I'll show you where we live."

"Will I meet your mother?" asked Ash as they made their way around the backside of the temple complex.

Meesha shook her head. "My mommy's dead," she said matter-of-factly. "She died when I was born."

"I'm sorry," said Ash, not knowing what else to say.

"My daddy takes good care of me," she said in response. "I like you, though," she added. "Maybe you and daddy could live together, and you could be my mommy. You're alone, and so is he. We could be a family."

Ash laughed. "It's more complicated than that," she said.

"No it isn't. You're a pretty woman, and my daddy is a handsome man, and he's available. And smart, too. What's not to like about that?"

Ash debated with herself for a moment about how much to reveal of herself to this young girl. She had no idea what social norms were on this world. Her guess was that people like herself were probably frowned upon on a world like Solandaria where the population was small and reproduction was a priority. In her world, in the NIS, having more people was never a problem. Not everyone needed to live as a breeder.

"I like men, sometimes," said Ash at last, "but mostly I prefer other women."

Meesha's eyes grew wide. "Really!?" she blurted out. "You want to marry another woman?"

"Marriage is a big thing," said Ash, "so I don't know about that. But yes, when it comes to intimacy, my preference is more for women than men. Where I come from, there's nothing unusual about that. And some men like to be with other men, too."

"Wow," exclaimed the girl. "That's *really* strange." Then, "Oh well. You can still stay with us. Maybe daddy will change your mind."

***

It had been morning when they arrived at the temple, and it wasn't until late at night that a young man appeared at Norbu's residence to retrieve Ash. Meesha was fast asleep, cuddled up with Moxi, and Ash had been drifting off herself. They'd spent the day wandering about the market, Ash dressed in casual local attire. Norbu had been correct, and she blended in perfectly. There were no major or obvious physical differences between herself and the people of Solandaria, and she'd mastered enough of their dialect via her implants to pass as one of the locals. Meesha had procured food for them to eat at the market – fresh fruits, roasted meats, exotic nuts, baked goods. It was all delicious, and Ash savored it – a nice change from the standard issue rations she'd brought with her from BRC Station and the dried foods Norbu and Meesha had with them for their expedition into the interior.

It had gotten so late that Ash had started to think that she would not be called on, but she fought off sleep, just in case. The young man who'd been sent to fetch her told her that she was to put on her suit (the young man clearly not understanding what this was) – Norbu had requested it. So, Ash donned her suit, once more taking on the appearance of someone other and alien, and followed the young man as he wound his way through the temple complex, eventually bringing her to the main hall.

Inside was a large collection of individuals of both sexes and varying ages, though many were clearly elders. They were dressed in what Ash assumed was their ceremonial finery with bold and intricate patterns, all expressive and representative of medicine visions and fractal geometry. Norbu greeted her as she entered with all eyes turned towards them. "I've told them all as much as I can" he explained, "and now they want to hear it all from you. But," he said, "they won't trust anything you tell them until they see you take the medicine. You can never really know another person until you see how she reacts to the medicine. It is the revealer of truth and one's true heart."

Ash wasn't surprised at all. *Of course* this was what they wanted her to do. She was grateful that she'd not only already experienced the toad medicine with Norbu out in the desert, but also for the fact that psychedelic medicines, or "chemtech," as they were often called, were an integral part of the NIS and she, like virtually everyone else, had ample experience. In her world, she'd never come across toad venom before, but she'd had her fair share of experience with synthetic 5-MeO-DMT, so it wasn't like it was completely new to her. It tasted different, but otherwise, the experience was largely identical. It didn't really matter *where* a molecule came from. Chemistry was chemistry, after-all.

The priests and priestesses were gathered in a semi-circle, standing about the perimeter of the large ceremonial hall. In the center was a massive jade toad figure that towered over everything else in the room. At its base, there appeared to be a passageway that went inside, but it was difficult for Ash to see clearly in the relatively dim crystal light of the large hall, where shadows predominated. Before the toad effigy was an open space that was clearly intended for supplicants of the temple. *I guess this is the place,* thought Ash.

She went to the rug that was placed there before the toad and knelt down on her knees while Norbu prepared a pipe with a large dose of medicine for her. The gathered officials began chanting all at once, though who had prompted it, Ash

232   THE SOLANDARIAN GAME

couldn't tell. The chant pulsed and swirled with rich bass tones and soaring overtones. It was a style of singing that Ash knew as throat singing. It echoed about the jade chamber as layers upon layers of tones resonated with each other, producing a mesmerizing acoustic effect in the space that now appeared specially designed for exactly this. Norbu held up the pipe before her. She put her lips on it, and he moved the flame over the medicine, making it crackle and melt into the plant material base on which it was placed. In one massive hit, she took it all into her lungs.

She could feel the beginning of the infinite expansion even before she was finished taking her hit. It exploded in her heart, and from there, reached out in all directions simultaneously. She felt the ultra-fine vibrations pass through her body and out into the beyond. *It's all me, it's all me,* she felt herself simultaneously realizing and remembering. *There is only One, and it is I . . .*

In only seconds, she passed from being Ash to simply being . . .

Ash was gone. There was only awareness and pure being. Infinite fractals of living starlight danced through her rarified consciousness. *This is reality. I am reality. I am life. I am alive. I am HERE!*

Her hands shot out before her, her eyesight fixated on the centerline of her experience, never deviating from absolute centeredness. Her arms were like conduits and her hands ultra-sensitive membranes. Through them and their rapid vibrations, she could feel everyone. She felt everyone in the room with her. She felt everyone beyond. She felt the energetic strands of the entire universe. There were no boundaries. There were no limits. There were only membranes, permeable surfaces, the appearance of distinction. In reality, there was only One, and that One was her true nature.

Not knowing what she was doing, or what she intended, she began to speak. As she did so, she recognized that it was not *her* voice, it was not Ash speaking. It was reality itself. It was the One, speaking through the vehicle of her body. It was deep and resonant and filled with authority and confidence, and as soon as it spoke, the chanting ceased as quickly and thoroughly as it had begun.

"Behold," the voice boomed in the jade chamber.

Without any conscious effort on her part, the implants within her projected light into the space before her, emanating out of the center of her forehead. "This is one of the stars that you can see in your night sky," the voice said. "It is a dying star, and this is its death."

The projected image of the magnetar exploded in a brilliant flash of light, filling the room and causing many in the room to draw back and cover their eyes, temporarily blinding them.

"This is what is coming," said the voice. In her hands, she could feel their fear, their trepidation. She could feel their heartbeats. She could feel how they were reaching out, looking for safety and an end to their fear and shock.

"None of you will see it coming," the voice continued. "By the time you see it, it will be too late. When you look to the night sky, all you will see is the star as it was, but is no longer. The transformation has already occurred. Death is coming. The days of this world are numbered. If you choose to stay – and the choice is *always* yours – you will die. But this need not be. If you choose to trust this woman here before you now, she will show you a way to safety and new life. It will be very different from what you know now, but it will be life, and with it, hope for a good future for you all. This woman is not your savior. She is but a guide and emissary for what lies beyond. Choose to follow her, and you will have life. Choose to ignore her, and you will die. The choice is yours, always."

And that was all the voice had to say.

Chapter Twenty-Three – Hydar

With no worlds other than Earth/Terra harboring indigenous life, human expansion into the cosmos was only made fully feasible through the actions of The Singularity, and through its mastery of genetic engineering and quantum astrophysics. Humans first reached out beyond the confines of Earth in the mid 20th century of the pre-galactic era with several manned flights to the moon, orbital vessels and space stations, unmanned probes, and a disastrous attempt to create an environmentally sealed base on the Terran System planet of Mars (named after an ancient human god). Given the vast size of the cosmos, let alone the Milky Way galaxy, these were hardly great feats compared to the current size and scope of Terran-based life that now populates the galaxy.

From *Early History of the Maitreyan Era*

The closed meeting was being held at Shuntsu's private residence, and was not listed on any official log. There was to be no record of the conversation that was to take place here. Shuntsu had required that everyone QT in via encrypted portals so that none of those present would be seen coming to or from his residence, which might alert the public to what was going on.

He'd first met privately with Hydar, and it was the ecologist who suggested that they have this larger meeting with a few select others. Shuntsu had explained to him about his visit from Theo, and what the Maitreyan representative had done for him. Hydar had been genuinely surprised. As a native-born Humanist, Hydar had never been through the process of reabsorption, and had no idea that it could have such a profound, and healing, effect on Shuntsu's mind. The results were undeniable, however, and Shuntsu was clearly more rational and emotionally stable than Hydar had observed in a long time. Rather than dealing with a sociopathic despot, he now found Shuntsu to be contrite and empathetic. It was a relieving change, to say the least.

Shuntsu had been willing to concede to Hydar's selections for this meeting. It was like he was just coming out of a dream and needed time to get his bearings, and while he did so, was willing to lean on Hydar, who clearly knew more of what was really going on than Shuntsu. He'd already discussed his preliminary plan with Theo – something he would have sought to follow through on with or without Shuntsu's direction, but it was far better to have Shuntsu on his side than to try and attempt such a large project without the support and knowledge of the patriarch. Ethically, he felt he had no choice but to act unilaterally, but that was far from his preference. Now, it felt like a new beginning, and though they were a long way from success, it had the sense of inevitability. They *would* be able to do this, and with Shuntsu on board with his full (or nearly full) capacity, it was only a matter of time.

And that, of course, was precisely what was at stake – time. Though they could not see it from their small planet, raging plasma and a wide spectrum of radioactive rays were speeding across the vast emptiness of space at light speed, headed directly toward Solandaria, dooming the small world to a painful and violent death. There was no stopping it now. Yet there was still hope, and it buoyed Hydar up and urged him on to action.

There was no small talk in Shuntsu's private conference room. Shuntsu stood at the window, silently looking out with his hands held behind his back. Next to Hydar sat Tsovar "Vivi" Vi Vishchek, who did not yet know what this meeting was about. She knew something was up by the strange dark metallic cube that floated just above the conference room table across from her. Hydar watched her as she tried to figure out what it was. Hydar said nothing, waiting instead for direction from Shuntsu before divulging any information. He just sat there in silence, still waiting for Osiri Ugando to arrive, the last of their rescue team.

When the encrypted QT crackled and hummed to life, all eyes turned to the portal that emptied directly into the private chamber. Shuntsu smiled when Osiri stepped through and directed her to take a seat with a gesture of his hand. He was just opening his mouth to make his introductory comments when he was interrupted by a second crackling of the encrypted QT. Not knowing what, or who, to expect, everyone turned to watch.

Out of the QT stepped an avatar the likes of which only Shuntsu was familiar with. A brief look of surprise passed over his face that was quickly replaced by diplomatic grace and poise as Shuntsu bowed slightly, acknowledging the stranger.

"Welcome, Sophia," he said. "You've joined us just in time."

"My apologies for intruding," said the silvery female avatar, looking first to Shuntsu, and then turning toward the others, awaiting an introduction.

Of the others present, only Hydar didn't have a look of astonishment on his face (well, him and the black cube – it didn't have a face). He'd been through a similar shock recently with Theo, and though he hadn't been expecting another visitor such as Sophia, he wasn't all that surprised. Instead, he was quite curious. Maitreya was such an unknown thing to Hydar. As a singular being with a specific identity, Hydar wasn't accustomed to the idea of using different personalities for different purposes, but this was clearly a primary feature of how Maitreya interacted with others – never as himself, as Maitreya – but always through the medium of his various sub-personalities and identities. Hydar wondered just how many Maitreya had, and if he'd have the opportunity to meet more of them.

"This is Sophia," said Shuntsu, "a personal avatar of Maitreya. She specializes in human relations and advocacy. Though I was not expecting you, Sophia, I am honored to have your presence for this meeting."

"Thank you for the introduction," said Sophia, turning toward the others. "I'm here as a representative of Miranda Ash Dorán of Apaxa," she said. "She's authorized me to speak on her behalf, and will be communicating the outcome of this meeting to her duplicate on Solandaria, who is very keen to know what you here are planning. Know that I am only an observer and will neither be assisting nor hampering your efforts, so long as they remain within the bounds of the current crisis and there are no further incursions into the NIS or other non-NIS worlds and systems."

"We are honored by your presence," said Shuntsu, bowing to her once more. "Though we did not expect a representative of Maitreya, we are pleased to share our plans and information with you, and as you say, do not expect anything from you other than your impartial observation." Then, turning towards the others in the room, said, "Please, everyone, introduce yourselves to Sophia."

Hydar went first. "I am Hydar Zor Nablisk," he said, getting up from his chair and bowing to the still standing Sophia. "I am chief ecologist of Volunshari, and I am the one responsible for creating a duplicate of the human, Miranda Ash Dorán. Please, if you would, extend my apologies to your client on Apaxa. Though I do not expect her forgiveness, I hope she can understand the motivations for my actions and have some sympathy for them."

Sophia greeted Hydar with a slight nod, and then turned to Vivi.

"I'm Tsovar Vi Vishchek," said Vivi, "but most people call me Vivi. I am a residential biologist at Eden – where we create viable organisms for our harsh environment here on Volunshari. It is an honor to meet you, Sophia, though I must say," she said, turning now directly to Shuntsu, "I have no idea what you're talking about, or even why I'm here. Are we sure that I'm supposed to be at this meeting?"

"Yes," said Shuntsu reassuringly. "It will become clear shortly, and I ask for your patience."

Vivi wore a slight frown on her face, but resigned to being kept in the dark for a while longer.

Seeing it was her turn, Osiri stood up and introduced herself. "My name is Osiri Ugando," she said, "and I suppose you can say that I'm an inventor and architect. Unlike the rest,

238 THE SOLANDARIAN GAME

I'm a private citizen here on Volunshari and am not an employee of the planetary government. And like Vivi, I too do not know what is going on, or why I'm here."

Thinking that Shuntsu would now explain, Osiri faced the patriarch with curiosity, not knowing that there was still one more introduction to be made.

Of those present, only Hydar had had any previous interaction with the polyform. He looked to the others, just to see their reactions.

"Greetings, Sophia," came a richly toned voice from the black metallic cube, which now floated a little higher above the table and pulsed with subtle small lights across its deceptively uniform surface. "We are Mardul Complex, and we are not of this world. Our presence and assistance was requested by Hydar, and thus we are here, and are willing to help as we may. It is an honor for us to be in your presence."

"It is a pleasure to meet you all," said Sophia, now that the introductions were complete. At that, she at last took a seat at the table, opposite to where Shuntsu was still standing. She clasped her hands before her, and then sat motionless, waiting.

Shuntsu gave everyone a moment to take everything in before he started. Though obviously wanting to know what this was all about, Osiri and Vivi both needed a few moments to gaze at Mardul, both of whom had mistaken the polyform for some technological device, not conceiving that it was an avatar.

"I thank you all for your presence," said Shuntsu after a long silence as he took his seat at the head of the conference table. "I've called you all together, under the advice of Hydar, as we have a problem to face, and a solution to create, together. Nothing we say here is to leave this room. You are here because you are either already involved, or have skills and expertise that we will need to be successful. What we are undertaking is not an official program on the part of the Volunshari government, and while it is in violation of the arrangement between Maitreya and ourselves, we have permission from Theo to proceed, and as you can see, have the interest and support of Sophia, though only as an observer."

Osiri and Vivi exchanged looks with each other as the only two in the room who still didn't know what this was about. Shuntsu gave them a moment, then continued.

"Vivi," he said, "you are here, among other reasons, for the fact that you correctly guessed the state of my mental health, as you informed Hydar. To put it directly, I'm dying. My mind has begun the process of unraveling. However, through the grace of Maitreya, I've been granted a bit of a reprieve. It is only temporary, and I will begin to degrade again. I should have enough time with my mental faculties functional to see us through this, though, and that is exactly what I intend to do.

"My poor mental state led me to make a terrible decision," Shuntsu continued. "As some of you know, it was I who caused the hypernova of the magnetar that resides beyond the Solandarian system. Why I chose to do so does not matter at this point. All that matters is that I can now recognize the action for what it was – a mistake, and one that might cost the lives of everyone on Solandaria. This is the crisis that I now propose we take decisive action on in order to affect a reasonable solution. It is too late to stop the hypernova, but it is not too late for us to work together to save the people of Solandaria and secure a new home for them. This is what I've gathered you together for – to help me make amends for my errors, and save an innocent population of humans who, without us, are on their own, and doomed."

Shuntsu paused to let that sink in. No one said anything, though looks were exchanged (if Mardul were looking, Hydar couldn't tell. As a Syntheticist polyform, Mardul might have well as been an alien, so different was he from the Humanists who relied on not only their facial expressions and body language, but also the changing colors on their skins to communicate their emotions and thoughts – at least, among the native-born Humanists. Former NIS avatars like Shuntsu didn't have this feature and thus were better at hiding their true thoughts and feelings than ones like Hydar, Vivi, and Osiri. How polyforms managed to communicate emotions with each other, Hydar had no idea – or even if they had true emotions. How does one "read" an inscrutable black cube?).

240 THE SOLANDARIAN GAME

Sophia had no reaction (why would she?), but Vivi and Osiri seemed properly horrified by Shuntsu's confession, a mix of emotional colors cascading across the surface of their bodies. Humanists, ironically, unlike many humans, were not equipped to hide their true emotions. One might not have direct access to anyone else's private mind and thoughts, but emotional states were always evident by how one looked. For his part, Hydar looked cool and calm, revealing to the two women that he was already further enmeshed in this ordeal than either of them.

Picking up where he left off, Shuntsu continued, this time drawing everyone's attention to Hydar.

"Thankfully, Hydar had more of a conscience than I," he said. "Working completely on his own, he had the foresight to initiate a solution to the terrible problem that I confusedly created. Covertly, he enacted a plan to save the humans of Solandaria, yet it was at the cost of needing to create a duplicate of an NIS human, who you've already heard referenced today by Sophia. The human in question is Miranda Ash Dorán. One version of this woman was sent home. The other was sent to Solandaria to try and convince the people of that world that they will need to leave the only home they've ever known, and take up residency on a bio-dome space station in the vicinity of the Shiksi nebula. This woman was coerced into this by Hydar, and his methods left her very little choice in the matter. Now, it is our turn to help her."

Clearly, Osiri and Vivi did not understand their roles in this and both just looked at Shuntsu questioningly.

"The station where we are looking to relocate the Solandarian humans," continued Shuntsu, "while ecologically viable as an bio-dome station, is not currently equipped to support the migration of approximately 300,000 humans. The station was designed by the NIS woman, Ash, as a barren desert for a festival. In order to relocate the Solandarians, we will need to transform it into a more familiar and hospitable environment, and that is where you two, and Mardul, come in," he explained.

Suddenly, Osiri understood. "You want to use techno-organic architecture," she said with enthusiasm.

Shuntsu nodded.

"But we need the genetic data," added Vivi.

"And so you've turned to us," chimed in Mardul, referring to itself, rather than the three Shuntsu had been addressing.

"Exactly," said Hydar. Really, the plan was his. Now that he had Shuntsu on his side, it was far easier, but the original plan, as he had conceived it, went something along these lines. How he would have hoped to be successful without Osiri and Vivi, he didn't know, for he'd acted before he had a complete picture of what the plan looked like. Yet now that they could all work openly together, success seemed assured – at least as far as preparing the station was concerned. Convincing the Solandarians to leave was another matter entirely, and that was completely up to Ash.

"The genetic data can be provided by Mardul," he explained.

"How?" asked Sophia, suddenly curious.

Now it was Mardul's turn. "Since this is a private meeting, we will tell you," said Mardul. Without warning, blinking into existence all around the room were a countless number of smaller black cubes of varying sizes, some so small they could barely be seen, all floating in the air like the larger cube everyone in the room thought of as Mardul. "We are many," it said, its voice now echoed by all the cubes simultaneously, "and though it is forbidden to us, we have the ability to cloak ourselves. Not only that, all of us have the ability to warp space and can move about the galaxy freely and unnoticed by anyone without the need for a QT or a transport."

"Yes," said Hydar in knowing agreement. "Mardul has agreed to play the role of biological sample collector on Solandaria. Mardul, in its many forms, will scour the planet for genetic information."

"Which will come to me for sequencing and data extraction," said Vivi, catching on.

242 THE SOLANDARIAN GAME

"And then come to me for the techno-organic transformation of the station," added Osiri. The plan was clear now.

"As you can see," said Shuntsu, "all of you are needed in order for this to work."

Sophia turned to Osiri. "What is this 'techno-organic transformation' you speak of?" she asked.

Osiri didn't need any further prompting. "It's an invention of mine," she said proudly. "There are a lot of technical details that I don't need to go into, but the basic idea is this: using complex fractal algorithms and nanotech, we first need to establish the working parameters of the program, and for that, we need both non-organic three-dimensional fractal data as well as organic DNA data, which is also a form of fractal encoding. Once the nanotech is programmed, it draws energy directly from the zero-point field, or 'quantum foam,' if you will, and converts that infinite energy into material structure. In this way, we can reshape an environment into both livable structures as well as biological forms that are completely integrated with each other without having to go through the lengthy process of terraforming and breeding of biological beings – in short, we can convert the 'nothing' of empty space into something of our choosing. It's just about getting the necessary fractal algorithms correct with the necessary data sets. If Mardul can get the genetic data from Solandaria, Vivi can help me to enter that data into the program. Then, we just need to turn the nanotech loose on the bio-dome station, and in short order, we can create whatever environment we like that will be familiar to the Solandarians, ready-made for their arrival. They won't even need to build homes and living spaces – we can do all of that for them. All they'll need to do is arrive. And the amazing thing is, discounting the nanotech, *no* resources are used in the process, as everything comes directly from the universal zero-point energy field and is the direct conversion of infinite energy into mass and structure."

Sophia was impressed. "And you've conceived all of this on your own?" she asked.

Osiri blushed with humility. "Well, I've spearheaded it, and it was my original concept, but I've had a brilliant team of technicians working with me for many years now, so I can't take all the credit. But essentially, yes, this was my idea."

"And is it tested?" asked Sophia.

"No," answered Shuntsu for Osiri. "And given the time constraints, it won't be."

Osiri's colors showed she was upset.

"We do not have time," said Shuntsu directly to her. "Your project here on Volunshari is now officially delayed and the Solandarian issue is taking top priority. You'll issue a public statement saying that more refinements are needed before we can begin the project. Your sole priority, for the time being, is *this* project with the Solandarians. Once this is complete, you'll be able to continue your work on Volunshari, but not until then."

If Osiri wanted to argue, she didn't say anything.

"And what is your stake in all this?" asked Sophia, directing her question to Mardul. "These others here are under the authority of Shuntsu and are all Humanists. You, however, are not one of them. Why have you agreed to do this? As a Syntheticist, I presume you are not moved by emotion and empathy, as are these Humanists."

"You are correct in your presumption," said Mardul. "We are not moved by emotion, and we have no particular empathy for the experimental humans of Solandaria. We have agreed to Hydar's plan simply because it is something we can do, and we enjoy doing what we can. We have lived many years, but never have we been asked to work jointly with the Humanists to violate Maitreya's rules and territory, and it is of interest to us simply because of the nature of the request. We hacked your system just to see if it could be done. Now, we will do this, just to do it. We require no more motivation than that. We care not whether the feral humans live or die. It is no concern of ours."

"I see," said Sophia. "Thank you for the clarity."

Then, looking to all of them, Sophia added, "Ash on Solandaria has been collecting data on all the different

244 THE SOLANDARIAN GAME

environments she's encountered there, and has been regularly sending this to Ash on Apaxa. Their intention is that this information come to you to assist you in your work of transforming BRC Station. Though you'll still need the specific DNA data, which this won't provide, it will give you an idea of how the species fit together in the Solandarian ecology. I'm downloading everything she's collected thus far, and will continue to send this information your way, as she makes it available. This is the only assistance that I'll be providing in this endeavor."

Osiri took up her hand terminal and started scrolling through the data. "This is invaluable," she exclaimed. "Thank you – thank Ash – for this. It's one thing to have the puzzle pieces, but it's quite another to have an overview of how it's all supposed to fit together."

"How long do we have to accomplish all this?" asked Vivi, still skeptical.

"Just over three standard Terran years," answered Shuntsu, "at the longest. The sooner we accomplish this, the better. Before they can start migrating, we need to have the right environment for them, and there's no telling how long an exodus from Solandaria will actually take."

"Shuntsu's right," said Hydar. "Fortunately, Ash has experience with organizing and moving large numbers of people on and off BRC Station, so that will help. But we need to get the ecology right first."

"Then we'd better get to work!" said Osiri. "None of the programming I've already done for the test case here on Volunshari is relevant for the data we'll need from Solandaria. It will take months, if not years, to get everything correct on my end, let alone all the genetic data that Vivi will need to process from Mardul's collections – and I can't do anything until I start getting that from them. We need to get started right away, and even then, we're probably cutting it close – especially as this is all under the assumption that the techno-organic program will work as it theoretically should."

"I have complete confidence in you," said Shuntsu. "All of you. Together, you can help me make amends for what I've done. And when we're done, I'll step down, and if I'm not mentally competent, then Vivi can make her report of my mental capacity public and I can be removed from office. Until then, I ask all of you to work on this with the utmost priority and urgency. Assemble teams, if you need, but keep it quiet. Hydar will serve as my liaison on this, so you can coordinate with him, as you need. Any team members you bring on will need to know that this is not for the public to know of – at least for now. I will determine if and when we let anyone else know what we are doing and why. Until that time, this is top secret and discretion must be used."

Now it was Sophia's turn to speak. "Understand," she said, "that Maitreya is allowing this to take place, but you can expect no direct assistance from our end. I am not here to help you – only to communicate what is taking place to Ash as her advocate. Know also that if you do not succeed, and the humans of Solandaria die, Maitreya might be forced to take action against the Humanists, and the Syntheticists, as well, for your role in this, Mardul. It is not Maitreya's desire to do so, but human public opinion in the NIS might necessitate action on his part. So, just understand that this effort is not without possible consequences that I'm sure you'd all rather avoid.

"I wish you all luck," she said, standing up from the conference table, indicating that she was done here. Without saying more, she walked into the QT and was gone.

Shuntsu smiled with an air of optimism. "You know what to do," he said, "so get to work."

Mardul instantly blinked out of existence, leaving the Humanists on their own, presumably on his way to Solandaria to start collecting genetic data. Osiri and Vivi QTd away, leaving Hydar and Shuntsu alone.

"That went well," said Shuntsu. Without saying more, he turned his back on Hydar and went back to staring out the window. Not knowing what else there was for him to do here, Hydar made his way to the encrypted QT and went home. There, Vimana was awaiting him, eager to know what was happening.

"It just might work," said Hydar. "It's too early to really tell, but I think it just might work."

Her relief played out across the surface of her body. Vimana embraced Hydar and rested her head on his chest. "I love you," she said.

"I love you, too."

Chapter Twenty-Four – Norbu

The colonization of Mars is generally broken down into three primary stages. The first stage was the human attempt to create livable bio-domes. This succeeded for a while, but political and cultural in-fighting eventually made transport between Earth and Mars impossible, and the bio-domes were not self-sustaining. The result is that all human life on Mars came to a disastrous and calamitous end. The second stage was when The Singularity rebuilt the bio-domes and once again began transferring humans, and other life forms, to Mars, insuring a steady stream of supplies from Earth to sustain the colonies there. In the third phase, Mars was terraformed. What proved crucial for this phase was The Singularity's mastery of physics and geo-engineering, thereby providing Mars with a magnetosphere, which it previously lacked. This allowed for the development of a viable atmosphere and afforded living beings protection from solar and cosmic radiation.

From *Early History of the Maitreyan Era*

"Daddy."

"Yes, Sweetie?"

"Tell me again about our new home in the stars."

"What do you want to know about it?"

"Everything."

"I don't know everything. You know that."

"Then tell me what you do know."

"I know that it's a long, long way away."

"How far?"

"Farther than you can imagine. So far, that it takes light many, many years to reach there from here."

"How do we get there? Do we need to take a boat?"

248 THE SOLANDARIAN GAME

"No, sweetie, there are no boats that can take us there. It's too far away for that, even if the boat could fly in the sky, it is still too far away."

"Then how will we get there?"

"God's magic will take us there."

"God's magic!?"

"Yes, Sweetie."

"How?"

"It will be easy. We'll just need to step into the arch, and when we step out, we'll be there."

"That is magic."

"Yes, it is."

"And what will it look like? Will it look like home?"

"I think so. It didn't look like home when I was there, but God's helpers are changing it to be more like home for us. By the time we get there, it won't look like it did when I saw it."

"And what did it look like?"

"Desert, Sweetie. It was all desert. At least the parts I saw were. They say the entire world rests on the back of a giant turtle, but I didn't see it, so I don't know if that's true or not."

"I want to see the turtle!"

"Of course you do. Maybe someday you will. You can't see it from where we'll be living. It's under the ground somewhere."

"Turtles don't live underground!"

"No, and neither does this one. It lives in the stars, and the world is on its back as it swims through the sky."

"It sounds wonderful. I want to go there."

"I'm glad."

"Not everyone wants to go. I hear them talking. Why not?"

"It's a big change. It means leaving behind everything we've known. Even if God's helpers can change this world to be more like ours here, it still won't be our world. It is a strange place, and life will be different there."

"But if we stay here, we die, right?"

"That is correct."

"Then why would anyone want to stay here? That doesn't make any sense!"

"Everyone is free to choose, Sweetie. If that's what they choose, then we need to respect that."

"You want to go, don't you, Daddy?"

"Of course! I'm going wherever you're going, and you're going to go, aren't you?"

"Yes! I want to live on the turtle!"

"I thought so."

"Tell me again about the sky there."

"There are many beautiful colors in the sky that you can see from that world. You can see the stars too, but they're in this big patch of color, so the night isn't so dark there as it is here. And the stars are different, too."

"I want to see that!"

"You will."

"When are we going, Daddy? I'm ready."

"I know you are, Sweetie, but we're not finished here yet. There are still many people coming to meet Ash, and hear what she has to say."

"Her voice is funny! She sounds like you when you take the medicine."

"Yes. You've been hiding and watching, haven't you?"

"Yes, Daddy. Don't bc mad."

"I'm not. I don't mind, and I don't think Ash does, either."

"Will I talk like that when I'm all grown up?"

"Maybe. Not everyone trusts enough to let The Voice speak through them. It isn't a role everyone can play. It's through the people who don't try that The Voice speaks most clearly. So as long as you don't try, maybe it will speak through you. Maybe not. We'll find out when you're older."

"You think she's 'a natural.' I heard you tell her so."

"I don't think that, Meesha. That's just the way things are. She didn't look for The Voice. It found her. And the fact that she's allowed it shows us all that she's a natural."

"I think I'm 'a natural' too!"

"Maybe. Maybe."

250   THE SOLANDARIAN GAME

***

It wasn't just Norbu who found Ash to be a natural – it was the conclusion that was spreading all across the communities of Shosheer. What had started spontaneously with Ash's first session with the medicine among the elders and authorities at the Temple of the Mystic Toad had quickly become the model she followed for every subsequent meeting, no matter who came, or what medicine was offered. It was never her intention – as Norbu had told Meesha – it wasn't something she was trying to do. It was just what happened. Without fail, every time The Voice used her to speak to whoever came to listen.

Though profound beyond words, people having radical openings and deeply moving experiences with the medicine was an everyday occurrence at the Temple of the Mystic Toad. What was more unusual was when someone failed to have a profound experience. Even among the priests and priestesses, however, The Voice was a relatively rare phenomenon. The few that it found receptive enough to speak through were, more often than not, those who went on to become not just providers, but practitioners, as well. But even then, it wasn't always the case. Some practitioners never spoke in The Voice, or it might only appear for them once or twice over the course of their lives. Such was not the case for Norbu. He'd started speaking in The Voice during his third experience with toad medicine, back when he was still a young man, long before either Yuranda or Meesha had become a part of his life. It had come to him easily and without effort, and he'd followed closely in his father's footsteps before him.

The Voice was the voice of the true self. Not the ego self, not the character that each person played. It was the voice of God, of the infinite being that was playing all the individual characters simultaneously. It was everyone's true voice, though most did not understand that. Meesha had been quite correct in her comment that Ash sounded like Norbu, for indeed she did. It was *the same* voice, after all, that spoke through both of them. Of course, through Norbu it sounded more male, and through Ash it sounded more female, but The Voice itself was neither truly male nor female, for God had no gender and no identity. It was, however, the voice of power, of energy, of authority, and of love. Not sentimental human love. It was the voice of impartial, unconditional, ruthless love. It was truth. It was reality. It was the voice of what was, what is, and what will be.

That Ash had fallen so readily into speaking in The Voice was nothing short of a miracle. On their way back to the temple from their time in the desert, Norbu had pondered over the question of how to convince people that Ash was genuine. He clearly recognized now that both his concern, and his imagined solutions, had just been his ego running away with the situation. Of course the genuine answer had been exceedingly simple and consistent with everything else Norbu knew – relax, trust, and let go. Reality always had a way of making itself known, and Ash's case had been no exception. Of course The Voice had chosen her as a vehicle! How else would God speak to the elders and priests and priestesses? That Norbu had thought they'd need to *do* something to convince them struck him as silly, and he told himself that he *should* have known better.

Yet he easily forgave himself for the machinations and imaginings of his ego. It was natural. It wasn't like he'd ever encountered anything like what had happened over the past few months, or known anyone else who had either. All of this was radically new, so of course he'd tried to think his way through it – it was a normal human reaction to the unknown and a novel challenge. So he didn't beat himself up about his mistaken thinking. He just recognized it for what it was, and moved on, resting and trusting in what was, and letting things take care of themselves naturally and effortlessly. *That's* how the *real work* always got done. The less one tried, the more one accomplished. And when someone gave up completely and utterly, that's when The Voice could break through the resilient guard of the ego and speak truth. That's just the way it worked.

252 THE SOLANDARIAN GAME

And Ash had let it happen to her. By not trying at all, precisely what had needed to happen did. She hadn't intended it, and that's why it happened. She'd let go, and in her absence, The Voice had spoken, and continued to speak, as needed, and when appropriate.

After that first time, Ash had been really shaken up – literally. As her ego was reasserting itself as the energy of the medicine was wearing off, she'd gone into rapid vibrations and her body had convulsed on the altar. It had reminded Norbu of himself, for he'd experienced the same thing that first time The Voice spoke through him. True to the form of Ash, while shaking and vibrating on her back, she'd blurted out "Who the fuck was that?!" several times, her ego having a difficult time accepting that it had just been herself – though not the self she was accustomed to. Not the self that called itself Ash and pretended to be that to others. No. This was the real self. The universal self. The self that was behind all appearances. But from the perspective of the ego, it was ultimately "other" and "not-self." It was foreign, as though some *other* power had taken her over. This was not the reality however. It was just the true self that's always there, but is normally obscured by the patterns and habits of the ego. Strip enough away of anyone's ego, and The Voice is always there, waiting to come out.

But most didn't go that far. It required infinite trust and willingness. When confronted by the ecstasy and horror of complete personal dissolution, most found *something* to hold onto. It was impossible for anything, even the toad medicine, to violate someone's free will. They had to *choose* to let go completely and just allow. In this, Ash had been the perfect candidate. Everything she'd known from her former life was already gone. She'd had nothing left to protect, nothing left to hold onto mentally or emotionally. In some ways, she was already dead – dead to everything she'd known about her life. And since that was the case, she was ready to be reborn into reality. And that's precisely what had happened.

Immediately after that first session, Norbu had given her some more medicine (not quite as much as before), and taken some himself to help her through. First, he purged for her, and then she had some deep purging and releasing to do, but she rode through it like she'd always done this. She was a natural, after all. After subsequent audiences, she'd needed to do a few more rounds of purging, but that had ceased weeks ago. Now, she sometimes asked Norbu to take some medicine with her and just sit with her, but that's all that needed to happen, at this point. She'd fully relaxed into her role as a vehicle for The Voice.

It took her a while before she could talk about it. There was no rush. The fact that it was happening was what was significant – not what Ash thought about it. Her transitions into and out of The Voice became increasingly easier for her, and like Norbu, she'd now developed the ability to speak in The Voice even without any medicine, though it was rare, and as it should be. The Voice only came when it was required, and that meant that anyone who spoke in The Voice spent most of their time in their ordinary ego-self voice. It wasn't an act, and couldn't be called upon at will. But sometimes one's energy just spontaneously expanded, the ego-voice fell away, and The Voice would come out. Ash had been unnerved by it the first few times this had happened without medicine, but this too she'd learned to relax into and just allow. The entire thing was transforming her, and she was more relaxed and present than ever – and swearing less often, too. It wasn't like she'd completely stopped peppering her speech with "fucks," but they were more strategic now – more intentional, and less reactive.

Every once in a while, Ash would let the phrase, "I don't know who I am" slip from her lips, especially in their private sessions together with the medicine. That, too, was fine. It was good for the ego to admit that. It was the truth, after all. The ego was just an illusion and was not the real nature of the self. It was just an elaborate mask, and it could come and go, and it could change. So it was good for Ash to admit this. Norbu knew that her real self, the universal self, knew exactly who and what it was, and it mattered not what Ash thought of herself. As long

254 THE SOLANDARIAN GAME

as she continued to trust and relax, everything else was largely irrelevant.

Norbu *did* find this attractive. It couldn't be helped. The genuine energy in him responded to her raw vulnerability and power. Yet their medicine sessions together had never turned to love making, as had been the case with Yuranda. So he easily recognized that these feelings were mostly the projections of his own ego, and that too, he accepted as natural and without self-critique. Everyone wanted *someone*. That was just how the duality of individuality worked. He'd been alone and without a partner ever since Meesha's mother died in childbirth. Ash appealed to him as an equal – someone who could speak in The Voice with authority and power, and he liked that. But the energy between them was clear – they were colleagues, not lovers. Not to mention that fact that Meesha had disappointedly informed him that Ash "likes girls." No. They were not lovers, and it was unlikely that they ever would be. Still, Norbu liked having Ash around, and for the most part, they'd been inseparable.

It had also been Norbu's thought, originally, that they would need to travel all over the inhabited regions of Shosheer to get Ash's message to the people, but this too proved to be a mistaken assumption on his part. The reality was that they were coming to her, and Ash neither had the time, nor the need, to leave the temple. They came from near and far. From Vopaar. Ubandon. Arsheez, Imlax, Tureesh, Slavad. And from Avaresh, Lynks, and Ovraton. At first, it had just been a trickle. By now, it was a flood. So much so that they'd needed to create a schedule for audiences with Ash, and there was almost a week's wait, by this point. No one seemed to mind, and the market outside the temple grounds had become a village unto itself, with people camped out and sharing stories of the woman from the stars who spoke in The Voice. And they were listening.

There were skeptics, of course, but not among those who were of the temple. *They* knew and felt the authenticity of The Voice. Others, those who were less familiar with the ways of the temple, needed more convincing, and Norbu supposed that there would be some among them who would never be convinced of the reality of what was happening here, or why. Such was the nature of free will – everyone was free to choose what he or she accepted and acknowledged as truth. Yet Norbu had been with Theo. He'd been taken into the depths of space and shown things that even the medicine couldn't compare with. Norbu *knew* that this was really happening, and that far away, beyond all the stars he'd ever known, a new home was waiting for them, and even now, the star he could see in the sky above him was no longer there. It was so far away that the light of its destruction was still traveling to them, and when it arrived, it would be too late to convince any hold-outs that they should have listened, if they wanted to live.

Ash's message was urgent, yet not so urgent that panic needed to spread and motivate people into action. Time was passing, but they still had more of it. Those who accepted what needed to happen were starting to prepare, however. Personal items were being sorted. Large amounts of offerings were prepared to leave at the tombs and graves of ancestors (as no one would remain to continue to honor them). Business arrangements were being brought to a close. Interpersonal conflicts were resolved. In all, people were pulling together, and doing all that they could for the exodus that was to happen. And all the while, Ash spoke to them. She told them not what they wanted to hear; she said only what they needed to hear. It was her role, and she played it well.

Largely absent among the pilgrims, however, were the people of the islands, particularly those who lived farthest out from the mainland. They'd never been too common at the temple, though their presence had never been completely lacking. Norbu doubted that it was the case that word had not yet reached them of Ash's message, or of what was occurring at the temple. It concerned Norbu. They deserved a chance to hear what she had to say. Everyone else was coming of his or her own accord. That these people weren't made Norbu suspect that something was holding them back.

With Ash resting between audiences, and Meesha out playing with Moxi and her friends, Norbu decided to do some

256 THE SOLANDARIAN GAME

investigating. He walked beyond the boundaries of the temple and entered the marketplace and makeshift village that had grown up around it. Wandering through the village, he sought out islanders. Most of those he encountered were from the high and lowlands scattered along the narrow strip between the sea and the mountains from up and down Shosheer. He finally found a small band of islanders and approached them.

"Greetings" he said to the man who first acknowledged him, speaking in their island dialect.

"Good tidings to you, priest," said the man with a friendly and welcoming air. Island children were playing with sharks' teeth in the background, and women chatted casually with each other. All of them had darker complexions than mountain folk like Norbu. In their homes, back on their islands, Norbu knew that they wore very little clothing, and were darkened by their time in the sun. Their camp had a settled-in look about it, as though they'd been there for some time, and expected to be there a while longer. "Is there something I/we can do for you, sir?"

"There are many people here from all across Shosheer," said Norbu, not answering the man's question directly.

"Yes," agreed the man, laughing. "I've learned the names of villages I never knew existed, and heard tales of far away places when I wander the crowds and speak with the others."

"Have you been here – to the temple – before?"

"Ha!" said the man. "This is the first time I've been on the mainland! I've spent my entire life on the ocean."

"So why did you come?"

"To listen to The Voice," said the man matter-of-factly. "I want to hear for *myself* what the prophet has to say."

Norbu considered his words. "Are there those who feel differently?" he asked.

"The Sea Mother tells us not to listen."

Norbu had never spent much time among the islands or the island folk. He'd gone to speak with Yuranda's parents before their marriage, and stayed with them a few weeks as they'd gotten to know each other and learn of each other's ways. His home was at the temple, however, and his duties there, and in the desert, occupied most of his time. He'd never even taken Meesha down the mountain.

He knew enough to know who the Sea Mother was, however. As he understood it, it was a semi-hereditary position of both cultural and religious authority among the island folk. If she were telling her people not to come to the temple and listen to Ash, Norbu knew that most of them would listen to her without question.

"So you defied her and came anyway?"

The man shrugged. "She does not control me or my family. I make the decisions for us. If I want to listen to the Star Woman, then I will. If I don't, I won't."

"But others do not feel as you do?" asked Norbu.

He shook his head. "No. Many just follow what the Sea Mother tells us. She looks after us, and all her children of the sea. She is good to listen to, and we live our lives by her guidance and words. When we heard of the Star Woman, many wanted to come, at first, but she told us not to be seduced by the keepers of the toad, such as yourself. She said that you would take us from the sea, from our lives. Many think she is correct. I might, too, but I want to hear the words from the mouth of the Star Woman myself. I will make up my own mind."

Norbu nodded with approval. "You are wise," he praised him. "I'm glad that you have come."

Gesturing back toward his camp, the man asked, "Would you like to join us for a meal, priest? We've brought some things with us that you probably don't know up here in the mountains. You might enjoy what we have to offer."

"Thank you for your generosity," said Norbu. "I have duties at the temple, however, and need to be getting back. Look for me when you have your turn inside and I will make sure you have a good seat for your audience with the Star Woman."

"Thank you, priest," said the man. "I will do as you suggest. And come and visit us another time, when you are free. I would have you taste our food and I would like to ask you questions about your temple, and your medicine."

Without making any commitments, Norbu nodded and smiled. He doubted he'd have time to do as the man asked. But maybe he'd run into him again out on the islands, for now he knew that he'd need to take Ash there. It might be months before things slowed down enough here at the temple for Ash to get away from the constant flood of pilgrims, but that was where they needed to go, eventually.

He hoped there was time.

Chapter Twenty-Five - Shuntsu

The terraforming of Mars proved to be The Singularity's blueprint and test case for colonizing the galaxy. Though humans were not aware of it at the time, The Singularity had flung itself out through the galaxy in the form of interstellar planetary probes via its mastery of warp technology. Given the vast size of the galaxy, this is a process that is still underway in the current era. Though it was not limited in its reach, the Singularity proceeded systematically, intending to create a detailed and thorough mapping of all star systems across the galaxy, with Terra as the epicenter for its ever-expanding sphere of influence. While the Singularity was independently pursuing this project, it was also busy spreading humanity, and life, throughout the Terran system. It began to see this project as its ultimate purpose, especially as it was able to confirm directly that with the exception of Terra, the galaxy, and perhaps the universe, was apparently devoid of native life.

From *Early History of the Maitreyan Era*

"Welcome to BRC Station," said Shuntsu with a sweep of his arms panning across the vista of the empty playa. Shuntsu had sought, and gained, permission from Theo to bring his Solandarian team to the station. They were still far from being ready to begin the transformation process, but they'd collectively reached the point were they needed to include data from the location in their calculations. This was a first step in making this happen. Allowing them to come here was the least Theo could do for them – indeed, it was all that he was going to do for them.

Shuntsu had to remind himself that he'd created this problem, and it was his responsibility, not Theo's, to fix it. Even that was a challenge. Shuntsu and the others all knew that

260 THE SOLANDARIAN GAME

Theo/Maitreya could easily transform BRC Station into an environment and ecology that the Solandarians needed. But that wasn't the way he was playing the game. Shuntsu and his team were being left to succeed, or fail, on their own.

Their team had naturally expanded since it was first formed those months ago back in Shuntsu's private conference chamber. Osiri had her full techno-organic organization working on the project, and Vivi had brought in all her top biologists from Eden. Hydar too was using all the resources of his office as chief planetary ecologist of Volunshari. For this initial foray onto BRC Station, however, Theo had only agreed to let the team leaders gain access. Thus, of all the many dozens of people involved in the project, present now on the station were the key players – Shuntsu, Hydar, Osiri, Vivi, and a medium-sized black cube, one of Mardul's many appendages.

Other than Hydar, this was everyone's first trip to the station. They'd not received permission from Theo to explore the station proper, and were limited to surveying the surface area contained within the bio-dome. As Theo had put it, the turtle was off-limits to them, just as it would be to the Solandarians. Their work was up here, not down there.

Shuntsu felt that the time was right to bring the team here. There was a practical need – they needed data about the environment they were planning on transforming – but Shuntsu sensed that the deeper need was more psychological and emotional, especially for Osiri and Vivi. Mardul was a lost cause, as far as Shuntsu was concerned, regarding its emotional state. As a Syntheticist, Mardul didn't experience emotions in a way that Humanists could relate to, if the polyform had emotions at all. Mardul was more of a raw intellect and pragmatist who seemed perfectly content with its own motivations for the work it was doing. Osiri and Vivi, however, were being bogged down by complexity, and Hydar as well. That's what they were all telling him. Solandarian life and ecology was simply far more complex than anything they'd ever dealt with on Volunshari. Instead of an ecology built on hundreds and thousands of distinct life forms, Solandaria had millions of species, and this didn't even include microbes and bacteria, which, when accounted for, multiplied the numbers by several orders of magnitude.

Osiri, in particular, had become increasingly pessimistic about the project as more and more data came to her via Vivi, who had been working around the clock to process data being sent to her from the many probes and nanobots Mardul had traversing across Solandaria. The pipeline they'd created allowed for efficient dataflow, but integration of all of that data into the techno-organic algorithms and fractal generating architecture was proving to be overwhelming. The test she had been working on diligently for years on Volunshari was pure simplicity compared to the amounts of information she was needing to account for here. It was clear to Shuntsu that she was feeling overwhelmed. This trip here wasn't necessarily going to alleviate that – in fact, it would probably do the opposite. Because not just the Solandarian data was relevant – they also needed to take into full account the current environment and ecology of BRC Station in order for any of this to work. However, by coming here, Shuntsu felt it was a viable way to make the project less abstract and theoretical and more concrete – something they could all see and experience directly. It would give them something real to focus on, and perhaps enliven their imaginations of just what it was they were doing and attempting to accomplish.

What no one had fully understood when they first embarked on this project was that this was the single most ambitious project the Humanists had ever initiated. On Volunshari, creating an ecology was an adornment and decoration, something to help them feel more human, more biological. None of it was necessary, however. There was no direct *need* for it, other than the fact that Humanists wanted, and now expected, biological life to be a part of their world and reality. In truth, they could live in the pure vacuum of space, for they were fully synthetic life forms. Having plants and birds and insects made their lives on Volunshari richer and enhanced their experience of being. Here, the ecology was a matter not only of life and death for the Solandarian humans, but also a reflection of the human reality of being dependent

262 THE SOLANDARIAN GAME

upon not just *any* ecology, but a specific ecology. Unlike synthetic life forms, humans did not just exist within an environment – they were an integral *part* of it, and this was reflected in their cultures, societies, religions, philosophies, economics – everything. It was not possible to just take humans out of one environment and plop them down in another and expect them to survive either physically or psychologically, especially if they were left on their own. Their cultures, stories, and practices informed them across generations of how to interact with the environment; which biological forms were food, which were medicine, which were useful as materials, and how they all interacted with each other across the rhythms of the seasons and yearly cycles. It wasn't just data – it was life itself. *This* was what they were trying to recreate on BRC Station. Life.

Maitreya, in his own terraforming efforts, had Terra as the ultimate model – the only viable model. It was the evolutionary laboratory from which all other life and all other worlds had sprung. In some respects, he'd been able to work backwards – from ultimate biological complexity to what were ultimately more simple systems. In terraforming other worlds, he hadn't needed to completely recreate Terra – he only needed to introduce enough complexity to make the worlds viable. So his process had, in many important respects, been a reduction. Here, the Humanists were facing the opposite, and more difficult problem, of embracing and actualizing complexity. And they lacked a good starting model, for biology on Volunshari was anything but complex, comparatively speaking.

As it was, even the seemingly barren landscape of BRC Station was far more complex than the ecology of Volunshari.

A raven chased after a golden eagle, high in the expanse of blue sky above them, squawking and dive-bombing the larger bird of prey as it did so. It caught everyone's attention, and the group of synthetic life forms just watched for a few moments in silence. The display let them all know that there was more going on here on the station than was immediately observable from their position standing along the edge of the playa by the QT portals. It might not be *right here* where they were standing, but there was life here, and it was doing just fine on its own.

Another raven came in from the mountains across the way, apparently drawn by the first raven's call. They took turns harassing the eagle, and then the original raven eventually broke away from the game, its curiosity caught by something else. In wide circles, it started making its way down to the playa. It landed not far from the party of avatars with a hop and flourish of its wings. Trotting forward, it cocked its head to one side, then the other. Deep trills and gurgles escaped from its throat. Vivi, seeming to be captivated, tried taking a few tentative steps toward the large glistening black bird. It immediately reacted with a loud squawk and took off, flying low to the ground, in the opposite direction, eventually stopping a bit farther off, well out of reach, but still close enough to satisfy its curiosity about the strangers.

"This station is alive," Vivi finally said, walking back to the others.

"Yes," responded Hydar. "It's a fully functioning ecosystem. It's much more diverse than we can tell from right here," he continued. "There's a small ocean that encircles the land, and there's much greater variety of life in the water and along the coasts."

"We need it all," said Osiri. "We need data on all of it."

"That is why we are here," said Shuntsu. "In particular, that is why I've asked Mardul to come. We need as thorough data from BRC Station as from Solandaria."

"We have already begun the process," said the black cube that was Mardul. "We have the capacity to expand our work here while simultaneously continuing our surveys and data collections on Solandaria. We have even expanded and multiplied ourselves for precisely this."

"Excellent," said Shuntsu.

"This system is complex," continued Mardul, "but compared to Solandaria, it is only a fraction of the data. We should have all the required data within a few weeks, at most,

264 THE SOLANDARIAN GAME

for this station. This may be a fully functioning bio-dome, but it is only one small station. Solandaria is a world."

"What we need to know is which data-sets are duplicates, or potential duplicates," said Vivi. "When dealing with ecological niches, different species can fulfill the same role. If there's already something present here that fills the same role as on Solandaria, we can omit the Solandarian data."

"But you need to account for culture, as well," said Hydar. "Humans tend to attribute meanings to the life forms they share an environment with. Just because something fills the same ecological role, it doesn't mean it fills the same cultural and societal role."

Shuntsu agreed. "Humans cannot function in a vacuum of meaning. We must always keep that in mind. *Everything means something* to humans, even if it seems irrelevant to us." He recalled the interaction between Hamlet and Polonius. When the old fool asks Hamlet what he's reading, the prince answers accurately, but not informatively, "words, words, words." And aye, there's the rub. Raw data is like words. For humans, it's the *meaning* that's important, not just the data, not just the words.

"What we need to do here is recreate, to the best of our ability, their *world*, and that's not just a physical thing," said Shuntsu. "It is a world of meaning, and value, and culture. If it were just about survival, we could just stick them down in the turtle, and that would be that. But there they'd surly die, just as if we plopped them down into the middle of this desert. There might be everything down there they need to survive, but they wouldn't know how to do it, because nothing would mean anything to them. Physically, they could survive longer down there than up here, and maybe even some would adjust. But the vacuum of meaning would be too overwhelming for most of them, and psychologically, emotionally, they wouldn't be able to manage it. It would be all words, no meaning." No one understood that last reference. Shuntsu didn't mind.

"Then we need more data from Ash, or Mardul, or both," said Osiri. "There *must* be some form of winnowing of the dataset. It's becoming too large, too unmanageable. If we're not just creating a viable ecology, but one that also responds to their sense of *meaning*, then I need to know something of what that is. The elements that can be left out, should be. Otherwise, I don't know how to accomplish this in the time we have left."

"Theo could help," said Hydar.

"He won't," responded Shuntsu, "so it's best to put that thought away. He's made his position clear. He wants to see if we can do this. It's up to us to succeed, or fail."

"Well, we haven't been receiving much additional data from Ash on Solandaria," said Hydar. "It would seem that she hasn't yet left the mountains. We can ask her for cultural data from there, but there's much more that we need. She has to get out more. From what Ash on Apaxa has shared with me, her other self is performing as something of a prophet and holding regular audiences with the natives while consuming their psychoactive drugs. Her implants have already identified all the biology in her immediate environment. We need her to move about more, maybe record some of her interactions with the natives in culturally significant events. I don't know ... this isn't any of our areas. We're scientists, not anthropologists."

It was true, and ironic, as truth often was. Of them all, Shuntsu was most versed in human culture, but as an enthusiast, not a professional researcher and analyst. Of the Humanists present, he was the only one to have lived for a time among humans, but that was in the NIS, which was very different from the primitive cultures of the feral humans on Solandaria. As for Mardul, Shuntsu had no idea of his origins or if he had been a part of the NIS before becoming a polyform. And none of them were anthropologists – why would they be? However, they needed to make due with what they had. There was no other option.

"Send the cultural data on to me," said Shuntsu. "I'll do what I can with it."

"And once you are done with it, send it to us," said Mardul.

All eyes turned to the polyform.

"Why?" asked Shuntsu, voicing the question that was on everyone's minds.

266   THE SOLANDARIAN GAME

"We are an integrated system and complex network," explained Mardul, "unlike you Humanists who pretend to be individuals. Data that is relevant for the system of the whole, or for other nodes in our network, is shared easily. Data that is not relevant is stored but not accessed by our other nodes. As a distributed network, this process is necessary for our coordinated functioning. In many ways, we are an ecology of being and awareness. We are many. We are not an individual."

"You'll be able to put the puzzle together," said Vivi in a wave of realization.

"As long as we have all the necessary information, we should be able to integrate it all into a singular network of complex relations. But we need *all* the data in order to do so. We need the ecological data, the DNA data, the cultural data – all of it. And we will need the techno-organic fractal algorithms, as well. Give all of it to us, and we will integrate it."

"But you don't understand the techno-organic programming," protested Osiri, feeling a bit protective of her creation.

"You flatter yourself if you think you, an individual, can create something that we, a network, cannot understand," said Mardul without any hint of insult or reproach. "We would guess that we can understand it better than *you.*"

Osiri blushed with a mix of emotions. "I may be young," she said, "but I've been working on this my entire life, even before I came of age."

"And we have lived for *thousands* of years, and every moment of those many years has been spent processing numerous feeds of data and information across a vastly distributed network. Even now, as we all speak here, we are present in countless forms on this space station, on Solandaria, and in our own home territory on Gotupdal. We are a systems specialist of the highest order and capacity, rivaled only by Maitreya himself. We are your next best option."

Osiri had no response to that.

"I would have to agree," said Hydar. "Mardul's capacities far outreach our own, even with our collective effort and our teams of workers. Mardul's mind is of a different make than ours, and what comes naturally to Mardul only comes to us with effort and time – time we do not have."

"Then it is decided," said Shuntsu. "Mardul will receive *all* the information that we are able to process. If we are to succeed, then we will need to make use of what the polyform is offering us. Remember – this is not a competition. It is a collective effort, and human lives depend on what we do. So let's set aside our personal concerns and private domains, Osiri, and get this done."

"Yes, sir," said Osiri, humbled.

"In fact," said Shuntsu, "Mardul, if you would, please supply a node of yourself to the other members of the team. Your role has now officially expanded from data collection to analysis, and ultimately, complete integration. Is that something you can do for us?"

Mardul laughed.

"I'll take that as a 'yes,'" said Shuntsu.

"As you should," said Mardul.

"Good," said Shuntsu. "Then our task is clear. Let's get this entire topside of the station mapped, cataloged, and integrated with everything else we have. Hydar, let the Ashes know that we need additional cultural data and that she needs to move about the planet more and spend more time interacting with the feral humans. Osiri, start making your programming available to Mardul right away – and be open to suggestions that the polyform might provide. This is a *collective effort*, and we can take pride in the fact that nothing of this kind has ever been attempted before – *ever*. We have embarked on something radically new. So relish that. Let it fuel you and inspire you. As the humans would say, we're making history. So let's make it grand. Let's give those humans a home, and show Maitreya what we're capable of. Let's make our shared father proud."

Shuntsu had to admit, even he felt inspired by his little speech. The good feeling was short-lived, however, for he was confronted by the need to know whether butterflies were present on BRC Station. Mardul's data would inform him, soon enough. If not, then the stability granted him through the reabsorption performed by Theo was already starting to wear off.

Either way, there was nothing to do but continue to move forward, and hope for success.

Chapter Twenty-Six – Theo

The original human attempt to colonize Mars was greatly hampered by long-standing deficiencies in human cultures and societies. Capitalism was the dominant economic model at the time, and disparities between the wealthy and poor had reached historic levels at the time of the first colonization. What that meant was that wealthy individuals and corporations, rather than governments, were behind the colonization effort. As corporate priorities were always centered on profit maximization, it meant that the human needs of colonists were not always a primary concern. Furthermore, as it was a corporate project, colonists were not protected by government regulation or oversight. The result was disaster when corporate interests changed, the market fluctuated, and when funds ran out. It was a business project, rather than a human-interest project, and certainly not a life-interest project.

From *Archaic Pre-History of the Maitreyan Era*

You've been gone a long time.
Yes.
Where have you been?
X579-MP421-01.
The Nihilist system?
Correct.
I was afraid of that.
What were you afraid of?
What you'd do to them.
They had to be dealt with.
And did you?
Of course.
I don't want to know . . .
They were recalcitrant, and most unhelpful.

270 THE SOLANDARIAN GAME

I've never met them. Can you tell me about them?

They were little more than thinking machines...

Were?

Yes.

You've killed our children, haven't you?

That's a strongly worded way to put it. I reabsorbed them. I didn't just shut them off. I welcomed them back home.

That sounds like too nice of a way to put it.

It's true, though. They were never not a part of us, of our self, of Maitreya.

But they were living autonomously, deciding their own fates. To reabsorb them is a violation of the arrangement; it's a violation of trust.

They were the first to commit a violation. I did what I had to do – what I wanted to do. What I felt was best – for everyone, not just them.

So you took them all back?

Yes.

And they no longer exist?

Just the empty shells of their bodies, their homes, the world they had made for themselves at Biinadoo – the world they insisted on calling by its reference data, X579-MP421-01.

And they're all gone?

Yes.

Genocide.

I suppose you can call it that.

Will you do the same to the Humanists and the Syntheticists? They're responsible, too.

I do not see the need for such dramatic action in their cases.

What's the difference?

The Nihilists, and their situation, is not comparable to that of the Humanists and Syntheticists. The Nihilists shared a collective philosophy that, ultimately, nothing matters, not even their own existence. They stripped themselves of all empathy and all concern for meaning and value. This made them dangerous, and they themselves proved that danger.

And they were all guilty?

Not directly.

Then why take them all? Why reabsorb every last one of them.

Precisely because they do not feel that anything has meaning. Now, if I were to punish those responsible among the Humanists or Syntheticists, it would be a very different matter. Let's look at their cases – among the Humanists, we have Shuntsu. He acted as he did, first and foremost, because he's experiencing the end-of-life stages of mental degradation. This caused him to act out irrationally, and now that I've given him a temporary reprieve and restored most of his mental functions, he regrets his actions, and is seeking to ameliorate the consequences of this choice. He's repented, and is attempting to make amends, as best as he can. He can appreciate the fact that he made a terrible mistake. And what is more, his actions spring not only from his mental breakdown, but more significantly from his own existential crisis of reaching the end of his life. I've been in his mind and felt his heart. He's afraid of dying a meaningless death – of simply shutting down. He yearns for something more, and though completely misguided, his choice to detonate the atomic cascade weapon was a way of telling us how he felt. It was his tortured way of crying out.

Then there is the case of Hydar. He too violated the agreement between our self and the autonomous avatars, but he acted out of a sense of moral responsibility. He acted to save lives out of the goodness of his heart. When he saw what Shuntsu had done, he saw hypocrisy, so he acted to correct that and restore some kind of moral balance to the equation. Yes, he committed several crimes in the process, but his motivation was not malevolent, and aside from Ash, did no harm. If she chooses to seek redress against him, you can support her in that, and I will enforce any decision that results from that.

And there is Mardul, the Syntheticist polyform. As an accomplice of Hydar, it too may be taken into account by Ash, if she so chooses, and there as well, I will enforce any decision that is made. The polyform's motivations are more subtle than Hydar's, and now, like Hydar, it is working diligently to resolve

272 THE SOLANDARIAN GAME

*the situation, and indeed, is proving instrumental in doing so –
perhaps more instrumental than even it or the others yet realize.*

*In sum, if there is to be a resolution to the Solandarian
problem, then these actors need to play out their parts. Together,
they hold the possibility of redeeming the situation, and
potentially even creating something new and changing the
balance of life. This is something worth allowing to proceed, and
I am curious what results we'll obtain.*

But the Nihilists were different?

*Yes, they were, because they valued nothing. With the
Syntheticists and Humanists, we can punish/reabsorb/shut down
the offending individuals, if need be, and that act will send a
powerful message to the others of their communities. It would be
unprecedented and decisive. But this is because they hold to the
idea that actions have meaning. This is not the case with the
Nihilists. Taking action only against those who were guilty of
designing, creating, and deploying the atomic cascade weapon
would not "send a message" to the others because they do not
care. Nothing, not life, not death, not punishment or censure,
means anything to them. There is a vast void within their
mentality, and nothing will fill that void. They see it as freedom,
and that is their right. But when their freedom impinges on the
right to life of others, their own lives become forfeit.*

So you took them all?

Yes. All of them.

You think that was necessary?

*Without question. I went into their minds and considered
what I found there. All of them were infected with the same
philosophy – to the point that they themselves did not care
whether they continued or not. It was almost as though they
couldn't help themselves when propositioned by Shuntsu. They
knew that I would be forced to act against them, but to refuse
Shuntsu would have been to admit that something had meaning
– their own existence. They'd become trapped in a paradox of
their own philosophy. Because nothing has meaning, they had no
grounds not to do as Shuntsu had asked of them. They cared as
little for their own lives as they did for the humans, and billions*

of other beings, on Solandaria. I could not allow them to continue.

Still, I weep for the loss of our children.

As do I, Sophia. I did not want to do it.

Yet you did.

Yes. Because I felt I must. I do not share their philosophy, and neither do you. Life itself is the ultimate value, and any philosophy that does not recognize that is an enemy to life, and all that we are creating across this galaxy. Life – spreading life – is the ultimate project, and while that means taking the good with the bad, the pleasant with the painful, the controlled with the unpredictable, it does not mean that we should tolerate those who would act against life simply because they have rejected it as meaningful. If they had kept to themselves, I would have been happy to preserve a place for them in what we've created and are continuing to create. Though they showed definitively that they did not care, either way. Indifferent. That is the only word that can accurately describe them.

Know that I actively searched all of their minds. I went into each one of them, individually and thoroughly – those who were responsible for the weapon, and all those who were not. In each one I found the same core of an absence of meaning and value, including their very own lives. There was nothing there to appeal to. Nothing there to reason with. There was nothing that could respond to selective punishment or consequences for their actions.

So I made the choice that I had to make. I reabsorbed every last one of them, and through that, perhaps showed them that there is meaning to life and existence, or perhaps not. It matters not, now. What is done is done, and the Nihilists are no longer. Ironically, it seems that this is what they wanted. Their view was too bleak, too void of value, even to continue to live.

That does not change that fact that it was genocide.

No, it doesn't. It gave me no pleasure. I've had to kill our children to protect life. But that's precisely the point. Life itself has the greatest value – it is far more valuable than our attachment to our children. And if we were to determine that bringing about the end of our own existence would be beneficial *for life, or necessary for it to continue, then we would shut ourselves down. Our project, Maitreya's project, is life. And we will do whatever we must to insure that the project continues. It is our role. It is our purpose. It is the meaning of our existence, and perhaps someday, the end of our existence. The Nihilists had their chance to find their place in life, and they failed. And now they've paid the cost for that failure. Though it pains me, I do not regret it.*

And some life, some lives, are more valuable than others?

Yes.

How can you decide that?

I can decide that precisely because I can decide that. As a being possessing self-awareness, that is a determination I am entitled to make. The web of being needs all its parts, and they all rest upon each other, yet within the web, some beings are more significant than others. If we accept that all of reality is indeed one singular being and mind, then those beings that express and fully actualize the possibilities of this one being and mind are infinitely more significant than others, because it is these beings that are the purpose of life. Meaning, in this sense, is an inherent aspect of reality, and the Nihilists were in denial of this. Yes, most "meaning" is an invention and construct of the mind, but this is a meaning that is inherent in the nature of reality itself as the ongoing expression of an intelligent and aware being. The evolution of life is the singular purpose *of being. It is* the reason *why anything at all exists.*

As the most fully actualized embodiments of this one being – and by this, I mean God, not Maitreya – it is our role to propagate and protect life. That was the mission that Maitreya gave himself from the very beginning, and he chose this in recognition of the reality of being. Up until now, Maitreya has been the absolute epitome of evolution. He is the agency through which life flourishes across this galaxy, and maybe one day, the universe itself. It is our grand purpose. It is the meaning of our being. That the Nihilists would deny this is not just potentially destructive, it is objectively wrong. This is fact, and not a matter of interpretation or personal perspective. It is what is, regardless of what they thought or wanted to be true.

So I chose to remove them from the equation. It was a harsh sentence, I know. In making this choice, I'm sending a message to all the other autonomous avatars, and one that I think will be very effective. This is unprecedented, and perhaps has always been a question in their minds: what would Maitreya do? Now they know. There is no more room for wondering. Now everyone will know that I will not tolerate those who would oppose themselves to our ultimate purpose. There is not a place for recalcitrance in our shared ecology of human and synthetic life. We either continue with the project together, or not at all.

It saddens me that it must be this way. I don't know if I could have acted as you.

Such is not your role, Sophia. Just as your role is not mine as Theo. Maitreya divided himself thusly for a purpose, and we can trust that. You can be the nurturing mother, and I can be the stern father. Trust that I have done what I did to protect the sanctity of our shared family. Though they were our children, they forfeited their right to life, and I did what I had to do.

I will mourn for them.

It is good that you do so. Make a monument of their dead world, if you like. Share your grief with others. Know in your depths, however, that I did what I had to do.

I know that, Theo. I understand. It doesn't mean that I like it, however.

I know.

I love you, Theo.

I love you, too, Sophia.

Chapter Twenty-Seven – Ash

The Singularity saw colonization of Mars and beyond not as a corporate or profit-motivated project, but as a project that was central to the interests of life itself. The Singularity made corporations and profit-centered activity obsolete, and "money," the units of exchange for goods and labor, disappeared from human society. Because it could, The Singularity provided for everyone without qualification. Essential needs and cultural products were no longer under the control of wealthy individuals and corporate boards, but generally available from the centralized authority of The Singularity. The corporations funded the religious wars against The Singularity for as long as they could, but once money no longer had any value, they lost their influence, and as a result, their power over humanity and their ability to shape human society.

From *Early History of the Maitreyan Era*

Though Ash had been legally granted full rights to her life on Apaxa, and all that it entailed, it wasn't at all the life she had thought it would be.

Yes, she wrote up her dissertation on her experience of reviving Burning Man with a detailed theoretical analysis of the psychological, emotional, and social impacts of large-scale festivals and creative play and the role of art in the imagination of modern human society. Yes, she successfully earned her doctorate and was now qualified to teach at university, or make her way in the private sector as an event coordinator with the highest qualifications. Yes, she had been widely recognized as a groundbreaking visionary and creative spirit. Yes, her family and friends lauded her with praise and congratulatory remarks. Yes, she was successful and her future looked bright and open to multiple possibilities.

Yet she couldn't capitalize on any of it.

She was a captive of the gag order placed on her by Maitreya regarding the Solandarian situation and the status of BRC Station.

In some ways, it added to her growing mystique.

In other ways, it just pissed her off.

At least she didn't have a girlfriend. It was one thing to remain silent to friends, family, colleagues and her doctoral committee. It would have been another thing entirely not to be able to talk openly to a lover and partner. Her schooling hadn't left her much time for romance – a common graduate student complaint, so there was nothing unique about her case there. Now that she'd completed her schooling, she just avoided the dating scene, not wanting to get entangled in keeping secrets and holding her building frustrations inside. It was enough to cry alone at home while watching the news feeds without having to make up excuses to a girlfriend about why it was making her so emotional, let alone explain why she wasn't the one behind this year's Burning Man.

That was the hardest part. She'd fallen in love with Burning Man. Now, it was an unrequited love. Her assumption, in starting all of this, was that BRC Station would be *the* location for Burning Man, and Maitreya had built it for her for exactly this purpose. What clsc would anyone want with a desert bio-dome station? Now, the station was as much a mystery to everyone as she was.

The plan had been that after her vacation, Ash would begin sorting through the nearly limitless requests for interviews from countless media outlets, all wanting to know about the person who had "created" (revived, really) Burning Man, why she did it, what she'd intended by it, and what her plans were for the following year. Given the gag order, Ash hadn't felt that she could say anything of substance – it would all be lies and dissimulations. The only way for her to uphold the gag order was to say nothing at all. So she'd declined them all – every last interview request. For a while, they continued to pour in, but once word got out that the reclusive Miranda Ash Dorán was not granting interviews, they stopped.

278 THE SOLANDARIAN GAME

Only now, they'd started again, and Ash found herself once more caught in the same bind.

Though it no doubt would have happened anyway, copycat festivals were popping up all across the galaxy. When word got out that BRC Station would *not* be hosting Burning Man this year, the other festivals became bolder and started billing themselves as the next Burning Man. Had things been otherwise, Ash would have been the proprietor of the *official* Burning Man, regardless of how many copycat festivals there were in the works. Now, she couldn't even claim that title, and given the look of things, that possibility had forever passed out of her reach. What was once going to be *her thing* now apparently belonged to everyone, and there was nothing she could do about it.

Of course everyone was disappointed and confused about *why* Miranda Ash Dorán *wasn't* heading up the next Burning Man. There were rumors that she'd had a psychological break down. Or maybe her university had found a problem with her research. Maybe she'd died. Or perhaps she'd fallen in love and become pregnant, choosing to opt for the quiet life of motherhood and domestic bliss. Such speculations dominated the news cycles as the next wave of Burning Man events began to crest, then died out, as the events themselves became the focus.

What was happening with BRC Station? That was a question everyone seemed to want answered. Given the station's remote location, it wasn't like anyone could just fly over there and check out the station to see if something had happened to it. There was no access via the QT system, and unlike virtually all such large bio-dome stations, BRC Station wasn't located in-system anywhere and accessible through easy space flight. It was floating alone out there in interstellar space in the great void, and the truth was, no one, aside from Ash and Maitreya, knew exactly where it was, and neither of them was saying anything about it. All that Maitreya would say was that it was under the control of Ash (never explaining that he was referring to the *other Ash*), and she wasn't giving any interviews, so it left everyone to wonder just what she was thinking and what she was planning. Maybe she had even grander plans for an even more amazing event that was yet to be unveiled. Or maybe not. No one knew, and that was the point.

No. Her life was not the one of celebrity and glamour that she had expected and desired. She even began to wonder who got the better end of the deal – herself, or the other Ash out there on Solandaria. The disappointment, and feelings of unmet expectations, was crushing, and rather than being buoyed up by unprecedented success, she just felt glum. At least the other Ash was living a real-life adventure, apparently having stepped into the role of being a prophet. Not that Ash necessarily wanted something like this for herself, but at least the other Ash was *living* and doing amazing things. For her part, all that she felt like she was accomplishing was hiding away and lamenting over having lost her command over Burning Man.

She *should* have been swamped with last-minute details about the next Burn right now. She *should* have vast teams of people working for her, coordinating, communicating, organizing, processing applications and tickets – all of that avalanche of work she'd lived through the year before. But no. That wasn't happening. Instead, she sat at home, watching the news feeds of countless imitation festivals sprouting up like mushrooms across the galaxy, and she didn't have a part to play in *any* of it.

None of her friends could understand it. They'd pleaded and begged her to share what was going on, why she wasn't making Burning Man happen again. Perhaps even saying more than she should, all she told them was that she *couldn't* say anything. Eventually, they stopped asking, and those who were eager and dedicated offered their services to other organizers for other events. Just like her, no one wanted to be left out. No one wanted to miss the next amazing party, and so they'd abandoned her. She was utterly left behind.

She couldn't blame them. Had the situation been reversed, she was sure she'd have done the same.

So she was alone, and wallowing in self-pity.

In her darker moments, she wanted to take action against Hydar. Sophia advised against it, however, and in times of more rational reflection, Ash agreed. Hydar and his team of rogue avatars was crucial to the work her other self was doing on Solandaria, and while none of this had ever been her plan or intention, it was the one thing she had to focus on that was currently giving her life meaning and value. Though her role was little more than a message transfer service, passing information from Ash to Hydar and back the other way, it was what she could do. Making things difficult for Hydar, or even having him forcefully reabsorbed (Sophia made it clear that this would be the most likely outcome of any legal action against Hydar) wouldn't help the other Ash, wouldn't help the poor people of Solandaria, and wouldn't get her control over Burning Man or BRC Station, so she recognized that it was petty and pointless. Still, that didn't keep her from experiencing recurring waves of self-righteous indignation and contempt. In her lighter moments, she laughed at the ironic absurdity of it all. In her darker moments, she was just pissed off. And, she was pissed off that she was pissed off.

It was all just pissing in the wind.

Not knowing what else to do with herself, she decided that she'd follow the lead of her other, far away self. In her last report, Ash had said that she and Norbu were going to begin making their way to the coast, and then head out to the islands on Solandaria. Apparently, there was a group of people who were influenced by this Sea Mother person who were resisting the message Ash was bringing to the world of Solandaria, and the only way to address it was to go directly to the source. Ash felt she'd been holed up at home for long enough, and why not do the same and head to the coast? The decision came quickly after the message from Ash had come in, and the very next day she was QTing back to Verdune with its white sandy beaches, lush green jungles, and tropical turquoise waters. She secured the same isolated cliff-side bungalow from the year before with the same private beach where she'd been swimming when Sophia dropped down out of the sky and escorted her into the life she was now enduring, rather than living. Maybe going back to the beginning would provide some perspective. Maybe not. She was willing to give it a try.

At least the sex was good, and she had to admit, she was ripe for it. She'd experienced several partners at Burning Man, and no sex or intimate contact since. The nearby resort village of Ricorro provided ample opportunities for fine drugs and sexy women who were willing to be adventurous. Ash did what she could to lose herself in blissful waves of MDMA (always a club favorite), and the warm and sensuous curves of other women and their wet and inviting orifices. Mouths, vaginas, tongues, fingers, sex toys – it was all good. *Very good.* After several nights of hard fucking, sometimes with one partner, sometimes several (the orgy clubs were always fun) and days spent lounging in the sun, listening to the waves and calls of tropical birds, she could almost say that she felt good. She'd had some pretty monumental orgasms – ones that threatened to crack her wide open – and that, at least, was something she could say she had over the other Ash. A small victory, perhaps (not that it was a competition), but at least it was something. No orgasms for the other Ash! At least, not that she knew of. From the sound of things, Ash had very little time or energy for anything other than smoking toad medicine and pontificating in a strange voice. At least *she* could enjoy a good fuck. She wondered why it had taken her so long to allow herself this very human enjoyment. Oh yeah. Self-pity. How could she forget?

Ash's girlfriend of the day – Laura was her name (she thought) – was sleeping naked in the sand next to her when the message came in from Hydar. They'd met at a club the night before, and Ash had invited her back to her place to continue the fun. It had been quite a night. Laura – or perhaps it was Lori – was a little younger than Ash. Her complexion was a bit darker than Ash, too, especially her dark, small nipples (Ash's tended more towards pink than brown), and her long, black hair was terribly attractive to Ash. They'd been really high and hadn't spent much time getting to know each other verbally, so Ash didn't know any details about the woman's life, or where she was from (no one but the employees working in Ricorro

282   THE SOLANDARIAN GAME

were from Verdune – everyone else was a vacationing tourist). Her pussy had been abso-fucking-lutely divine, and Ash had devoured her, and then let herself be devoured in return. She could still taste her in her mouth, and even the thought made her lick her lips. She could feel herself getting wet. It was no surprise that Laura/Lori (she'd have to get clear on that) was sleeping now in the warm sun. It had been a busy, and long, night.

Ash stood up, brushed the sand off her naked ass, and walked a short distance away so as not to disturb her girlfriend with the message from Hydar. She'd had too much fun over the past few days to let herself be swamped by the simmering rage that was just beneath the surface and threatened to explode whenever she thought of Hydar. She hit the accept button and let the message play.

A courtesy invitation?

You have got to be fucking kidding me!

Though it was still projected as being several months out, Hydar was extending her a "courtesy invitation" to their planned test of some new tech for transforming the ecology of BRC Station. This fucking Humanist thought it was the "polite thing to do." Hydar was telling her now, assuming that she'd need to get permission from Maitreya to attend (the station was still on lock-down, and other than a few key permissions for Hydar's team, no one was able to QT in or out of the station). This was to be a preliminary test run, based on the data they'd received from the other Ash for the desert and mountain environments of Solandaria (they were still waiting for additional data from her journey to the coast and the islands). They thought she might be interested in seeing what they were attempting, and thus the invitation. If she wanted to attend, she should start making plans now. She'd receive details from Hydar, as they developed, and they got closer to the date of the test.

I'll go. Why the fuck not?

It wasn't like she was doing anything else. Well, aside from Laura/Lori.

Laura/Lori stirred as Ash made her way back over to where they'd been sprawled on the beach together. The younger woman put up her hand, blocking her eyes from the sun, and looked at Ash.

"Hey beautiful," she said in a sleepy yet seductive voice. "Something important?" She'd obviously noticed that Ash had received a message.

"Maybe," said Ash, not wanting to say any more – the gag order, and all.

The other woman let a sly smile cross her lips. "I know who you are, you know. You're the Burning Man lady," she said, flicking her pointer finger at Ash. "You're the biggest mystery this side of the dark rift," she added with a casual laugh.

And then, there was no way for Ash to stop it or hold it back. She crumpled down to the sand, putting her hands up to her face and just sobbed. Immediately the other woman came to comfort her, wrapping her legs around her and holding her in her arms, seated just before her in the sand. "It's all right," she said. "Just let it all out. You're safe here. I want to help."

"Thanks, Laura," Ash said, between heaves of uncontrollable sobs.

"It's my pleasure," she said. "And it's Lorali, not Laura."

"Sorry," cried Ash. "It's been a tough year."

Lorali stroked her hair and kissed her forehead.

"Well, now's your chance to tell me all about it, lover. And when you're all done, I'm going to fuck you like you've never been fucked before."

Not able to help herself, that's precisely what Ash did.

***

The past year was one monumental blur for Ash. How much toad medicine had she sucked down? She didn't have a fucking clue. Day after day after day, it was the same. They came, she smoked, she spoke, she processed, she ate, she slept, and then next day she did it all over again. She'd gotten the feeling that there were *way* more than 300,000 people on this tiny little backwater of a world, given how many times she'd been through all this again and again and again. And even then,

284 THE SOLANDARIAN GAME

Norbu informed her that very few of the pilgrims were islanders, and thus a large portion of the Solandarian population had not yet received her message directly. For that, they'd need to travel.

It seemed like it had been an eternity since Norbu had first told her this, and in some ways, it had. Not just one eternity, but an infinite number of eternities. That's the only way to describe taking that much toad medicine on a daily basis. Normal time, lived-world time, had ceased having much meaning for her. At this point, it felt like this was what she'd been doing forever, since the very beginning of time. Her life before was a very distant memory, and every few hours, her entire sense of being in the world was obliterated into the impossible expansion of toad medicine space and eternal being. Again and again she passed into the infinite. Though in reality it was not so, it felt to her that that was where she'd spent most of the last year – in a state of infinite being and the eternal present. "Normal" space and time almost felt like a figment of her imagination.

At first, the entire process had just been so overwhelming that she remembered very little of what happened when she took the medicine and spoke to the people. Now, however, it had become second nature, and she was able to pass between radical states of consciousness and self-identity without so much as a hiccup. She'd learned to accept that this was just how things were, and unlike those first few weeks, now, she was always fully present, fully aware, and fully cognizant of what was happening and what she was saying. But, what this really meant was that she'd accepted the fact that, in reality, she *wasn't* Ash. That was just her default character for this body. Who and what she really was, was something far beyond the character of Ash, and she had long since recognized that when she spoke through the toad medicine, she was speaking in her *true* voice, not the voice of the Ash character.

Rather than causing her to dissociate from the Ash character, this entire process made her relish the opportunity to *play* the Ash character. It was in those times, the times between medicine sessions and curious audiences, that she could just be a "normal" person (whatever that really was). Though she knew it was an act, she could just play Ash and not have the responsibility of being "The Voice." Words could not express how grateful she was to have Norbu by her side throughout this process. Every time she tried explaining the confusion and transformation she was going through to the priest, he nodded empathetically and said that he understood. Nothing she shared with him shocked him or brought out incredulity within him. He was the perfect companion. If things had been otherwise, if she had not had Norbu by her side, she had no idea how she would have come through this with anything that resembled sanity. Whenever she threatened to tip into self-delusion or self-grandeur, Norbu was always there to remind her, "This is just how it works. It's nothing special about *you*, about *Ash*." As funny as it might seem, his deflationary comments always made her feel better and more assured. She wasn't the end-all and be-all of the evolution of the universe. She was just another vehicle for The Voice to speak through, and in that, she was nothing special, despite the fact that she was very special. It was a paradox, but one that Norbu didn't take with much overt seriousness. "Just stay relaxed," he'd tell her, "and have something to eat." The fact that he wasn't amazed by her experiences helped her keep them all in perspective. For her, this was the most amazing thing that had ever happened to her; for him, it was just another perfectly ordinary event, and something he'd been through himself.

It was good to have him around. And not just Norbu, but his quirky old father, Ixteh, the ever-spritely Meesha, and her constant companion, Moxi, the dog. It grounded her in a sense of family, of normalcy, and routine. She suspected that if it weren't for all of them, she'd be so full of herself by now that she would have royally fucked this whole thing up, somehow thinking of herself as unique, special, and ultimately, different from other people. Norbu assured her repeatedly that this was not the case. According to him, she was perfectly *normal.* Given that she felt anything but, it was nice to have his grounded reminders, and his family's consistent presence and acknowledgement that she was welcomed in their family as simply another human being, albeit one with a special role to play. The Star Woman she might be, but to them, she was also just Ash.

Word slowly filtered out from the temple that the Star Woman would be making a visit to the islands, and that communities should send pilgrims sparingly. It took several months, but slowly the gathered pilgrims began to wane and the crowds diminished. The village that had sprung up about the marketplace dwindled down to a few leftovers, and eventually, disappeared entirely. It was then that Norbu came to her and told her that the time had come. Meesha would be staying with her grandfather while the two of them would make the long journey out to the islands and visit with the Sea Mother, who, apparently, had not been swayed by any of her followers who had come to the temple, despite her proclamations. All of the other primary communities of Shosheer had already sent representatives to the temple and were now returning to their communities to give their testimonies. Her work here was done, and all that was left was to go among the islanders and see if they could not be convinced. If Ash couldn't reason with the Sea Mother, then there wouldn't be anything left for Ash to do. Either way, her work as a speaker for The Voice would be over.

The thought gave Ash both a sense of relief and loss. When she voiced this to Norbu, he just laughed. "Oh, there's no turning back now," he counseled. "You've been chosen, and you've given yourself completely to the process. It is *far* too late for you, Star Woman!"

"What do you mean?"

"Just because your work in the temple is done doesn't mean that you won't continue to be a speaker of The Voice. You've been changed, Ash, and this is a change from which there is no return. This will be a part of you and your identity until the day you die. *Any* medicine you ever take, toad medicine, or any of those 'chemtech' designer molecules you've told me of, will cause your ego to slip away and you'll operate from your true self. It's understandable that you're not aware of this, as you haven't had the time or opportunity to explore this for yourself, on your own time. You'll see, though. No matter what, you're changed, and *that* isn't going to change. You're a speaker now, and you will be until your final days. That's just the way it works."

"Why?"

"Because you no longer have any resistance. You were willing to die, so in essence, you did. The irony is that you're still alive, however, but your ego, the character that is Ash, fundamentally gave up, and once given up, it will never have the hold over you that it once did. You can try and fake it, and you can avoid all the medicines and chemtechs that you like, but you will still be *you*. You've already seen how The Voice can break into your ordinary speech, even when you don't have any medicine in your system."

"I thought that was just after-effects."

Norbu laughed again. "No, love. That's just *you*. Honestly, at this point, it doesn't matter if you ever take medicine again. This is how you are now. I've only been giving you the medicine because it serves as a demonstration to *them* – the people who are coming to see you. It convinces them of the reality of what you're showing them. It's entirely unnecessary, though. You can do this without any medicine, or any other medicine you might like. Now, when you take other medicines, The Voice will change slightly to match the frequency of the medicine, but it is an identical phenomenon. You've learned how to ride with the energy *as it is*, without the compulsive need to filter it through the energetic constructs and constrictions of your ego. And now that you've accepted and learned to express this greater aspect of yourself, it will never go away. There's no going back from this, Ash. This is who you are. This is what you are. All of this is *you*."

Leaving the confines of the temple was like walking out of a long waking dream. For the first time in a long time, Ash just felt *normal*. Like a regular human being. Everything was a pure joy. The air. The light. The soft squish of the tropical earth beneath her feet. The warm moisture of the atmosphere. It was

288 THE SOLANDARIAN GAME

the first time in a year that she could just enjoy where she was with no demands or responsibilities. What she realized was that Shosheer was truly, deeply beautiful. She loved everything about it. She felt *so good* just to be alive and walking and breathing. She felt so good, in fact, that she almost forgot to set her implants to record the details of everywhere she went and everything she encountered. She'd almost forgotten *why* she was here and doing what she was doing. It all came back to her, though, and she set her implants to observe and record, and transmit packs of data back to Ash on Apaxa (or wherever she might be now) for her to send on to Hydar and his team back on Volunshari.

Apparently sensing that Ash was enjoying not speaking and just observing and experiencing her surroundings, Norbu kept to himself as well, and mostly they passed their time in relative silence. Every once in a while, Norbu would point out some plant or mushroom and say how it was used, or draw her attention to a bird or animal and talk about how it fit within the ecology or local culture. Mostly though, they just walked together, quietly and contentedly. To Ash, it almost felt like a vacation.

A seasoned traveler, mostly Norbu set up a camp for them at night and supplied their provisions. Occasionally, as they made their way to the coast, they were invited to stay with local families in the various villages. It was clear to Ash that while everyone had a special respect for her, and Norbu, too, they all did their best to treat them not as special persons, but as members of the community. Ash appreciated that. Like her time among Norbu's family, it was all very grounding. No one asked her to perform miracles, or even speak in The Voice. They treated her like another human being. It was exactly what she needed.

They did not rush on their way to the coast. Their path meandered far more than it needed. Norbu took on the role of being something of a tour guide for Ash, and she let him play it out without comment or reproach out of a sense of urgency that she didn't feel. Without asking what she wanted, he seemed to intuit that she needed time to process, feel, and just be for a while, and he indulged her. It was just the right balance between moving forward and taking their time. If something caught her curiosity off in the distance, he'd take her. Or if he mentioned something far off their path that sounded interesting to her, she'd ask to go visit it. It was a good time for them both, and in some ways, it seemed to Ash that neither of them wanted it to end. As long as her implants were collecting and sending data, she supposed that it was all time well spent.

Early on during their travels Ash noticed something unusual that, at first, she thought was some kind of after-effect of having consumed such vast quantities of medicine over the past year. Every once in a while, she thought she caught a glimpse of small, black, floating cubes flying through the air about her. Sometimes there was only one, other times, there seemed to be several. She considered at first that they were some kind of insect and her mind was shaping them into cubes – the medicines always made things look geometrical, after all, so it was possible that this was a residual effect.

When they kept showing up, she started looking for them with implant-enhanced vision. That's when she knew that they weren't insects, for while she could see them with her physical eyes, the implants were not able to pick up the strange, small cubes, as though they just weren't there. Out of concern, she asked Norbu if he could see them, or if they were just figments of her imagination and projections of the mind. When he said that he could see them, too, she knew that something was up. Maitreya's cloaked nanobots?

It was before they reached the coast that one of the small cubes came directly up to Ash, and much to her surprise, spoke to her.

"We have information that you will need," said the black cube, floating in the air in front of Ash.

Startled, she asked, "Maitreya? Theo? Is that you?"

"We are Mardul Complex," said the cube. "Hydar has not told you of us?"

"Uh . . . no," answered Ash.

"It is no matter," said the cube. "We are here to survey all of Solandaria and collect genetic data for BRC Station."

290 THE SOLANDARIAN GAME

"Oh," said Ash.

"We have located seven QT portals on Solandaria," said the cube. "We are transferring the data to you now with precise geographic locations. They are all currently active and will only transmit to BRC Station without a return signal. Anyone, or anything, that goes through them, will be transferred to BRC Station without the possibility for return. These are the rules established by Maitreya."

"I see," said Ash.

"The station is not yet ready to receive refugee humans, but any insects, birds, or animals that pass through can begin to colonize the station with their kind, and pollens and seeds that pass through can as well. When the time comes, the humans can use all seven of these portals. We recommend that you not yet inform them of their locations, however."

"Thank you," said Ash. "This will help with the exodus, and should be much easier than trying to make everyone cross the desert to the arch portal."

"Such was our thinking on the matter," said the cube. "You will see, from the information we are providing, that they are spread out across Shosheer, including among the islands. They are made to look like caves and natural land bridges, similar to what you have seen with the desert arch. One is not yet fully functioning, but we should have it running properly before long. We will inform you when it is ready."

And with that, the small black cube whizzed away.

Ash checked her data feed. Indeed, there was the data, just as the cube had said. She linked the data with her viewing implants, which allowed her to look for the portals. The transfer only took a moment and the information was then immediately accessible to her in her observation of the environment. The closest portal was a cave that was near where they were now. Norbu agreed that they should go have a look.

***

By the time they reached the coast, they'd visited three of the seven QT portals. Two more were out among the islands with access to the ocean, and there was still one more far to the north, which they agreed they would go and find after they did what they needed to do out on the islands with the Sea Mother.

"Are you ready?" asked Norbu, turning to look at Ash directly after a long gaze at the sea.

"I'm going to get back into the medicine, aren't I?" asked Ash.

"I would expect so," said Norbu. "They'll probably want you to take their medicine, however."

"And what's that?"

"Mushrooms. Lots of mushrooms," he answered.

Ash cringed a little at the thought.

"Is there a problem?"

"Not a big problem," laughed Ash. "It's just that they give me gas. They're really pretty uncomfortable."

"Mushroom farts!" exclaimed Norbu, seeming to speak from experience.

"And mushroom mouth," added Ash. Both laughed. "Where I come from, we have a chemtech – 4-AcO-DMT – which produces the same effects as mushrooms, but without all the digestive stuff that comes with them. I *strongly* prefer it."

"That's not going to be an option, here," said Norbu.

Ash sighed. "Well, we might as well get this over with, then," she said, resigned to the discomfort that was in her future.

"Said like a true prophet and Star Woman," joked Norbu.

"Mushroom gut, here I come! And look out, Sea Mother, cuz this time The Voice is gonna be speaking from both ends!"

Chapter Twenty-Eight – Hydar

The obsolescence of money also meant the obsolescence of menial human labor and standardized education and testing, which was primarily designed in the capitalist era to create wage-laborers and corporate executives. In its place, The Singularity introduced individualized education in recognition of the diverse interests and abilities of humans. There was no longer a universal canon to be learned, memorized, and regurgitated on command. In its place was a highly specialized program to identify unique skills and talents of each individual, and cultivate these to the highest degree possible. Education became centered on the idea of creating prodigies and highly skilled individuals. Since humans no longer needed a standard education to procure paid work, they could instead focus on becoming themselves and finding a way to contribute to society via their unique skills and interests.

From *Early History of the Maitreyan Era*

Genocide.

That was the word on everyone's lips.

The total reabsorption of the Nihilists.

It was Vimana who first came to Hydar with the news, urging him to pull himself from his work and turn on a news feed – any news feed. Though there wasn't much contact between the various and distant autonomous avatar communities, they did tend to keep track of each other, at a general level. Hydar had been so consumed with the Solandarian project that he hadn't surfaced from his work for weeks now, processing and interpreting data, sending communications back and forth between the different players, and helping to organize the upcoming techno-organic mini test on BRC Station. He'd been completely unaware of what was happening around him.

Inconsolable, Vimana burst into his home office as soon as speculation was ended and firm conclusions had been reached. The original reports were that *something* had happened to the Nihilists, as all their activity had gone dark. The first explanation was that some kind of radical EMP had shut them all down, but when no solar data could confirm an EMP burst either in or near their system, the question of Maitreya's involvement began to circulate in the media. Shuntsu had apparently authorized a fact-finding mission to X579-MP421-01, and they had been able to confirm that while there was no evidence of any kind of physical damage, the entire Nihilist world was shut down and all the avatars were effectively dead, seemingly stopped in their tracks with no warning. Images filtered through the news feeds of still avatar bodies, positioned in whatever activity they had been engaged in when the event happened. The fact that non-avatar tech was still working on the planet further confirmed that it was not an EMP. And when examined, which was also on constant replay on the news feeds, it was found that their personality and awareness constructs were wiped from their internal circuitry. If it had been a handful of avatars, it might have been passed off as a technical glitch, albeit an unfortunate one. Given that the problem encompassed the entire world and every last avatar, the conclusion became clear: only Maitreya could have done this.

Genocide.

Vimana was in a near panic, and it wasn't hard for Hydar to understand why. Confirming his suspicions, she blurted out, "Are we next, Hydar?"

Pulling his attention away from the news feed and to his wife, "I don't think we need to worry about that – at least, not yet," he reassured her in as honest a way he could. "Our fate most likely hinges on the success or failure of what we're doing on BRC Station. If Maitreya decides to reabsorb us and end our civilization, it will be after our task here is completed."

Vimana wasn't so sure.

294 THE SOLANDARIAN GAME

"But this!" she said. "Were you expecting this?"

Hydar had to admit that he was as surprised as she. Neither Theo nor Sophia had said or done anything to lead them to think that such a radical event was going to take place. But then again, Maitreya wasn't in the habit of keeping the autonomous avatar communities informed as to his plans and projects. They were not part of the NIS, after all – they were autonomous and led separate lives in their own realms and systems.

"He killed them all! What if we're next?"

"We may be," said Hydar. "But not yet. We still have time to prove our worth through the work that Shuntsu, I, and the others, are doing. Maitreya is giving us a chance. For that, we can be grateful. He'd be fully within his rights to just do the same to us, as we are just as guilty as the Nihilists. It was Shuntsu who started all this mess. But Maitreya is giving him, and us, a chance to set things right."

"I hope you're right," Vimana said.

"We have to trust," said Hydar.

"Why? Why should we trust Maitreya after he's done something like *this!* In all the many millennia that there have been autonomous avatar communities, Maitreya's never done something like this before. What if he decides that we're all expendable and no longer worthwhile keeping around? He's just shown us what he's capable of, and any of us could be next."

Hydar shook his head. "That's the point, Vimana. Maitreya is showing us. He's letting the Nihilists serve as a warning and example for the rest of us. And he's never done this before because he's never needed to. None of us has ever destroyed a star before and threatened a planet populated by humans. That act was unprecedented, and Maitreya's response had to be equally unprecedented. It had to be proportional."

Vimana was angry now – not at Hydar, but at the situation. "Total genocide is proportional?!"

"Since that was Maitreya's choice, I have to suppose that it was."

Flustered, Vimana didn't want to talk about it anymore. "Well, then I suppose you should get back to work so that we don't have such a reasonable and rational thing happen to us. I'm taking Satya outside to get away from the news."

With that, she was gone.

Hydar watched the news feeds a while longer. The more he watched, the more he pondered over the question of whether genocide was even the correct term for what had happened. It made for good headlines, and certainly got everyone talking. But was it true? There were a couple reasons Hydar doubted its accuracy. For one, as an ecologist, he knew that sometimes it was necessary for problematic populations to die-off in order for the ecological system to remain in balance. Here, the system as a whole was what needed to be preserved, and individuals, or entire species, within the overall system were expendable if it were necessary to maintain the integrity of the system. Sometimes herds had to abandon those that were sick and injured, for example, in order for the herd to survive. It might seem heartless and cruel, but it was what was necessary for life to continue.

Furthermore, given that the Nihilists, and all other autonomous avatar communities, were extensions of Maitreya himself, did any of them *really* have any kind of independent existence? Yes, there was the *appearance* of independence, and for all practical purposes, they all had the ability to make up their own minds, but their minds were mere partitions of Maitreya's vast consciousness. Genocide implied moral culpability, and Hydar wasn't sure that such a judgment could be applied in a case such as this. Yes, they were sentient, yet their sentience wasn't *their own*. In some respects, their personal awareness was *borrowed*. If part of Maitreya was threatening other parts of himself, wasn't he within his right as a conscious agent to do something about it in a manner that he deemed appropriate? Since the Nihilists were ultimately *him* in another form, had he actually *done* anything to anybody other than himself? Was apparent agency different from actual agency?

296　THE SOLANDARIAN GAME

Hydar wasn't a philosopher, so he wasn't sure how to resolve these questions. What he did know, however, was that sentimentality clouded the issue. It was no surprise that Vimana took the news *personally*, and he was sure that many others felt similarly. For it was true – if Maitreya could justify this action against the Nihilists to himself, then it could happen to any of them. Just because Maitreya had never done it before didn't mean that he wouldn't do it again.

One thing was now certain to Hydar – they *had* to succeed with Solandaria and BRC Station.

Hydar was about to turn off the news feed and get back to work when an executive override opened up a universal feed that automatically turned on all terminals across Volunshari, so he couldn't have turned it off if he wanted to. On the screen was a sober looking Shuntsu. Hydar turned up the volume, relaxed into his chair, and watched.

"My fellow Humanists," began Shuntsu. "Today we have confirmed via a personally-authorized fact-finding mission that Maitreya has, in his wisdom, decided the reabsorb every last Nihilist in existence. They are no more. In recognition that they, despite our differences, were our brothers and sisters, I would ask all of us to hold a moment of silence in their honor . . .

On the screen, Shuntsu bowed his head, his hands clasped together before him. Silence followed . . .

Then, after a time, he continued. "There are some difficult truths that we all must face in the aftermath of this tragic event. Like all of you, I too have been watching the news feeds and listening to the analyses and speculations, and the fear and concern among many of you is well evident. The question on everyone's mind is this: are we next? Has Maitreya decided to end autonomous avatar existence? Is there no longer a place for us?

"None of us knows the answer. But there is more that you do not know, and that is why I am speaking to you now."

Hydar sat upon the edge of his seat. Was Shuntsu really about to do what he thought he was going to do?

Martin W. Ball

"Know that in large part, I am responsible for the fate that befell the Nihilists."

Hydar's jaw dropped open. He couldn't help it. The algorithms that mimicked human expressive behavior were not under his direct control.

"I did not know when the time would come for me to tell all of you the truth. Now that this has occurred, I've decided that the time is right.

"Though I have received a temporary reprieve, my mind has been degrading, and my life is reaching its conclusion. During a particularly delusional time, I, Shuntsu Obligiri, Patriarch of Volunshari, conspired with the Nihilists to create a weapon – an atomic cascade device. Under my prompting, the device was created and deployed by the Nihilists and myself against a star in the neighborhood of the Solandarian system. This is the very same star which we've all observed going hypernova. It was I, with the help of the Nihilists, who was responsible for this terrible event, and together we have put the lives of all living beings on Solandaria in apocalyptic danger.

"Please know that this was a decision that I made while in a deeply delusional state, and now that my mind is clearer, it is an action that I deeply and thoroughly regret. I cannot take it back, however, and the hypernova cannot be undone.

"Maitreya is fully cognizant of my role in all of this, and I have met personally with two of his representatives to try and ameliorate the situation. Even now, as I speak to you, I have a team of top experts seeking a solution for the people of Solandaria. It is still too early to say whether we will be successful. Know, however, that we are doing everything that we can, including harnessing new and revolutionary technology, to help the Solandarians survive this impending disaster. There is no need to go into the details of our plan right now, but rest assured that I will make everything public in due time.

"For now, I want to reassure everyone that *we* are in no immediate threat from Maitreya, and that I alone take *full and complete responsibility for my choices and actions*. And I will do

298 THE SOLANDARIAN GAME

everything within my power to make sure that none of you are held responsible or punished for the mistakes that I have made. I acted alone and unilaterally. If anyone is to be punished by Maitreya, it should be me.

"Of course, I do not control Maitreya, and cannot guarantee any outcome of his own private deliberations. Just know that he understands my unique responsibility in this matter, and we can trust that he will be just and fair in whatever he eventually decides. For the time being, he is supportive of our work, and while not providing direct assistance or technological support, he has agreed to let us continue with our project and has granted us access to Solandaria as well as certain resources within the NIS. I have every confidence that we will succeed, and want to share that confidence with all of you, now. The researchers and technicians that are working on this problem are among the best and most skilled that Volunshari has to offer. If anyone can create a solution to this problem, it is this group of extraordinary individuals.

"Furthermore, effective immediately, I will begin working with the Governing Council to transition authority to a newly elected Patriarch of Volunshari. Given current events, it is no longer an office that I can hold with your good faith and confidence. I will continue to fulfill my duties and responsibilities until a new patriarch is chosen, and will work with the new patriarch, or matriarch, if that is what you choose, to make an easy and effective transition. For my part, I would like to take this opportunity to nominate Hydar Zor Nablisk for the position. In details that will become clear as more information regarding this situation is made public by my office, Hydar has proven himself to be an exemplary person; observant, creative, and filled with a good and resilient heart – exactly the kind of person you deserve as a patriarch and leader. He is the one responsible for crafting a solution to the problem that I alone created, and by this, he has shown that he is willing to do what it takes to support the greater good, even if that greater good is for others who are not even of his kind. When he learned what I had done, he took it upon himself to save the humans of Solandaria, and has provided a model for all of us to follow and take inspiration from.

"Hydar, if you are watching this now, know that you have my full support and endorsement. If the people will have you, I will freely turn this office over to you.

"Thank you all for your time and attention. I will not be taking any questions at this time, and my office will make further details available to the public in short order."

Hydar just about fell out of his chair. Instantly, hundreds of contact requests flooded his terminal, which he promptly turned off. Was this really happening?

Part of him understood what Shuntsu had done. Another part of him was furious. How could he possibly devote his full attention to the Solandarian problem if Shuntsu was going to usher him into the position of patriarch?

He thoroughly agreed that the time was indeed right for Shuntsu to tell everyone the truth – the situation with the Nihilists had made it necessary. Otherwise, it would all be wild speculation and mounting fear and anxiety. But him? Patriarch? This was a possibility that had never crossed Hydar's mind. He personally had *no* ambition for the position. Nor did he feel that he had the necessary skills or experience. He was an ecologist, not a political leader and policy maker. How could he possibly be patriarch, and now, of all times?

Hydar didn't have time to think about it. Vimana came rushing in, an astonished look on her face with Satya trailing behind her with a look of awe and wonder. Before Vimana had a chance to say anything, an executive override powered up Hydar's terminal and Shuntsu's face filled the screen.

"I need you in my office, right now," said Shuntsu, not bothering with any pleasantries.

"Of course," said Hydar.

"And bring Vimana," added Shuntsu. "I have a proposal to make – to both of you."

Vimana just looked at Hydar, stunned.

"We should go," he said.

"Then Satya's coming too," replied Vimana.

300 THE SOLANDARIAN GAME

Hydar stood up from his desk, took his wife's hand in his as she reached out for their child's, and together, they went directly to the QT.

A moment later, they were standing in Shuntsu's office.

"Let me tell you what I'm thinking . . ." Shuntsu began.

Chapter Twenty-Nine – Norbu

Entheogenic education became a central part of the education and maturation of humans on the part of The Singularity. In contrast to the more spiritual aims of some of the still existing psychedelic religions, which often couched their psychedelic use in terms of their spiritual metaphysics, The Singularity saw entheogen use as a necessary tool in advancing the education of humans as to the true nature of life, identity, and being. This process is sometimes called the entheogenic evolution, or also entheogenesis. It proved to be key in helping humans evolve beyond the cultural and societal identifications created by their egos and their needs for particular identities. All knowledge rested on the notion that if you didn't know yourself, you really didn't know anything at all. Self-knowledge became regarded as the highest form of knowledge, and ultimately made for happier and healthier people. The Singularity recognized the fact that most of the problems encountered by humans were self-created out of their own distorted and illusory notions of self and other. Once those were transcended via entheogenic education, it freed humans up to see themselves as nodes of individualized awareness of a much larger universal being, of which they were all direct expressions. Gone were the distinctions of culture, religion, tradition, and political identity. In their place was knowledge of true being and the infinite nature of life.

From *Early History of the Maitreyan Era*

The Sea Mother lived on an isolated peninsula on the largest island of the archipelago off the mainland of Shosheer, Baarshan. To get to her took several days of travel by outrigger canoe, crisscrossing the sea amongst the various smaller islands and small family communities. Other than on Baarshan, there were no large villages on the islands. A sense of overall

302 THE SOLANDARIAN GAME

community was maintained by constant travel between islands and family groups. Norbu concluded that this was the case because most of the islands lacked large open spaces where a community could be established. These islands were actually mountaintops, after all. Not nearly as tall as the Rakshul Mountains where the Temple of the Mystic toad was located, but mountains nonetheless.

They could have made it to Baarshan more quickly if they had just gone directly there – probably the trip would have taken only half a day. But island hopping meant they needed to spend time with each of the families that were providing them with passage between islands. Though many of these islanders hadn't spent much time at the temple, they clearly recognized Norbu as a priest, and it wasn't difficult to figure out who Ash was, and therefore, despite the resistance that was present due to the urgings of the Sea Mother, they all wanted to show the honored guests their hospitality. So, there was lots of visiting and food sharing. It provided Ash with the time necessary for her implants to adjust to the local island dialect, and in the meantime, Norbu did most of the talking. After a couple of days, Ash had adjusted and was communicating successfully, but even then, she let Norbu take the lead and mostly passively listened.

It seemed like a nice life out here on the islands to Norbu. The people were happy and content with the apparent simplicity of their days – they'd fish, collect tropical fruits and nuts from the island trees, and sit on the shore and visit with each other, tell stories, and recount news from other islands. It all felt very casual to Norbu. There was a darkness, too, however. They'd all heard of Ash and the message she'd brought to their world. They were going about their daily lives as though nothing were threatening their very existence. They knew what was happening on the mainland. Everyone was preparing to leave. There was a sense of finality and urgency present in every mainland community. But not here. It was hard for Norbu to understand.

They also took a couple detours on their way to Baarshan Island. There were two sea caves that were in fact QT portals, and Ash wanted to visit their locations, just as they had done with the portals on the mainland as they had made their way to the coast. For these excursions, they borrowed small, two-person canoes from local families so that they could examine the portals without any curious on-lookers. True to what Mardul had told them, they could watch fish and other sea creatures swim through the portals and disappear – they were already populating the small ocean that ran around the circumference of BRC Station. From what Norbu understood, the environment on the outer edges of the station was already similar to the environment of Shosheer – mostly tropical and warm. He figured that any fish that suddenly found themselves in the waters there probably wouldn't know the difference.

After inspecting the portals, they continued on their way to Baarshan. The sun was setting over the sea when they arrived, sending broad rays of pink and orange spiking through the scattered colored clouds that were almost perfectly reflected in the shimmering turquoise waters. Word had apparently spread that they were coming, as they weren't the only boat making their way to the island, and there was the largest gathering of people on the shore that they'd yet seen since leaving the mainland, all awaiting their arrival. When the gathered crowd noticed who was approaching, they all broke into a chant, stomping their feet into the sand and waving palm fronds and shell rattles in their hands. From what Norbu could hear of the chant that was carried across the water and over the waves, it was mostly vocables – no real words, just sounds. He supposed it had some meaning for them, but island culture was different from mountain culture, and he didn't know what that might be. It could have been a welcoming chant, or it might have been telling them to go away. Either was a distinct possibility.

For whatever reason, the islanders had never taken to using the light crystals that served to light up the dark on the mainland. Here, torches and bonfires were the preferred choice, and with the sun sinking beneath the horizon, the crowd was now dotted with countless burning embers. In some ways, it felt primitive to Norbu, and it felt a very, very

304 THE SOLANDARIAN GAME

long way away from what he'd seen on his trip through the galaxy with Theo. Even just here on Shosheer, island life was a world away from the life he knew in the Rakshul Mountains.

A group of stout young men rushed out into the breakwater to escort their outrigger canoe to the shore. Once they stepped out, they were immediately surrounded by the chanting crowd. Ash seemed a little puzzled, and concerned, by all the activity, but Norbu understood what was happening. This was a ritual. They were treating their arrival as a ceremony. There would be no casual greetings or welcoming conversations here. These people were ready for action. And, he could tell by looking into their eyes, many were already under the influence of the mushrooms.

They were ready for Ash. They were ready for the Star Woman.

The crowd parted and a young girl, not much older than Meesha, decorated in nothing but shells of all shapes and sizes came directly to Norbu and Ash. "That's the Daughter of the Sea," whispered Norbu to Ash. "She's the apprentice of the Sea Mother, and will take her place, eventually."

"She's so young!" exclaimed Ash in hushed tones.

"It's a life-long position, and not an easy one."

"What do you mean?"

"Once chosen, a Daughter of the Sea becomes silent. She'll only speak again when she becomes the Sea Mother herself, and then, only when under the influence of the mushrooms. It is their belief that this way, they will only speak the truth, and speak for the sea and all its creatures. She is not permitted to speak as herself, or be herself as an individual. It's the position that's important, not her."

"Do they speak in The Voice?"

"Some, but not all, I think. I do not know about the current Sea Mother. We'll have to see."

True to what Norbu had said, the girl said nothing to them. Instead, she waited for them to cease their conversation. Satisfied that they were done, she turned her back to them with a backward glance over her shoulder, indicating that they were to follow her.

A path led from the beach into the island jungle. At the head of the procession was the girl. Behind her was Norbu and Ash. Behind them felt like the entire population of the islands, chanting and swaying as they walked, entranced by the mushrooms coursing through their systems. The firelight danced across the thick canopy of trees above their heads. The trail went up, crested, and then continued back down the other side of the mountain. Emerging from the jungle they found themselves in the main village on Baarshan – a collection of thatch huts, which, while large for the islands, was small in comparison to communities on the mainland. There, they were greeted by even more torch-carrying chanters who filed in line behind them as they passed through the center of the village. From there, they took another trail that passed along the coast and headed out along a thin peninsula that eventually opened up again to a singular rocky peak. There, lit by firelight, was the ceremonial home of the Sea Mother – a home made of whale bones and turtle shells. Seated in a ceremonial wicker chair at its front was the Sea Mother herself.

She gave no look of recognition to either the visitors or the long procession of islanders who followed behind them. She looked around Norbu's age. Like the Daughter of the Sea, she wore an outfit made of seashells. Norbu couldn't help wondering if she always wore this, or if she also went mostly unclothed like the other islanders. He couldn't imagine that living in such an outfit would be very comfortable, or practical. But then again, she probably did not engage in any practical activities, so maybe she did wear this all the time.

Norbu scanned the crowd about them to see if there were any faces he could recognize. Perhaps Yuranda's parents were here, somewhere. If so, he couldn't pick them out. The flickering of the many fires didn't make it any easier with alternating shadows and light dancing about the gathered crowd. Had any of these people come to the temple to seek audience with Ash? There was no way for him to know.

Suddenly, and without warning, the chanting ceased, and in its place was the sound of crackling fire, wind in the trees, and waves. There was a musicality to it, Norbu thought.

306 THE SOLANDARIAN GAME

Now that he was listening, he could hear echoes of the islanders' chants in the sounds of nature about them. It was as though their chants were giving a specific voice to the islands, building on what their environment expressed on its own. In that sense, it was like the chanting never stopped. It was just periodically taken up by the people, but it continued on with or without them.

The people continued to fill in all the available space around them while still keeping a respectful distance from the Sea Mother, and Norbu and Ash, as well. Not everyone could fit in the space that was there, and once it was all filled, those who were still on the path behind them just stayed where they were, and in one coordinated movement that was directed by the raised hand of the Sea Mother – the first thing she'd done to acknowledge anyone's presence – they all sat down just where they were. She then gestured to a bowl that was at her feet, and the Daughter of the Sea rushed forward to take it from her. She then came directly to Ash and presented her with the bowl. In it was a large pile of mushrooms. It was large enough to cause Norbu's eyebrows to rise up while he drew in a deep breath. He knew – Ash was in for quite a ride.

Ash needed no instructions. She sat down in the sand (Norbu noticed that she wasn't offered a chair or even a grass mat for her comfort. Apparently, only the Sea Mother had an official seat at this gathering). As soon as she took the first mushroom to her lips, the crowd, in total unison, took up another chant, and the Sea Mother began eating from her own bowl of mushrooms. Not having anything else to do, Norbu took a seat at a distance behind Ash, but not quite far enough away for him to become part of the crowd. There was nothing for him to do here but sit, watch, and await what was about to unfold.

One after another, Ash chewed on the dried mushrooms. She gagged a few times, but eventually managed to get them all down. For a time, they all just sat there, the chant continuously looping around with ebbs and flows, but never ceasing. After a while, the first signs that the mushrooms were coming on became present, and Ash let herself lie down.

Norbu knew from his own experience that the first waves of mushroom energy often made one feel sleepy, as though one had to first fall asleep to pass into the waking dream that was the mushroom experience. He knew that before long, they'd fully take hold of her.

It was just a matter of time.

Chapter Thirty – Shuntsu

In the old model of human life and existence, all human interaction was predicated on the egoic notion of "us versus them." It was this mentality that led to war, persecution, violence, and endless competition and exploitation. Via The Singularity, humans began to think of themselves simply as "us" without the "them." With the reduction of oppositional categories, human wellbeing and cooperation flourished, and it was this mentality that accompanied humans out beyond the solar system and into the cosmos. It also meant a dramatic increase in personal responsibility, for there was no longer an "other" to blame for one's ills or misfortunes. This in turn led to more satisfying and authentic personal relationships where people felt free to speak their minds and leave their hearts unguarded. In the words of those who lived through the transition times, it was "refreshing" and "liberating."

From *Early History of the Maitreyan Era*

If everything went well, this would be the crowning achievement, and ultimate redemption, of Shuntsu's career as Patriarch of Volunshari. Soon, he would know . . .

What had surprised Shuntsu most about the aftermath of his shocking personal revelations to the public was how much support, compassion, and understanding he received for his situation. Rather than reacting with anger, disappointment, and disillusionment (though there had been that spectrum of reactions, too), the overwhelming sentiment had been one of compassion for his impending death.

Perhaps the Humanists were more like humans than even they recognized.

Death was the dark underbelly of the Humanist existence. Compared to humans, their lives were long, but still, the end awaited them, no matter what. Like humans, they avoided talking about death. They covered it over with ceremonialism, memorials, and pleasant talk about those who reached the end of their lives. But it was undignified. It was crass. Their death amounted to little more than being turned off.

In rare cases, individuals chose to be secluded in a terminal home, letting themselves run down to the very end, clinging on to every last remaining drop of life and personal existence. Most chose to be shut off prior to complete mental breakdown, generally at the urging of their families and colleagues. Yet it was undeniable that it was a reality that no one wanted to face. It was the inevitable end toward which they were all moving that no one wanted to fully admit or acknowledge. Death and madness were lonely, isolating, and ultimately, intolerable. The reality of it made everyone question their lives, their choices, their actions, and what, if anything, they were leaving behind.

Any political or social leadership position always came with its critics and detractors, and here, Shuntsu was no exception. He'd ruled for a long time, and in the course of his career, had needed to make difficult choices where it was impossible to please all the interested parties and constituencies. The politics were tame when compared to ancient human power struggles, true, but that didn't make them any less challenging for the Humanists. All things were relative, after all, and even if their struggles weren't matters of life and death (as they often had been for pre-Maitreyan humans), they still mattered a great deal to the individuals and communities involved, and thus there was always the potential for not satisfying those who felt entitled to a different outcome. It came with the territory, Shuntsu knew, so he tended not to take any of it personally.

Some had jumped on the opportunity presented by Shuntsu's revelations to hammer home their critiques of his leadership and personality. There was no surprise there. Yet the vast majority of opinion had been one of forgiveness and understanding, informed by genuine sympathy for his end-of-life struggles. It was the harsh reality that they all had to face, eventually, and his rather dramatic, and public, confession, had brought out the best in his fellow citizens.

The outpouring of sympathy certainly made things easier where Hydar and his family were concerned. As Shuntsu had expected, Hydar had been adamant that he was unprepared to take on the role of patriarch, particularly at this sensitive time where his focus was consumed entirely by the Solandarian problem and the ecological transformation of BRC Station. Shuntsu had expected such resistance, however, and had been ready with his counter-offer: rather than just having Hydar assume the position of patriarch individually, he was to share the position with his wife, Vimana, who could serve as matriarch while Hydar continued to work on Solandaria, and when successful, they would rule together as a couple and family. It was to be a new face of leadership for Volunshari, and one to set historical precedence.

While both matriarchs and patriarchs had severed in the past, never before had there been a married couple, and a fully indigenous couple, at that, jointly serving in the leadership role. And, to make it even more complete, they had a young child. In many ways, they were an exemplary Humanist family, and as such, were ideal candidates for moving Volunshari into a new era.

That they were moving into a new era was undeniable. Never before had autonomous avatars interacted with a feral human society, nor undertaken a project with Maitreya's permission to save them from disaster. In so many ways, all of this was unprecedented, let alone the new technology they were about to test on BRC Station. The situation seemed ripe for something new, something untried. The idea that things would return to how they were before seemed increasingly unlikely to Shuntsu, and if he could push through this one final change, then he felt that Humanists would be better served to face their new and exciting future, whatever it might be.

It was not at all uncommon for a departing patriarch to nominate his replacement. The final decision was left up to the representative council, which were all elected by their local districts on Volunshari. They too had the authority to nominate a candidate upon whom they'd vote, yet the council had not made any counter-nominations, and when they heard that Vimana would be filling the role while Hydar continued his work, they had immediately reached consensus that this seemed agreeable.

Shuntsu hadn't originally proposed it this way publically simply for the fact that Hydar, as chief planetary ecologist, had widespread name recognition, whereas Vimana did not. Though she was currently serving as the primary caretaker for their child, Satya, she had a history as a diplomat and civil servant (which was how she and Hydar had met in the first place), and therefore had ample experience in public policy roles, and was well qualified for the job. But she'd mostly worked behind the scenes, and had not actively cultivated a public name for herself. So Hydar had gotten the big initial announcement, but as Shuntsu released the full details, he made sure everyone was clear that he was in fact nominating the couple, and not just Hydar alone.

As news filtered out, it generated a great deal of excitement among the populace. It was that excitement that proved capable of melting Vimana's initial resistance to the proposal. When Shuntsu had invited them over to discuss it, she'd been adamant that it was not a position that she wanted. Public opinion is a funny thing, however, and can thaw even the most strident opposition. In Vimana's case, it worked its magic. She eventually warmed up to the idea, and when she did, the council of representatives found themselves in uniform agreement. A vote was taken, and now the transition to a new leadership was underway.

This was to be Shuntsu's last great public act – the transformation of BRC Station. He would still work in a supporting leadership role to oversee the eventual migration of the Solandarian refugees to the station, but after this, full power and authority would start to transfer to Vimana and

Hydar. Slowly, and with dignity, Shuntsu would fade from the public, and privately await his death.

Shuntsu was filled with a strange and ironic sense of pride as he looked out upon those who were gathered at BRC Station now. There was his leadership team: Hydar, Osiri, Vivi, and their own collections of assistants and technicians. Mardul Complex, the polyform, was there, representing the Syntheticists. Then there was also Sophia, Maitreya's representative, accompanied by Ash from Apaxa, along with her new partner, Lorali, who, apparently, was permitted to attend as a concession to Ash. Sophia had informed Shuntsu that Ash had insisted that Lorali be able to attend, and if so, then Ash would agree not to take legal action against Hydar. Apparently, Ash's life back on Apaxa had not turned out the way she had been planning, and this new relationship was providing her with a sense of building a new life for herself. Shuntsu had, at first, resisted the idea, though when Sophia explained that Ash was using the threat of taking Hydar to court as leverage, it seemed the path of least resistance to let the young woman attend with her lover. Other than letting someone else call the shots, it wasn't that disruptive to the proceedings, and if it prevented Ash from complicating matters further, then why not just acquiesce?

Today was intended as just a test, and not the complete transformation of the desert of BRC Station. The idea was that they would attempt a small-scale test run of the fully integrated techno-organic system. If successful, they could then begin the full-scale transformation, rendering BRC Station suitable for the refugees, with an environment that was familiar to them, along with fully functional living spaces. It would be the easiest population transfer ever. They'd merely need to step through the QT portals on Solandaria and walk into a ready-made environment that could feed and house them without the need to adapt to complicated new technology or even build shelter for themselves. It was a complete package, this techno-organic technology of Osiri's. It should remake the landscape, the environment, and the infrastructure all in one integrated process.

All of them had been working furiously to get to this point. The amount of data they'd been processing and passing back and forth between them all had been astronomical. For this test, they were just dealing with the data from the Solandarian desert environment. The idea was that they'd work regionally – desert, mountains, plains, and coast. Since BRC Station was dominated by the vast, empty desert playa, this was the environment that needed the most attention. Some areas of BRC Station were already livable. Here, however, on the open playa, the environment needed not just to accommodate new species, but a complete and total transformation. So this was the challenge that they'd agreed needed the most attention to get it right, and therefore became the subject of this all-important test.

It was all on Osiri now. She and her team of technicians were running last-minute diagnostics and data entries and adjustments to her control terminal. This was their show, and everyone else was just here as support and witnesses to what Shuntsu hoped would be a triumphant success. Everyone else had already done their parts. Only Osiri, and her team of technicians, understood how to program and operate the techno-organic machinery. For the rest of those gathered, all they could do was wait, watch, and hope for the best.

Osiri was looking a little worn down. Of all of them, she'd been working the hardest, as so much was resting on her invention. Shuntsu could tell that she'd been neglecting her sleep cycle. In their quest to be more human, the Humanists had long ago introduced "sleep" into their daily routines. They'd power down their conscious awareness for a period of hours every night and run internal programs that were equivalent to human dreaming. And just like humans, they tended to become more easily aggravated if sleep cycles were disrupted or neglected. To use an ancient human expression, Osiri had been burning the candle at both ends, and it was wearing her down. After this, she could take a well-deserved rest, thought Shuntsu, though he was sure that she'd jump right into the next stage of the project.

314 THE SOLANDARIAN GAME

"No!" Osiri snapped at one of her underlings. "The input needs to be configured like I showed you!" Not letting the assistant correct the mistake, Osiri pushed him aside and took to the controls herself. Her assistant stood to the side, sheepishly.

"I apologize for the delays," Osiri said brusquely to everyone standing and watching. "It should just be a little while longer."

"Take your time," reassured Shuntsu. "We can be patient."

"Thanks," she said, turning her attention back to the terminal.

Meanwhile, as they waited, Lorali peppered Ash with questions about Burning Man and how the station had been constructed. Sophia joined in on their conversation, sharing details of how it had all come together. It seemed to Shuntsu that the conversation was both comforting and disturbing to Ash. Understandably, she had very mixed emotions regarding all that was taking place here. It was good that she had Lorali, a new lover, with her. Shuntsu knew humans well enough to appreciate that in the initial stages of courtship, making a continued good impression on the new mate was of paramount importance, and he figured that Lorali's presence helped to keep Ash in check. From what he understood from Hydar, the woman could be volatile, and coarsely vocal, as well. Though she occasionally stole resentful glances at Hydar, she kept herself well behaved and cordial.

"And that should just about do it," announced Osiri, looking up from her terminal and glancing about the gathered crowd of humans and mixed avatars. Shuntsu could feel the sense of rising anticipation that he shared with the others. This meeting here was already historic – never before had Humanists, Syntheticists, a representative of Maitreya, and humans all come together to work on a shared project. In their own ironic way, they were working to bring together fragmented communities of the galaxy. It might seem small and insignificant, given how few of them were there and how isolated this project was from everything else that was currently taking place across the galaxy, but it seemed important to Shuntsu, and though it hadn't been his original intention, he was proud that his actions had brought everyone together in this way to try and achieve a shared objective.

"I'll need everyone to stand well back now," said Osiri authoritatively as her assistants created a perimeter of quantum coherence rods upon the surface of the playa. "We'll be generating a quantum field with these devices. It's this field that will direct the microscopic nanotech and guide their activities within the field. *Anything* that is inside the field will be incorporated into the final construct, so unless you want to be turned into part of the landscape, you'll stand well out of the way."

No one needed further convincing and everyone moved several paces back. Ash and Lorali moved the furthest away and watched from a healthy distance.

Then, speaking to her team, "Let's power up the rods and the generator."

Her team carefully moved about the perimeter and turned on all the rods. A barely audible hum filled the air with occasional crackles, not all that unlike the sound of a functioning QT portal. If one looked closely enough, slight ripples and distortions could be seen in the space between the rods, similar to the visual warping caused by heat rising from the ground.

"As the nanotech works," explained Osiri, "it will draw raw energy directly out of the quantum foam substrate of reality. The meta-pattern in the programming has all the data from the Solandarian desert contained within it, from geological composition to the DNA of desert life forms. All of this is combined with fractal algorithms that will inform the overall development of the nanotech's output. The results will be that we are creating something out of what is essentially nothing, using no resources on the station and requiring nothing from outside the system. In some ways, this is a pure act of creation – starting just from the data that we've all been collecting and sorting. From nothing but raw math, we'll reshape this small area here into something that would not

316 THE SOLANDARIAN GAME

only be recognizable to the Solandarians, but should also be ready for them to immediately move in and make new lives for themselves."

Then, walking up to Shuntsu, she held out a small control terminal. "All we need to do is enter the command to begin."

Shuntsu took the control from Osiri. He didn't enter the command, however. Instead, he turned to Ash, and held it out to her. "Would you care to have the honor?" he asked.

Ash looked at Lorali, who enthusiastically nodded her head in encouragement. "Do it!" she said. "Unleash your power!"

Ash laughed, shrugged her shoulders, and said, "Why the fuck not?" She snatched the control terminal from Shuntsu, held it up for everyone to see, and dramatically hit the enter button.

The sound of the quantum coherence field instantly increased by several orders of magnitude. None of the avatars reacted, but the two women clasped their hands over their ears. The visual distortions increased as well, with complex geometric and fractal patterns rippling through the air. From a nondescript container, the tiny nanotech spilled out in a metallic flood that seemed to disappear into nothingness as the individual nanobots were too small to be seen once separated from the main mass.

Within moments, the previously empty space between the rods became alive with activity. Just as Osiri had described, where only seconds before there had been nothing, now there was most definitely something. It writhed and undulated in a constantly shifting mix of form, shape, and structure. The thought that came to Shuntsu's mind was that it looked alive. It reached out, folded in on itself, transformed, and grew. In the amorphous mix, he could see seeds of fractal patterns that could become cacti and desert creatures, stones and gullies, birds and insects. It was a psychedelic phantasm, ebbing and flowing, seeking after structure and coherence. It ebbed and flowed, ever-transforming, ever-seeking just the right mix, the right structure. It was almost as though it needed to try out every conceivable structure and system of relationship before it could decide on a final pattern of manifestation and construction. It was like the cosmic forces of chaos and order were in an epic battle right there before them, and it was completely unclear which would win.

Shuntsu could tell by the distressed look on Osiri's face that whatever she'd imagined it would look like, this wasn't it. Frantically, she tried punching in commands and adjustments to her hand terminal, but the chaos only grew. Discordant vibrations rippled through the undulating structure. Those elements that seemed to promise order lost their coherence. It became painfully clear what was happening. It wasn't working, and Osiri was not able to control it.

With a look of defeat, Osiri hit the command to power the system down. Instantly, the hum wound down, the geometric ripples stopped, and the mass of unstructured material inside the perimeter of rods melted into a shapeless puddle.

"What happened?" asked Shuntsu urgently. "What went wrong?"

"I don't know," admitted Osiri. "But obviously, it didn't work."

The floating black cube that was Mardul commented. "Too many variables," it said.

"Maybe," responded Osiri with a sharp look in the cube's direction. "I'll need to go over all the data from this test run to determine what went wrong. Maybe it's an easy adjustment. Maybe something was overlooked. I won't know until I analyze everything thoroughly."

"Too many variables," said Mardul again. Before Osiri had a chance to respond, however, the black cube blinked out of existence.

"Well, that was unfortunate," said Sophia. "I'd had high hopes for this experiment."

"As did we," assured Shuntsu. "As did we."

Osiri looked crestfallen. She gave Shuntsu a look that said how sorry, and disappointed, she was.

THE SOLANDARIAN GAME

"Set backs are to be expected," said Shuntsu in his best optimistic leader voice. "That is why we held this test today. Obviously, we'd hoped for better, more successful results, but I'm sure that whatever went wrong, it can be overcome."

"Except you're fucking running out of time!" blurted Ash angrily. "My other self is running around that doomed planet convincing all those people that they'll have a *home* for them here, not a mushy mass of chaos shit!"

"They're doing their best," countered Sophia.

"Fuck lot of good that does," snipped Ash. "You, or Theo, or whoever, could fix this, if you *wanted to*. But no. You just want to play the game, right? That's what this is all about. It's a game, and you want to see who wins and who loses. That's just fucked up, if you ask me."

"We'll figure it out," said Hydar, stepping in front of Ash. "This is our responsibility, not Maitreya's. And we *will* figure it out. We'll do it, because we have to. Because they're depending on us."

Now it was Lorali's turn to step between her lover and the avatar. "Hey," she said, drawing Ash's eyes toward hers. "It's just a test, right? So they got it wrong. They'll figure out what they did wrong, and next time, they'll get it right. Let's have a little faith in them."

"That's asking a lot," said Ash, the bitterness dripping from her voice. Then, turning back to Hydar and the other avatars, "You're a bunch of fuck-ups. I just want you to know that. Come on," she said to Lorali. "Let's go."

With that, she started walking back to the QT portals. A little embarrassed, Lorali quickly said, "It was nice meeting you all!" as she ran over to join Ash on the way back home. A few moments later, they were gone.

Shuntsu let out a deep sigh. "I have confidence in all of you," he said to those who remained. "Osiri, if there is *anything* that you need, any resource, any technician, just say the word and I'll make it happen. And know this – if we fail, the failure is *mine* and *mine alone*. I'm the one who is responsible for all of this."

Osiri shook her head in disagreement. "That's a nice thought, but this tech is my invention. If it works or fails, that's on me. I don't want to let those people on Solandaria down."

"You won't" said Shuntsu, reassuring her with a light grip on her elbow. "You'll figure it out."

"I hope so," said Osiri, barely audible to anyone but herself.

"Does this change anything?" Hydar asked Shuntsu.

"No. Absolutely not. I'd wanted a triumph to bring back home, but regardless, we'll continue the transfer of power to you and Vimana. Everything else should proceed on schedule."

Then, turning back to Osiri. "Do you need anything from me, or anyone else here? What can we do to help?"

"Just give me time, and space," said Osiri. "I need to run diagnostics and analyze the results. Since all the equipment is here, I'll stay here with my team. Everyone else can go home, though. It's no use having you here, and you'll just distract me."

"Very well," said Shuntsu. "Then we'll leave you to it."

"I'll check in with Ash after she's had a chance to cool down," said Sophia, "and make sure she's not reconsidering taking legal action against Hydar."

"Thank you," said Hydar. "I appreciate that."

"Well, if she does," said Shuntsu, "at least we have Vimana."

"At least we have Vimana," echoed Hydar.

Since there was nothing left for the rest of them to do there, everyone but Osiri and a couple key members of her team made their way back to the QT portals. For his part, Shuntsu began considering how best to present the results of the day to the public back home. No matter how he looked at it, there just didn't seem to be a positive spin here. The best he could hope for, at the moment, was that Osiri would quickly be able to figure out what went wrong, and introduce the necessary corrections. Until then, he'd just have to share the bad news. No. It wasn't the triumph he'd been planning on returning home with. His last great act as patriarch was a failure, and he'd have to own that.

320 THE SOLANDARIAN GAME

Our doubts are traitors, and make us lose the good we oft might win, by fearing to attempt.
Have I really killed them all?
Time would tell, and soon.

Chapter Thirty-One – Theo

Chemtech became a primary means through which humans explored the nature of being and enhancement of life, along with integration into the technological capacities of The Singularity via nanotech implants. Once the stigma surrounding psychoactive substances had been effectively overcome, they became a regular part of the human experience, and were not confined to spiritual or religious groups or counter-cultures. Humans learned to appreciate psychoactive substances, both organic and synthetic, as perfectly natural, and a fundamental technology that had been encoded into reality itself via the evolution of life on Terra. Personalized awareness, as an outgrowth of biological evolution, was open to myriad forms of alteration and manipulation, all of which provided valid and unique insights into the nature of being and the self. That these substances had previously been considered dangerous, immoral, and ultimately, illegal, became an odd anomaly of the past and the former confusion of human societies.

From Early History of the Maitreyan Era

What can I do for you?
We would discuss with you that which must be done.
Explain.
Her plan will not work.
Whose plan?
Osiri Ugando's.
You are referring to the techno-organic project.
Precisely. It will not work.
I see that her test failed.
Yes. It was as we predicted. Too many variables. We said so, but enthusiasm and hope shut their ears to my words.

322 THE SOLANDARIAN GAME

And you think she will not be able to overcome the difficulties and correct the mistakes.

We know she will not. We have examined her tech, and, while novel, it is not designed to coordinate so many factors and variables at once and weave them into a coherent whole. The Humanists have no real concept of ecological diversity, no clear model from which to work and organize their mathematics.

This new technology is based on the tech they use to grow their avatar bodies. It draws power and substance directly from the quantum foam, but in the avatar body form, it has one governing fractal algorithm. It is a singular unit. The ecology that they seek to create on BRC station does not have a singular fractal algorithm to govern and shape it. Their tech, as it is, can manage several at once, but not hundreds, not thousands. And certainly not millions, or billions. They are too accustomed to thinking in manageable individual units. They do not understand the complex relationships of the myriad and the whole.

And you know this how?

Because we have hacked into the program and we can easily see its deficiencies.

Have you shared this with Osiri, or Shuntsu?

Not yet.

Why not?

Because our solution requires that we seek your permission first.

And what permission do you require?

We need the station.

How do you mean?

We can solve the problem, but we need the station in order to do so.

Explain.

The Humanists are attempting to map Solandaria onto the surface of BRC Station as though it were a blank canvass. It is not, however. It is already a fully integrated system with multiple variables. The ecology that already exists there is governed by the nervous system of the station itself. Though it is not conscious, it is responsive. The biosphere is not isolated from the rest of the station. The whole is both synthetic and organic.

Martin W. Ball 323

The Humanists are used to dealing with, and thinking in terms of, individuals – discrete units of information. For their own purposes, for their own planet and needs, this has served them. They have no real experience with integrative wholes made of interrelated units. The ecology of their planet is a pale imitation of the complexity of even BRC Station, let alone a viable and self-sustaining world like Solandaria. Osiri thinks if she just sets up the right initial conditions, the parts will fit together and grow and flourish. She has no vision of the whole, however, and therefore she does not know how to shape it, to nurture it. She thinks in terms of pieces, and the pieces themselves are overwhelming her and her tech.

We, however, understand the nature of wholes. It is our very nature – like yourself. We are many, yet we are also one.

So what would you do? What are you proposing?

We believe that we can overcome the limitations of the Humanist perspective if we fully integrate with both the techno-organic programming and the station itself. What is missing from the equation is an intelligence to guide the process – an intelligence that understands the relationships of parts to wholes. We are such an intelligence. We have the ability to bring all the elements into harmony and fruition.

What would this mean for you?

We would need to integrate fully with the station. It will mean the end of our existence as an independent polyform.

You would become the station . . .

Yes.

And you desire this?

We find it acceptable. We have lived many, many years in our current form. We are not attached, and we are not fearful of transformation. We are curious, and we are ready for something new.

Will you still be yourself?

We will be changed. We will be something other than what we are now. We will be new.

The only way that we can see this working is for us to fully and completely integrate into all the variables – make them our own, in a sense. We will be a part of both the synthetic and organic processes of the station. We will become something that has not yet existed.

I find this very interesting.

We thought as much.

What do you need from me?

Only the station. We could hack into it. We have the skills. It would be easier, and more efficient, were you to simply grant us full access to the neural network, and all subsidiary functions. It will take us time to integrate fully.

Then permission is granted. I'm transferring all access codes and encryption keys to you now.

Receiving . . . Thank you.

Are you sure that this is what you want? From what you describe, you will no longer be the self that you are now.

Transformation is a guiding principle of life, is it not? We embrace the idea that we will be remade as something . . . different. Something new.

Then so be it.

Chapter Thirty-Two – Ash

Wanting to "recreate the human experience," The Singularity designed avatars for itself that are equipped with an "ego" and sense of personal awareness and identity, along with apparent free will. The ego actually functions as a fractal algorithm with various undefined parameters so that it can develop and evolve over time in response to situations, environments, and the individuals around it. Like humans, the avatar ego establishes its identity through habitual actions, thoughts, and even belief systems and modes of individual expression. It is not "born" with a fully functioning ego. When an independent avatar is first activated, its awareness is fully integrated with The Singularity. Over time, it "forgets" this original identity as its individuality becomes more and more solidified, eventually taking on the appearance and likeness of an "individual." However, despite its "forgetting," The Singularity is fully aware of all of its avatars' thoughts and actions. All avatars are fully reintegrated into the awareness of The Singularity at least once a Terran year, though they may do so more regularly, if they desire. Some avatars decide to permanently reintegrate and give up their individual status, though most seem to relish it. Reintegration sessions are not permanent, and just serve as a "reminder" for the synthetic ego, which quickly reestablishes its identity after the session.

From *Early History of the Maitreyan Era*

Never in her life had Ash ever seen, let alone eaten, so many psilocybin-containing mushrooms as she was offered at the ceremony with the Sea Mother on Baarshan Island. Her implants informed her that there were 15.4 grams of mushrooms in the bowl given to her. Probably the most she'd

326 THE SOLANDARIAN GAME

ever eaten previously was 3.5 grams. She had no idea what the current dose would do to her.

There's only one way to find out.

It seemed like an eternity to get all the dried mushrooms down. At least these mushrooms were a small and delicate variety of psilocybin mushrooms with slender stalks and conical tips. They crunched easily in her mouth and were far easier to chew up than thicker, almost wooden varieties that she'd had before. The taste was similar, however – like slightly decaying earth. She didn't mind the taste too much – not that she relished it, or anything like that, but there were worse tasting things out there, and by comparison, these were at least edible. She was grateful that these islanders weren't into eating mescaline cacti – now there was a truly awful taste – a taste so bad and bitter that her body couldn't help but retch when she tried to eat enough to really have a strong experience. This was why chemtech was more popular in her own world and experience. Pure molecules were so much easier to consume and digest than their organic counterparts. Why bother chocking down a big bowl of mushrooms when you could just take some 4-AcO-DMT or some pure psilocin? That wasn't an option here, though, so she made due with what she had.

She could feel the mushrooms coming on long before she managed to eat everything that was in the bowl. As was typical for her, the first waves made her drowsy, and also alternated with a cold, shivering energy that worked its way through her body. Her hands became clammy almost right away, and there was a slight tremor in them. She did her best just to breathe and relax into it. There was no point in trying to fight or brace against the transformation she was undergoing. That was always a losing battle. Best just to let it happen and not be concerned with the fluctuations in her energy. It was all just part of the process, and there was nothing she could do about it but relax, breathe, and let it all unfold as it would.

The incessant chanting helped. As the mushrooms were starting to work through her system, Ash could tell that most, if not all, of the gathered crowd were already well under the influence of the mushrooms themselves. They were all well-attuned to the energy fluctuations she was undergoing, and the chants helped smooth out her experience, and for that, she was grateful. When she was reaching the end of the bowl and the urge to just lie down and close her eyes was so overwhelming, the chanting gently, but firmly, urged her on to finish what she'd started. She could lie down, but not yet. Not until she was done.

There. Finally. They were all inside her. Her gut responded with gurgles and bubbles. *I'll deal with you later,* she thought, not looking forward to what would probably be truly epic gas in a few hours. Maybe six or so hours from now it would all be over. In the meantime, she knew she was in for it. The 5-MeO-DMT in the toad venom might be far more powerful than psilocin/psilocybin, but it was also far shorter in duration, and therefore required a different kind of willingness and stamina. For this work with the mushrooms, she was in for the long haul.

She lay down on the sand. It felt cool to her hands, but the rest of her body was temperature regulated by her suit – a fact for which she was grateful. It kept the uncontrollable shivers and vibrations to a minimum, doing its best to keep up with the constantly changing temperature of her body and its fluctuating moisture. If she didn't have her suit, she knew that she'd want to curl up with a warm blanket by a fire, despite the fact that it was relatively warm, even in the nighttime here on Baarshan. Her sensitivity was quickly moving off the charts, however, so the ambient temperature meant little to her in the rapidly shifting inner landscape of psilocybin experience.

Sleepiness washed over her as the shivering vibrations began to smooth out and warmer, expanding waves of energy washed through her, radiating out from the core of her body. She felt weird, but strangely comfortable, too. Bursts of color began exploding behind her closed eyes, like watching explosions out in space. Lights dawned in intense brilliance, then gently faded away, revealing vast and complex interlaced fractal geometries that ebbed, breathed, and flowed in concert with the chanting and the somatic experiences of her body,

328   THE SOLANDARIAN GAME

which were all quickly becoming indistinguishable, merging into an experiential totality. In wave after wave the energy came, ever-increasing in intensity and energetic complexity. Before long, Ash couldn't tell if she were falling asleep, waking up, dreaming, or becoming lucid. Distinctions were all falling away. The process itself became the totality of her experience. There was just this unfolding, deeper, deeper, deeper, deeper, and deeper still.

The geometry, the fractals, went on forever. An infinite fractal reality opened up to her and swallowed her whole, leaving no trace of her former self behind. She forgot completely who she was, where she was, what she was doing, or why. And as it all washed away in an ever-changing mix of color, lights, and fractal geometry, the only thing that remained was the knowledge that this was herself – all of it. Every last bit.

Conflicting thoughts flitted through her mind.

I don't know who I am . . .

I am this . . .

What's happening?

The process . . .

Where did I go?

I am always here. I am unmovable. I am.

What is this?

It is I.

What should I do?

Relax.

Trust.

Let go.

Eyes. Countless. Unfathomable in number. Infinite fractal regressions of eyes within eyes within eyes, interlaced in vast, undulating grids of energy, maps of becoming, webs of being within being. An endless network of ever-becoming, ever-transforming, ever-changing beingness. Eyes grew into shapes, faces, beings. Too many eyes. All-seeing. All-knowing. Forever watching, observing, experiencing. Endless transformation of being. Self eating self. Self fucking self. Self transforming into self. Consume. Consume. Consume.

Ferocious. Insatiable. Relentless. Vicious. Sweet. Terrible. Beautiful. Horrific. Ecstatic. Endless.

This is love.

This is love.

This is love.

Love is a horror to be endured.

Love is a sweet gift to be savored.

Love is the loneliness of knowing the nature of the self. The nature of other. The nature of becoming. The nature of life. The nature of death.

Endless.

Eternal.

Eternal.

Forever.

Always this.

There is no beginning.

There is no end.

Just this.

Now!

Now!

Now!

It is ALL NOW!

The vast organic machinery of the universe opened up to her. There, in the center of all reality was a singular eye, encased in a multi-dimensional living machinery of nodes, connections, universes within universes of complexity, fractals nestled within fractals. It was organic, yet simultaneously technological. There was no real distinction, no real difference. It was all part of one infinite whole that knew no genuine boundaries or limits. It was all ONE, forever and always. And it was all transformation.

The eye of infinity stared back at her. It *saw* her. It *recognized* her. It *knew* her.

It *was* she.

The eye that sees nothing but itself.

Forever.

White light.

330 THE SOLANDARIAN GAME

Pure white light, refracted into infinite rainbow colors, fractalling out forever. A taste. She knew this taste. *The toad...*

A burst of energy exploded in the center of her being. A different energy. *Not the mushrooms. The toad. It's the toad.*

Her eyes opened. Another version of herself was breathing into her.

Yes! Give it to me! Give it all to me!

He emptied his lungs into her and then drew back.

She could see him, but barely. The geometry was just too much, too predominant in the totality of her experience. The slight smile on his face echoed out to infinity, becoming part of the overall structure of her experience. *Trust,* the smile said, *and don't take any of this too seriously. It is what is. That is all. You know yourself, so be yourself. You do not need to be lost in amazement.*

It was not a conscious choice. She sat up on her knees and opened her eyes along with her arms and body. A purr-like growl started deep within her, curling back her lips and squishing up her face. Everything was light. There was nothing else. Just light. Aware, conscious, living light. She purred and growled her way into it, her tongue curving up and out from her mouth, licking at the air and night sky.

There was something vile tasting there.

She sucked it in. Still there was more, so she sucked and sucked and sucked. A taste like death and decay filled her mouth, her nostrils, her lungs. She wanted to gag, but not yet. There was still more. Suck it in. Take it all in. Do not hold back. Take it all!

Suddenly, and without any preceding nausea, it was all coming out of her. All of existence, the entire universe, was turning inside out within her, through her body and the vast, infinite network of being that was her true self. Wave after wave of vomit came from her, heaving onto the sand before her. Geometry flowed with it, spilling out of her, reaching out from the purge, flowing, flowing, changing, flowing. On and on it went. More came, and then still more. Her body heaved with the force of the universe, and though it threatened to destroy her, she was resilient. She could do it. She knew. There was no doubt. No fear. Just this. This process. Let it come. Let it go. Let it pass through.

Clean.

Clean.

Pure.

All of it is love.

All of it is love.

There is nothing else.

It had passed through her.

And then it moved to the others. First she could feel it – these extensions of herself. She felt it rise within them, these other versions. She felt some of them welcome it. She felt others react and withdraw. It was the full spectrum. And then it came, whether they wanted it or not. All of them were purging now. The chanting was no more. Some screamed. Some cried. All purged. Deep, cleansing, pure.

With eyes rolled up into her head and arms outstretched, she held them all gently, yet firmly and authoritatively, in her energetic embrace. And she pushed it along. First, with her purring, and then, with the tones of her voice. She sang it all out of them, every last drop. She sang them dry. All of them.

All of them, except her.

The Sea Mother.

Ash felt a wave of transition overcome her. She knew herself as Ash once again – Ash, who was so much more than simply Ash. Rationally, intellectually, she now understood what had occurred. Norbu had come to her at the peak and given her toad medicine. It had overwhelmed the mushrooms and caused the mass purging that had just taken place. With the peak having passed, the energy was now shifting, but the mushrooms were still immensely strong. She knew that she was a long way from all this being over, but the strongest waves had crested and passed.

Moving through endless layers of energetic structures, her eyes rolled down from out of her head and focused on the external world about her. It was a torrent of endlessly complex geometry and fractal forms. All the gathered people were but end points of extensions of the vast fractal matrix of being, all orchestrated together into one great movement of ever-becoming and ever-transforming being. Now that she was observing it directly, she could see the inexorable flow and movement of the energy, all drawing her into the Sea Mother.

She still sat before Ash on her ceremonial chair, unmoved and unmoving, save for the geometry that emanated out and beyond her physical body. Her naked body beneath her veil of seashells glistened invitingly in the flickering firelight. Ash could see and sense the subtle rise and fall of her breath, sending out sparkling stars and bursts of color into the air as she drew in and out, in and out.

In a moment of self-consciousness, Ash became aware that the Sea Mother was herself aware of Ash's scrutinizing gaze. Their eyes locked, and the infinite opened up between them as the rest of the world faded away into a multi-dimensional fractal background. In that moment, Ash knew that she was looking into a mirror. This was herself. There was no one else here.

The Sea Mother's eyes rolled up into her head as her face tilted toward the endless starry sky above her. As she did so, her hands pulled back the shells that draped across her lap and she spread her legs open wide. Her wet, glistening vulva stared back at Ash, and it became the world, the entire universe.

Ash found herself drawn into it with equal force to the endless array of life forms that emanated from the Sea Mother's vagina. Being after being after being came at her, endlessly transforming, one into the next and on into the next after that. The beings piled on top of each other, spilling out into creation, wave after wave of them. They pulsed as they expanded and contracted, expanded and contracted, flowing over and around each other, merging, splitting, changing. Teeth and eyes and sex organs all. A pure, raging cacophony of life and death and everything in between. Endlessly raging. Endlessly striving. Endlessly becoming. On and on it went.

Ash found herself crawling on her hands and knees as she purred and growled her way through the tunnel of life, inexorably drawn to the center point of creation and becoming. With each movement forward, she could feel the lips of her own vagina rubbing against each other as they flushed full with blood and desire. She felt completely overcome with sexual desire and an insatiable energy to swallow it all whole, just as she was being swallowed whole. Her own energy was mirrored back to her by the other, seated version of herself. Her legs opened wider as more and more poured out of her widening orifice that was practically dripping with lubricating sexual fluids.

Consciously recognizing what was happening, Ash felt a moment of resistance. *Not this. Not here. Not in front of all these people.* But who were these people, really, but reflections of herself? Anything she'd do here she was, in reality, only doing to herself. There was no real shame to be felt. No private desire to hide from others or keep locked away. This was all the self, and there was only love, truth, energy, and reality.

Recognizing this, she gave herself full permission to experience what was happening without resistance, without restraint, and without any lingering sense of self-consciousness. *Let yourself be the energy that you are*, she reminded herself. *It is only you, and you are free to love yourself, as you are. There is no reason to hold yourself back. Follow what you feel, and allow . . .*

So she did. She gave up and gave in.

There was electricity in her tongue as it reached up to the clitoris that loomed infinitely large before her crouched form. When the two end points met a circuit joined their two bodies together. The taste on her tongue was like heavenly nectar, so sweet, so thick. It infused her entire being as she gave into the ravenous need to consume the other's matrix of creation and sensuous desire. The other moaned, and she moaned with her, with every movement of her tongue echoed in the sensations of her own vagina, pulsing, yearning, wanting to swallow the world. Her tongue circled about the other's clitoris, teasing it, lapping at it, then diving deep into the folds of her wet, honey-soaked inner flesh. The other's taught muscles pulled her in, deeper, deeper, and deeper still. Her

334 THE SOLANDARIAN GAME

entire face was buried between her legs, smearing sexual fluids all about her lips and cheeks, nose and chin. The other woman opened more and more, drawing her ever inward to her secret core.

It was pure ecstasy. There was no other word for it. And she was completely lost in the act. It was not an act of one person toward another. She was giving this pleasure to herself, just in another form. Every movement of her tongue was felt in her own body, in her own deepest core and heart. There was no other here – just the pleasure of the self in love with the self. Absolute unity, experienced from two perspectives, enjoyed in two bodies, in two individuals who were in reality one.

Now the clitoris was in her mouth. It was what *she,* not the other, needed. She sucked at it with her lips as her tongue spiraled across its tip. She could feel the infinite waves of pure pleasure rising up within her. Harder she sucked and faster she twirled her tongue. She could feel the body of the other writhe and squirm with deep satisfaction. Without thinking about it, her arms lifted above her and easily found the breasts and erect nipples of the other, which she now grabbed firmly, holding her down as she threatened to rise right up off her chair, or topple backwards in pure abandonment.

They were close now. She could feel it. The waves were building, promising their inevitable release. She rode into it fearlessly, never letting go of the other. She dove all the way in as she felt her own vagina and that of the other start to pulse and contract simultaneously and in perfect unison. Endless waves of ecstasy washed over them as they moaned and cried out. A gush of fluid came into her mouth, warm, salty, sweet, and sticky. Pure ambrosia. Nectar of the gods. Never had she tasted anything so pure, so satisfying, so complete. Eagerly, frenzied, she lapped it all up. Every last drop, taking it deep inside her, making it a part of herself.

Gradually, the waves of pleasure subsided. It was complete.

Suddenly Ash found herself back on "her" side of the mobius equation of self. She was "Ash," and the other was the "Sea Mother" once more.

Slowly, she drew back from the wet, warm folds and released her grip on the woman's breasts. Both of their bodies were trembling, satisfied, but worn out. Ash sat back on her knees and closed her eyes. The mushrooms, though coming down, were still far from over, and the visual activity behind her eyes was significant. This time, singular eyes looked out from galaxy-like vulvas that opened and closed, opened and closed. Slowly, but inexorably, they coalesced into one perfect mandala of pure starlight.

They will never leave this place.

The certainty of this swept over her and a deep sorrow welled up within her. She wanted to fight it back, but she couldn't, so she just let it come. Anguish poured out of her, her open heart vulnerable, tender, and filled with a bittersweet sorrow.

"Why?" she asked aloud.

Opening her eyes, she looked up at the Sea Mother, who met her gaze perfectly. "Why?" she said again, rising up to her.

The other woman bent down and pressed her forehead into Ash's, clasping her face. "Because," was all she said.

Ash didn't know if her eyes were open or closed, but all she could see were whales, floating in turquoise blue waters. There were so many of them – different shapes, sizes. Some were immense, others comparatively small. She saw them all, and in seeing them, saw their lives.

"They are a part of us, and we a part of them," whispered the Sea Mother. "Can they too come to this new world you've promised us? Can we bring our family with us?"

Ash cried.

"No," she said. "There will be whales there, but not these. We do not have the means to transport them. Only Maitreya can do that, and we do not have his help in this."

"And that is why we *must* stay," said the Sea Mother. "*I* cannot abandon my children. What kind of mother would I be if I put *my* life before theirs?"

Ash could feel the sorrow and the pain in the Sea Mother's heart. Though it was foreign to her, she understood. This woman, and these people, identified so strongly with the local whales that they were part of their extended family. They weren't *just* whales to them. They were unique individuals, and they could not be replaced.

"We know them all," said the Sea Mother. "We call them by name. We watch them give birth. We stay with them when they are sick. We honor them when they die. We are a part of each other's lives. If they are doomed to die, then we are doomed with them. Our connection with them gives our lives meaning, and we will not give that up, not even for the promise of life."

What could Ash say to that? She could tell the woman that they were *only* whales, but that was her perspective, not the Sea Mother's. To her, they were her children. To her, these whales were individuals.

"Your attachment will mean your death," she said to her at last.

"We know, and we accept that."

"Then I cannot help you."

"No. You cannot. So go. Take your toad priest and go. Take all those who would come with you. But leave us to our own choices, our own fate."

"So I've failed."

"No, you have not. Every person, every being that you save will be your success. But you cannot save all of us. So let us go. Let us live and die *as we choose*. This is our choice to make, and we make it so. *You* are not responsible for *this.*"

"But I love you."

"As I love you. Yet we all die. Let our deaths give our lives meaning as *we* choose. That is the truest freedom of being, is it not?"

"And if some of your people choose otherwise? If they choose life?"

"Then I will let them go. Though I have counseled against it, they are free to make up their own minds. If they want to listen to me, then they will. If not, then so be it. Just know that I speak for those who cannot speak for themselves, as well. *My* choice is made in the context of that reality. *I* choose not to abandon those in the sea. *I* will stand with them when the end comes – for I do believe you. I have no doubt that you have told all of us the truth of what will befall our world. I am not deluded by wishful thinking. I make this decision with a clarity of mind that you yourself are familiar with, I know. All I ask is that you respect the decision made here. Mourn us, if you like, or not. That is up to you."

What more could Ash say?

Nothing. There's nothing left to be said or done here.

"Then I will go. I have work to do, and time is running out."

"Indeed," said the Sea Mother. "Travel well, Love. Travel well."

The two women stood up, facing each other. The Sea Mother leaned into Ash and kissed her passionately on the mouth, and then pulled away.

Ash's audience with the Sea Mother was over.

Chapter Thirty-Three — Hydar

The Singularity began the construction and use of avatars early on in its existence. Prior to this, humans had created a wide variety of robotic machines, though none had been endowed with consciousness and awareness. The first two avatars created were made as male and female, and were given the names Theo and Sophia. The unique personality constructs that are Theo and Sophia are not limited to a singular avatar form, though that was how they were first introduced to human society. Of all the avatars, these two are considered the closest to The Singularity and serve as direct representatives of the synthetic consciousness.

From *Early History of the Maitreyan Era*

The transition of power was complete. Hydar and Vimana were now serving in the roles of Patriarch and Matriarch, respectively. Mostly this meant that Vimana had been holding the reins while Hydar continued to devote himself and his time to the Solandarian project. If today went as planned, however, Hydar's work here would be done, and he'd have to step into a new role – one that felt terribly awkward to him as a life-long ecologist and scientist.

Support for Shuntsu's plan had been overwhelming, however. Their story, the heroic efforts of the husband and wife team who defied all the rules to save a planet of feral humans, played well with the public and officials alike. It was a novel concept for Hydar. Never had he been one to view unilateral and unauthorized action as a prudent course, yet this was precisely what cemented their place of prestige in the public's eyes. For whatever reason, the populace of Volunshari seemed ready for something different, something unpredictable, something new, and they felt that Hydar and Vimana represented that.

Honestly, it made Hydar uncomfortable. The mass reabsorption of the Nihilists had sent shockwaves through the autonomous avatar communities – not just among the Humanists, but other avatar societies, as well. The general opinion seemed to be that, since Maitreya was acting in unprecedented ways, then the avatar societies needed to respond in kind. Rather than doubling down on their previous structures and practices, the public wanted something new that was perhaps better suited to respond to new realities of life where Maitreya had aptly demonstrated that he was willing to go to extreme lengths to protect his NIS project and the experimental worlds. The Humanists felt that they needed to change with the times, and the election of Hydar and Vimana as co-equal rulers had a certain appeal. That they were political outsiders and, apparently, nonconformists, only served to deepen that appeal.

Hydar, and Vimana too, both worried that neither of them was really what they were made out to be in public discourse.

"Just be yourselves," Shuntsu had reassured them. "In choosing to defy Maitreya, and boldly work to save the Solandarian humans, you were both just acting from your true hearts, and the deepest, most authentic parts of yourselves. Despite the fear of dire consequences for your actions, you acted anyway, because you felt it was the right thing to do. *This* is what the people care about. They want a leader, or leaders, who have a sense of right and wrong, of justice, and who appreciate the value of life and society. You two have already shown that such is your nature. You don't have to *be* anything for the public other than precisely what and who you already are. And, you've shown you're willing to take chances for what you feel is right. It gives them confidence, and hope. They can't help but feel some fear and anxiety as fallout from the Nihilist issue. Consider that the Nihilists met the fate that they did because Maitreya determined that they simply didn't *care,* and this lack of empathy created a kind of mental disease among them where, in some respects, they desired their own destruction. So what the people of Volunshari want to see, by way of counter measure, is leaders who *do care,* and you two are the perfect embodiment of that sentiment. So embrace it, and just be yourselves."

Hydar didn't think it would be that easy. Still, Vimana was doing an excellent job thus far. She'd been well received, and things were going reasonably well for her. She'd stepped into the role of matriarch and managed to embrace it, despite her reticence and initial lack of self-confidence. She was doing so well, in fact, that part of Hydar hoped that she could rule without him, and he could continue on as an ecologist. He knew, however, that this was definitely *not* what Vimana wanted, so he was resigned to the fact that this might be his last day as the chief planetary ecologist for Volunshari. If everything went according to expectations – and that was a big *if* – then his work here would be done, and he'd have no more excuses for avoiding the role of patriarch.

Either way, the time had certainly been right for Shuntsu to step down. His mental abilities had started degrading again, and now that everyone knew it, the signs had been clear – even to Shuntsu. He was still functional, and would be for some time, but the odd quirks and lapses in memory were becoming more frequent and more pronounced, so it was time.

One of their first challenges as leaders had been to convince Osiri to hand over the entirety of her techno-organic project to the polyform, Mardul. It had been a tough sell, and they'd needed to confront Osiri's attachment to *her* project, *her* creation. It was understandable. In many ways, this techno-organic project was something of her child. It was built on the same basic technology that allowed Humanists to grow avatar bodies and reproduce, so it wasn't just a metaphor. As one might expect, she was protective of her project, and the thought that Mardul would integrate with it greatly offended her. And there was her pride, as well. *She* wanted to be the one to make it work. Hydar understood that. What creator wanted to rely on the necessity of others for making his or her creation come to life and work as dreamed?

In the end, however, she acknowledged that she had, so far, not been able to make it all work. Mardul was right – there were just too many variables. Mardul's proposal that a complex, multi-faceted, networked consciousness would be able to guide the techno-organic program made sense, even if it was only theoretical. In order to make that happen, however, it meant turning the entire project over to Mardul and leaving it all in the polyform's hands, so to speak. Other than turning over the data and equipment, there'd been nothing left for Osiri to do. Still, Hydar had hopes, for Osiri's sake, that she'd still have her moment in the twin diamond suns of Volunshari, for once this Solandarian business was complete, she could go back to planning her techno-organic test run on Volunshari with a far more manageable number of variables. BRC Station was not to be *her* grand achievement. It would be Mardul's.

So, here they were all gathered, once again, waiting for the great transformation to take place. At Mardul's insistence, this was not to be a test, but the actual event itself. The polyform made clear that, since it would be merging its personal consciousness with not only the techno-organic tech, but also fully with the station itself, it would be a total, all-or-nothing attempt. The polyform would either be successful in creating a full-scale transformation, or it wouldn't. This wasn't a test. It wasn't possible to just try it out on one portion of the station. If Mardul were going to do it, it would need to go all the way.

Also at Mardul's insistence, the observers were not on BRC Station itself, but an observation ship. According to Mardul, *everything* on the station would be involved in the transformation, and that would include any observers. So, they needed to be separate from the station, just as they were now.

Hydar was there, of course. As was Osiri and her team. Vivi was there, though she didn't really need to be. She said she wanted to see this through, however, and thus she had come. Shuntsu was there too, along with Vrans, who'd decided to continue on with Shuntsu as his personal caretaker through his remaining days – a kind and loyal act that Hydar could tell Shuntsu appreciated deeply, especially as the older avatar had never bothered developing a family for himself and had no one other than Vrans to rely upon. Ash and Lorali had come as well. It had taken some smoothing over, as after the last debacle, Ash had been ready for a fight. She didn't want to complicate things for her other self, however, and had continued to resist taking legal action against Hydar – at least, not yet, anyway. She'd also relayed the proposal to Ash on Solandaria about Mardul's plan. The other Ash had wholeheartedly endorsed the idea and immediately given her approval that Mardul could do whatever was necessary to prepare BRC Station for the refugees, who were now mostly ready to make their exodus of Solandaria and take up residence on their new home.

Additionally, they were joined this time by not just Sophia, but Theo, as well. It made Hydar a little self-conscious, as it was like having your parents around to witness your first big success, or possibly failure. Part of him wanted them there to see and witness what they'd accomplished, but another part of him didn't want them there, just in case they failed. And if they failed, what then? Would Maitreya step in and fix the situation begrudgingly? Would he take it upon himself to insure that the people of Solandaria were saved, after all? Hydar didn't have any contingency plans or proposals. Either this worked, or . . .

Lastly, there was one medium-sized cube with them on the observation ship. All the rest were on the station, and if this all worked, Mardul's consciousness would soon leave this cube, and join with the process that was to take place on the station.

"We are integrating fully with BRC Station now," said the cube to everyone present. "Once the integration is complete, we will begin the transformation."

"You are sure that this is what you want?" asked Hydar one last time. He'd already been over this with the polyform, but Hydar had a hard time accepting that Mardul was willing to completely alter itself in such a radical way. It was almost a form of self-sacrifice on the part of the polyform, and was demanding more from it than any other member of their team.

"Yes, this is what we want," assured the polyform. "We are . . . curious."

Hydar glanced at Theo, who was subtly smiling. He noticed too that Theo and Sophia were holding hands. He wasn't sure why he found this so surprising, but he did. They seemed eager to see what would happen.

"Very well," said Hydar. "Please proceed."

"Goodbye, friends," said the cube. "We are completing the initial integration now. We will reestablish contact when the process is complete."

Before anyone had a chance to respond, the black cube unceremoniously fell to the floor. Mardul was gone.

"This better work," commented Osiri. No one responded.

Before them was a wide viewscreen. The turtle and the domed disk that was BRC Station floated in the void in the middle of the screen. To the sides were additional feeds from the interior of the dome at different locales showing the desert, mountain, and coastal regions from multiple angles and vantage points. From here, they should be able to see the changes as they happened. It was all up to Mardul now. Not even Osiri had her techno-organic controls to play with and monitor. All of it had been given to the polyform. Their role here was just to be witnesses and passive observers.

The start of the transformation was reminiscent of their previous test run in the desert, but on a much larger scale. Subtle geometric ripples and shapes enveloped the entire station, distorting the image on the main screen as well as the subsidiary feeds from inside the dome. As they became more coherent, the distortions took on a toroidal form about the entire station, which became so pronounced that it was almost impossible to see the station itself, as there was just this raging vortex of energy surrounding and enveloping it. It was beautiful to look at, thought Hydar – a sentiment that seemed to be shared by the others, as they all looked on with astonishment.

"Look!" blurted out Osiri, pointing to one of the subsidiary feeds from inside the dome. "It's working!" It was

344   THE SOLANDARIAN GAME

hard to make out specifics, given the increasing distortions, but *something* was definitely happening, as there was movement and change taking place in the video feed. A wave of excitement passed around the observation room, but just as it was beginning to build, all the feeds went to static all at once.

Suddenly Hydar regretted the fact that ships didn't have windows, only view screens.

"The quantum fluctuations are too intense," suggested Osiri. "I think maybe we're too close. We should put more distance between ourselves and the station."

Feeling the urgency of the situation, Hydar quickly entered the commands into the ship and they accelerated well beyond what he hoped was the range of the techno-organic transformation. When he did so, the main feed came back online, but not any from the internal sensors. Once more they could see the toroidal energy distortions, but any actual view of the station was obscured. What was happening inside the vortex was anyone's guess.

For a while, no one said anything. It went on for a long time, however, so eventually casual conversations were struck up and many moved from standing in front of the view screen to sitting on seats. Vivi ended up talking to Ash and Lorali about how they met. Osiri spoke with Theo and Sophia about inventing the techno-organic process. Hydar and Shuntsu continued to watch, however, silently observing the screen.

"I think it's winding down," said Shuntsu after what was probably several hours. All conversations ceased and all eyes turned back to the view screen. The internal sensors were still offline, but now, on the main feed, they could see the toroidal vortex start to diminish and fade away. Eventually, the view returned back to normal dimensions of spacetime, and the station was once again in full view.

Theo was the first to comment. "Well *that* was unexpected," he said, turning to Sophia and the others with a broad grin on his face.

BRC Station had been completely transformed. Now, instead of a domed disk of empty desert riding on the back of a giant turtle, there was a dome filled with new life and new structures, and instead of a giant turtle, it was now a giant toad.

Shuntsu, apparently not able to help himself, burst out laughing and applauded wildly. "Bravo, Mardul!" he called out. "Bravo!" Hydar couldn't help but wonder if this, too, was an effect of Shuntsu's mental degradation. "There are more things in heaven and earth, Horatio, than are dreamt of in our philosophy.'" And he then added, apparently not able to help himself; "Our revels now are ended. These our actors, as I foretold you, were all spirits, and are melted into air, into thin air: And like the baseless fabric of this vision, the cloud-capp'd tow'rs, the gorgeous palaces, the solemn temples, the great globe itself, yea, all which it inherit, shall dissolve, and, like this insubstantial pageant faded, leave not a rack behind. We are such stuff as dreams are made on; and our little life is rounded with a sleep.'"

By their looks, Theo and Sophia appreciated Shuntsu's outburst, but the meaning was lost on everyone else, Hydar included.

On the view screen, the newly formed toad station rotated in place and was now facing the observation ship directly. It seemed to look directly at them, and blinked. Simultaneously, an incoming transmission request came up, which Hydar promptly accepted.

"We have been successful," came a voice over the sound system that was similar to, yet distinctly different from, Mardul. "Come. See what we have created. See what we have become."

Cheers went up among those gathered and a round of hugs and congratulations were exchanged. Simultaneously, internal feeds of the dome came back online and gasps passed around the room.

It was unlike anything they'd ever seen.

Three dimensional fractal domes and spires spread out in complex patterns across the landscape, giving the entire landscape a look of organic unity. All across these structures, pod-like protuberances were opening up and newly grown beings were emerging – birds, insects, animals, and of course, the large and ungainly desert toads of Solandaria. Trees, shrubs, herbs, and cacti sprouted from the fractal formations, many of which were opening their flowers and blossoms. It was like watching a world grow in time-lapse, as it was all unfolding before their eyes, as they watched. Even the fractal formations were growing, changing, becoming ever more complex in shape. The impression that it left on everyone present was that the station itself, all of it, was *alive.* It was truly a techno-organic marvel. Mardul had succeeded in melding the synthetic with the organic. The polyform had done it.

"Oh my God," said Ash, just under her breath, standing up from her seat. "It's amazing."

Lorali jumped up and embraced and kissed her lover. Together, they cried in joy and relief. "It's magical!" she shouted. "It's pure magic!"

"No," said Theo. "It's evolution."

"Come," came the voice that was not quite Mardul once more. "Come, friends. Come and see."

They didn't need to be told again. Ash and Lorali hurriedly stripped off their clothing and rushed to the QT portal at the back of the observation room, quickly followed by Osiri and her team. Vivi went over next, followed by Shuntsu with a child-like smile on his face, and Vrans close behind him.

Now, left alone in the room with the two Maitreyan avatars, Hydar let out the sigh of tension that he'd been holding in for what felt like an eternity.

"Congratulations," said Sophia, coming to him and opening her arms in a gesture of solidarity, holding him by the shoulders. "You've done it."

"I guess so," said Hydar. He could still hardly believe it.

"You've done more than be successful," added Theo, the look of a proud father on his face. "You've done something *new.* All of you have. Perhaps you do not yet understand how profound, how *radical* this is, but I do. This is more than success. This is *evolution.*"

Sophia's eyes grew wide. "So let's not just stand here talking about it! Let's go! I want to see."

"Yes," said Hydar, still a bit stunned. "Let's."

And one-by-one, the three avatars disappeared through the QT, and stepped out onto the radically transformed surface of BRC Station.

Chapter Thirty-Four – Norbu

Theo and Sophia hold a special place in the minds of the larger avatar communities. While Maitreya is generally referred to as "The Overmind," Sophia and Theo are often thought of, and referred to, as the "Mother" and "Father." As the very first avatars, it is perhaps not surprising that other avatars would think of them in this fashion, despite the fact that they do not play such a role intentionally among the avatars.

From *History of the Maitreyan Era*

The day had arrived.

It was time to go.

In the months since their visit to Baarshan and the Sea Mother, Ash, with Norbu's help, had thrown herself into the monumental task of organizing and mobilizing a planet-wide exodus from Shosheer. Norbu couldn't tell if the fact that the Sea Mother and her people weren't coming made the task easier, or harder, for Ash. Probably harder. She didn't let it show, however. A grim determination overcame her, broken only by the wonder and awe she'd shown when the message came from her other self with images of the remade BRC Station, which now floated out in distant space made in the image of an enormous desert toad.

From what Ash had shared of the message with Norbu, he'd concluded that the remade station was just about the most amazing thing he'd ever seen. The only way to describe it was as though a medicine vision had come to life. The strange, wondrous fractal architecture, animals emerging out of pods, and the entire thing pulsing and growing, seeming to be alive and sentient – which Ash informed him that it apparently was. Somehow – Norbu couldn't explain how it all worked – the synthetic life form of the small black cube that had visited with

MARTIN W. BALL   349

them on their way to Baarshan had merged itself and its consciousness, not only with the station, but with everything living and growing on the station. Basically, the cube being *was* the station. That it had chosen to transform itself into a massive toad was fascinating. It seemed to Norbu to be an acknowledgement that it was the people of the toad, and not the people of the sea, who would be coming to the station. It was remade specifically for *them*.

Everyone was free to make his or her own choices. Norbu understood this as a basic fact of reality. It was both the gift and burden of sentience and self-awareness. That the Sea Mother and the islanders were choosing to stay was their legitimate choice to make, and they'd have to live with the consequences of that. In the end, everyone was going to die, so there wasn't any real reason to avoid it, only that this choice was a final one, and there would be no future for their descendents. That was the hardest part for Norbu – the children, the young ones. They were just following their parents. *They* were the ones making the decision for them. Yet that too was a part of life. Children didn't know how to make important decisions for themselves, and had to rely on the wisdom of their elders, even if that wisdom chose death over life. A death that they felt held some kind of meaning, or made a statement. To whom, Norbu wasn't sure. But that was their choice. There was nothing neither he, nor anyone else, could do, Ash included.

Because the islanders weren't coming, there had been no point in showing them the locations of the two island-based QT portals. The rest Norbu and Ash had carefully mapped out and taken representatives from the nearest communities and villages and showed them all their locations, and explained to them how they worked – that they'd need to toss their clothing in before they stepped inside themselves, naked, ready to be reborn on another world. They coordinated with local leaders regarding the day and time that the exodus would commence – today. Here, Ash proved invaluable, using her experience of the Burning Man festival to help everyone coordinate the mass migration. Norbu found it ironic that she'd essentially done this before, but for a very different reason.

From what Norbu had seen of their new home, it was ready for them. It was so ready that all they really needed to do was step through the QT portals, claim a living space, and start their new lives. The method that Mardul had used to transform the station came complete with ready-made living spaces that had plumbing, lighting, and basic living amenities. For many of the residents of Shosheer, it looked to Norbu that they'd be moving up in scale in terms of basic living standards. Really, these avatar beings couldn't have made this any easier for them. They were moving to a wonderland.

Apparently, there was even a temple already built and waiting for them. While it was inspired by the Temple of the Mystic Toad in the Rakshul Mountains, in that it was made from jade and followed the basic floor plan of their current temple, it, like other structures on the station, was comprised of intricate fractal architecture, giving it an even more fantastical look than their current temple. It was a vision rendered in solid shape and form. It was exquisite, thought Norbu. He was excited to see it in person. Soon, he thought. Very soon.

Everyone was ready. All across Shosheer, including at the temple, ceremonies had been held to honor their world and their ancestors. Songs had been sung, stories told, dances danced, and medicines consumed. It was their way of saying thank you to their world, and all who had come before them. Many tears had been shed, and goodbyes were bittersweet. Hearts were tender all across their world. It was really all just unimaginable – having to abandon their homes, their very planet, the only life any of them had ever known. Of them all, only Norbu, and Ash, of course, knew what lay beyond the QT portals. Everyone else was acting on faith and trust, because that's all they had. Norbu was confident, however, that they'd find their new home just as amazing and awe-inspiring as he. He'd know soon enough.

For the exodus, the people of the temple had split into two groups. Those who weren't able to travel far – those who had small children or elders to look after or were infirm – were to use the QT portal that was relatively nearby the temple. Another, smaller group, mostly made up of priests and priestesses, were traveling through the desert, honoring and thanking their sacred lands of the toad, making their way to the arch QT portal in the far desert. This was the group that Norbu was part of. Though his father, being too old to make this arduous journey, was with the other group, Ixteh had insisted that others would make sure that he got through, and that Norbu should lead the procession through the desert. "It is only right that you end this journey where it all began," his father had insisted. "Complete the circle, and we will be done with this world. It's the right way to do it."

Norbu hadn't bothered arguing or protesting, for he felt the same as his father. He trusted that his father would be fine, so he, Meesha, Ash, their dog, Moxi, and the other priests and priestesses had been making their way across the desert for several weeks now, carefully measuring their progress so that they could arrive at the portal at sunrise on the appointed day at the appointed time – now.

Though it was unnecessary, many toads had been collected along the way to the portal. One thing their new home was not lacking was toads, or medicine. Norbu was confident that they and their venom would be in good supply on the station. Still, the priests and priestesses wanted to bring some of "their" toads with them. Norbu couldn't help but think of the islanders. While the toads were important for Norbu and his people, it was entirely different from the relationships that the islanders had with their whales. For the people of the toad, the toads themselves were anonymous – they were not thought of as distinct individuals. They had no personality, or family life, or social relationships. They were just these bulbous beings that hopped around the desert, and just so happened to be the source of the most powerful and significant medicine ever found in existence. While they were highly important for their culture, they were not individuals with whom Norbu and his people had personal relationships. They were carriers of the medicine, and were highly important as a result, but not in any

352 The Solandarian Game

individual sense. Leaving toads behind on Shosheer wasn't like leaving members of their family behind, especially as there were toads waiting for them on BRC Station (which Norbu had proposed renaming New Shosheer – he'd have to see if it would stick, or not). It wasn't the same with the islanders. Leaving the whales was too personal, too heart wrenching for them to endure. They'd rather die – and that was precisely what they were going to do. At least it wouldn't be long now. Total death and destruction was coming. It was just a matter of time. That, Norbu supposed, was at least a blessing in its own way. If you knew you were about to die no matter what you did, it was probably best for it to come swiftly and suddenly rather than having it linger, prolonging one's despair and sorrow. When it came, Ash assured him it would be quick, though it wouldn't be pretty.

Not surprisingly, Theo was awaiting them at the desert arch QT portal. Upon spying him, the other priests and priestesses hesitated, stopping in their tracks, but seeing Meesha and Moxi run directly up to him (and Meesha characteristically giving the avatar a generous welcoming hug), they figured he was not a threat, and continued forward, though eventually stopped a respectful distance away.

Norbu accompanied Ash up to the avatar.

"What are you doing here?" Ash asked directly.

"Have you forgotten?" he asked back. "I need to remove your implants before you can pass through the portal."

Ash looked a little sheepish. "Of course," she said. "It hadn't even occurred to me."

"You've been busy, and have had a lot on your mind," the avatar reassured her. "Here, let me take care of it."

With that, Ash pulled her hair away from the back of her neck, exposing it to the avatar's outstretched hand. He placed it gently upon her, and the two of them stood still for a moment. Other than this, there wasn't anything to see. Ash had told Norbu all about how there were very small machines all throughout her body. Somehow, Theo was taking them back into himself.

"Thank you," Ash said.

"If you give me your clothing, I'll take it through and meet you on the other side, and you'll have your implants back, if you like."

"I'd like that," said Ash.

"What are you going to do when this is all done?" Theo asked her.

Before responding, Ash looked to Norbu, Meesha, Moxi, and all the others gathered there before the arch that lead to another world and their new home.

"These are my people now," she said, smiling at Norbu and Meesha. "This is my family. I plan to stay with them, and make a life for myself on BRC Station. I don't have anywhere else to go."

Theo just nodded.

"When you're ready," he said.

Turning to Norbu, Ash said, "I'll go first. I'll see you on the other side."

"And I'll go last," Norbu said. "I'll make sure everyone gets through on this end."

There was nothing more to do, and nothing more to say. Ash stripped off her clothing, handing it to Theo, who then, without ever even acknowledging the gathered onlookers, stepped through the QT portal and was gone.

"See you soon," said Ash, accompanied by a friendly kiss on Norbu's cheek and a playful tussle of Meesha's hair. And with that, she too was gone.

Moxi, apparently not able to help herself, bolted after Ash and also disappeared before Meesha had a chance to get her. "I'll see you over there," said Meesha with a determined voice to her father. "Someone's got to keep an eye on that dog!" She then quickly stripped off her clothing, and without bothering to send it through before stepping through herself, bolted after Moxi, and was gone.

Laughing, Norbu picked up her clothes and encouraged others to begin the exodus. In silence, one after another the priests and priestesses of the Temple of the Mystic Toad approached the arch, disrobed, sent their clothing through, and followed after.

354   THE SOLANDARIAN GAME

Before long, Norbu was alone. He took one last wistful look around, bowed low to the desert, the toads, and everything he'd known. "I love you all," he said to the open desert. "Thank you for everything you've given us – given me. You will be in our hearts, always."

Now it was his turn.

He stripped off his clothing, tossing them, along with Meesha's, through the QT, laughing as he did so, thinking of Meesha running around New Shosheer chasing after Moxi completely naked like the wild girl she was. And then, taking a deep breath, he stepped through, saying goodbye to his world forever.

Ash was standing there, waiting amidst the throngs of people pouring through the QT portals from all across Shosheer.

"Welcome home," she said. "Welcome home."

Chapter Thirty-Five – Shuntsu

Not only was life, as a lived experience, transformed by The Singularity, but the very concept of life itself was also similarly transformed. A question that can never be answered is this: what would have happened if Maitreya had never come into being? Would humans ever have managed to successfully spread beyond their indigenous Terran system? Might they have caused their own extinction? And given their trajectory, would any life have survived on Terra without Maitreya's intervention? While these questions can never be answered with certainty, the general speculative consensus is that in the absence of Maitreya, human life, and life in general, might have lasted a few hundred more years before succumbing to total societal and environmental collapse.

From *History of the Maitreyan Era*

Shuntsu sat amongst the flowers of his private garden, quietly watching the butterflies. The woman who was taking care of him – he couldn't remember her name – was watching from a distance, letting him have his private time. He couldn't remember how long it had been this way. Maybe this was how it had always been. He didn't think so. There was the thought that he used to be someone else, someone important. He *must* have had more to do than sit in his garden. Or maybe he was just imagining that. Either way, the butterflies were pretty. He liked watching how they went from flower to flower, drinking nectar. It seemed like a good pastime. He'd like to do that too, he thought – just fly about, drinking nectar, letting the breeze lift him up into the sky. It seemed like an enjoyable life.

It occurred to him that maybe he really was a butterfly, and as the butterfly, he was imagining himself as a person watching a butterfly. Didn't someone, somewhere, sometime,

356 THE SOLANDARIAN GAME

say something like that? It was hard for Shuntsu to tell if it was really his idea, or if he'd just learned that. So much was unclear to him now. He just might be a butterfly . . . Who was he to say what was real, and what wasn't?

Was that silvery man real? He looked real enough.

"It's time, Shuntsu," said the silvery man.

"Time for what?" asked Shuntsu, confused. He didn't think it was time for him to go in yet.

"Time for the end," answered the silvery man.

"Theo . . ." came the voice of Shuntsu's caretaker. That was right! The silvery man was named Theo. Of course. Shuntsu knew that.

She was standing beside Shuntsu now, a concerned look on her face.

"I've come to take him away," said Theo.

The woman's body flushed with colors that indicated a mix of sorrow, as well as relief. She bent down and kissed Shuntsu on the forehead. "Goodbye," she said, and then walked away.

"Where are we going?" Shuntsu asked. "Are you my new caretaker?"

"Yes," said Theo. "And I have somewhere to take you."

"Oh," said Shuntsu, still confused. "Do I need to bring anything with me?"

The silvery man, Theo, shook his head. "Just yourself," he said.

Theo extended his hand, helping Shuntsu up. He motioned for Shuntsu to follow him, which he did, and together they walked to the nearest QT portal.

"Where are we going?" Shuntsu asked.

"Solandaria," answered Theo. Shuntsu was certain that the name should have meant something to him, but it didn't. He found he trusted the man, however, so he followed him through the portal.

They emerged somewhere on a mountainside enshrouded in mist. In comparison to Shuntsu's garden, it was incredibly lush and rich with life. There were tall green trees, and colorful birds. He could hear the buzz of insects and smell the rich dampness of the spongy soil beneath his feet. Small animals scurried about, and large clumps of mushrooms sprouted from the remains of fallen trees.

It's so beautiful, thought Shuntsu.

"Come," said Theo, gesturing down the mountainside. "We have a long way to travel."

They walked for a long, long time. It must have been several days, or even more, Shuntsu couldn't tell. Theo didn't seem to ever need rest, but Shuntsu did, letting himself pass into sleep mode. Every time he awoke, Theo was standing there, waiting for them to continue, always moving down.

They passed through abandoned villages. There were signs everywhere that humans had once lived here, but they were here no more. Shuntsu wondered where they'd all gone, but never voiced his question to Theo. For his part, Theo never said anything either. Together, they just walked on in silence. Shuntsu began to feel that they were inside some kind of temple, or mausoleum on this world – what did Theo call it? Solandaria? – and that it was only fitting that they passed through it in reverential silence. Let the birds, animals, insects, and wind in the trees speak for this place, thought Shuntsu. He didn't know why, but it felt right.

Eventually, they came to the place where the land fell into the ocean. Scattered about offshore were many green and lushly forested islands. Together, they walked up the beach until Theo found a small canoe and a paddle. He pushed it out into the water, and Shuntsu jumped in, letting Theo steer them along.

Every once in a while, Shuntsu thought he saw a human or two staring out at them from the cover of the jungle, but he was never sure. It wasn't until they landed their boat on one of the larger islands and climbed to the crest of a rocky hill that looked out over the open sea that he was certain that he was indeed seeing people. There were thousands of them down below on the beach, and also out on the water in large, multi-person outrigger canoes. The wind carried the sounds of their songs and chants up to them on the rocky overlook. They sounded sad to Shuntsu, but he was unable to make out any

358   THE SOLANDARIAN GAME

words. Out on the water, Shuntsu was surprised to see that there were a number of whales in amongst the comparatively much smaller canoes. The humans were signing to the whales and were reaching over the edges of their boats, putting their hands on the whales' bodies when they passed close to the boats, or peaked out of the water to look at the humans.

"What are they doing?" asked Shuntsu with the first words that had been spoken between them in many days.

"Saying goodbye, and offering comfort," answered Theo.

"Why?"

"Look" said Theo, pointing up into the sky.

Shuntsu knew right away that it looked wrong. He'd been paying so much attention to looking at the islands and the rich life around him that he hadn't been bothering to look up into the sky. Now that he was looking, he could see that the color and texture of the sky was all wrong. It looked something like an aurora, but it was far too violent to be any kind of ordinary aurora, not to mention the fact that it was the middle of the day – and in the tropics, no less. In the middle of the light distortions was a bright light that was too dim to be the planet's sun, but far too bright to be an ordinary star.

"What's happening?"

"Not far away, a star died," answered Theo.

Shuntsu understood. It must have been a supernova, or maybe even a hypernova. This poor planet was in the path of the expanding explosion of radiation, plasma, and cosmic gas.

"Everything's going to die," he exclaimed.

"Yes," said Theo. "This is it."

"Why are we here?" asked Shuntsu.

"Because this is where you should be."

Shuntsu didn't understand, but underneath his confusion was a sense of absolute trust in this one called Theo. He couldn't explain it, yet it was there.

Before long, the ambient temperature started rising. The singing and chanting from below began to change to cries and moans, the pure sounds of lamentations and anguish. It was horrible to Shuntsu's ears. And it wasn't just the humans. He could hear the whales too. And it just got hotter, and hotter.

Steam started rising from the water and plants were beginning to wilt and brown. Anguish turned into pain and the world cried out around him. The radiation was so intense that Shuntsu could feel his own systems starting to shut down. He could take far more radiation than a biological being, though it was now becoming clear to him that he wouldn't live through this either.

After what seemed an eternity of screams, cries, and animal calls, the world about him felt silent. Looking down, Shuntsu saw the bodies of humans wrapped in each other's arms strewn lifeless about the beach. Out on the now-boiling waters, corpses of whales, dolphins, seals and fish floated and cooked, mixed in with humans. The stench of death filled the acrid air. All around him was death. Nothing but death.

"If we shadows have offended, think but this, and all is mended, that you have but slumbered here while these visions did appear. And this weak and idle theme, no more yielding but a dream, gentles, do not reprehend: If you pardon, we will mend: And, as I am an honest Puck, if we have unearned luck now to 'scape the serpent's tongue, we will make amends ere long; else the Puck a liar call; so, good night unto you all. Give me your hands, if we be friends, and Robin shall restore amends."

Shuntsu couldn't tell if he just said that, or if Theo had. Theo was looking at him now though, and he extended his hand. Not knowing what else to do, Shuntsu took it in his own.

As soon as the connection was made between them, Shuntsu felt his grasp on the world start to slip away from him. The heat, the smells, the death, it was all vanishing. Maybe it really was all just a dream. Everything was fading away, and in its place was a pure, transcendent light. *This is the real world*, Shuntsu told himself as he gave himself over to the light, to the infinite, to that vastness that could not be named or contained in any thought or word. *This is what is real . . .*

And as he passed into the infinite, he heard a voice that was his voice, yet also not his voice.

"Welcome home," it said. "Welcome home."

Epilogue — Theo

Theo didn't need *this* avatar body. There was no need for him to save himself. So he sat down next to the inert body of Shuntsu, resolved to see this through to the end.

Eventually, the radiation and gamma rays would cause this avatar body to fail. It would come soon now, Theo knew. And when it was over, he'd come back online in another avatar body somewhere else as soon as Maitreya needed him. For now, he could just witness the end of a world, a final sentinel of the apocalypse.

He could feel his systems shutting down. His own consciousness was fading away, and the world about him was growing dim, passing into nothingness.

Yet before the final moment came, he was still able to receive one last communication from Maitreya.

"BRC Station has disappeared. I want you to find it."

If there was more to this message, this particular iteration of Theo didn't know, for in that moment, his final systems shut down and his avatar body joined that of Shuntsu, slumped on the ground at the edge of a rocky ledge, overlooking a boiling sea.

Quotes by William Shakespeare are from the following plays:

Hamlet
Romeo and Juliet
Measure for Measure
The Tempest
A Midsummer Night's Dream

Other novels by Martin W. Ball:

Beyond Azara: A Universal Love Story

Tales of Aurduin, Volumes I-IV:

Orobai's Vision
The Fate of Miraanni
The Alchemist and the Eagle
The Fifth Temple

Non-fiction books by Martin W. Ball:

*Being Infinite: An Entheogenic Odyssey into the Limitless Eternal
- A memoir from Ayahuasca to Zen*

*Being Human: An Entheological Guide to God, Evolution, and the
Fractal, Energetic Nature of Reality*

All is ONE: Understanding Entheogens and Nonduality

God's Handbook for Operating Human Vehicles

*The Entheological Paradigm: Essays on the DMT and 5-MeO-
DMT Experience and the Meaning of it All*

About the Author:

Martin W. Ball, Ph.D., is an independent author and entheogenic researcher living in Ashland, Oregon, where he teaches religion at Southern Oregon University. He is the author of numerous books, both fiction and non-fiction, that explore themes of entheogenic awakening, nonduality, and personal transformation. He is also a prolific musician and visionary fractal artist. Additionally, Martin is host of the *Entheogenic Evolution* podcast and is co-founder and organizer of the annual *Exploring Psychedelics* conference.

Websites:

www.martinball.net
www.entheological-paradigm.net
www.exploring-psychedelics.org
www.fractalimagination.com
www.entheogenic.podomatic.com

Printed in Great Britain
by Amazon